CADDY COMPSON

Major Literary Characters

CHELSEA HOUSE PUBLISHERS

Major Literary Characters

DAVID COPPERFIELD
Charles Dickens, *David Copperfield*

ROBINSON CRUSOE
Daniel Defoe, *Robinson Crusoe*

DON JUAN
Molière, *Don Juan*
Lord Byron, *Don Juan*

HUCK FINN
Mark Twain, *The Adventures of
Tom Sawyer, Adventures of
Huckleberry Finn*

CLARISSA HARLOWE
Samuel Richardson, *Clarissa*

HEATHCLIFF
Emily Brontë, *Wuthering Heights*

ANNA KARENINA
Leo Tolstoy, *Anna Karenina*

MR. PICKWICK
Charles Dickens, *The Pickwick Papers*

HESTER PRYNNE
Nathaniel Hawthorne, *The Scarlet Letter*

BECKY SHARP
William Makepeace Thackeray, *Vanity Fair*

LAMBERT STRETHER
Henry James, *The Ambassadors*

EUSTACIA VYE
Thomas Hardy, *The Return of the Native*

TWENTIETH CENTURY

ÁNTONIA
Willa Cather, *My Ántonia*

BRETT ASHLEY
Ernest Hemingway, *The Sun Also Rises*

HANS CASTORP
Thomas Mann, *The Magic Mountain*

HOLDEN CAULFIELD
J. D. Salinger, *The Catcher in the Rye*

CADDY COMPSON
William Faulkner, *The Sound and the Fury*

JANIE CRAWFORD
Zora Neale Hurston, *Their Eyes Were
Watching God*

CLARISSA DALLOWAY
Virginia Woolf, *Mrs. Dalloway*

DILSEY
William Faulkner, *The Sound and the Fury*

GATSBY
F. Scott Fitzgerald, *The Great Gatsby*

HERZOG
Saul Bellow, *Herzog*

JOAN OF ARC
William Shakespeare, *Henry VI*
George Bernard Shaw, *Saint Joan*

LOLITA
Vladimir Nabokov, *Lolita*

WILLY LOMAN
Arthur Miller, *Death of a Salesman*

MARLOW
Joseph Conrad, *Lord Jim, Heart of
Darkness, Youth, Chance*

PORTNOY
Philip Roth, *Portnoy's Complaint*

BIGGER THOMAS
Richard Wright, *Native Son*

CHELSEA HOUSE PUBLISHERS

Major Literary Characters

CADDY COMPSON

Edited and with an introduction by
HAROLD BLOOM

CHELSEA HOUSE PUBLISHERS
New York ◊ Philadelphia

Inset: Title page from the first American edition
of *The Sound and the Fury* (New York: Jonathan Cape
and Harrison Smith, 1929). By permission of
the Houghton Library, Harvard University.

Chelsea House Publishers

Editor-in-Chief Nancy Toff
Executive Editor Remmel T. Nunn
Managing Editor Karyn Gullen Browne
Picture Editor Adrian G. Allen
Art Director Maria Epes
Manufacturing Manager Gerald Levine

Major Literary Characters

Managing Editor S. T. Joshi
Copy Chief Richard Fumosa
Designer Maria Epes

Staff for CADDY COMPSON

Researcher Steve Mirassou
Editorial Assistant Anne Knepler
Picture Researcher Villette Harris
Assistant Art Director Loraine Machlin
Production Coordinator Joseph Romano
Production Assistant Leslie D'Acri
Cover Illustration Daniel Mark Duffy

Printed and bound in the United States of America

Library of Congress Cataloging-in-Publication Data

Caddy Compson / edited and with an introduction by Harold Bloom.
p.   cm. — (Major literary characters)
Bibliography: p.
Includes index.
ISBN 0-7910-9540-8.—ISBN 0-7910-1009-0 (pbk.)
1. Faulkner, William, 1897–1962—Characters—Caddy Compson.
2. Faulkner, William, 1897–1962. Sound and the fury.
3. Compson, Caddy (Fictitious character).   I. Bloom, Harold.   II. Series.
PS3511.A86Z74 1990
813'.52—dc 19
89-31351
CIP

CONTENTS

THE ANALYSIS OF CHARACTER

Harold Bloom

"Character," according to our dictionaries, still has as a primary meaning a graphic symbol, such as a letter of the alphabet. This meaning reflects the word's apparent origin in the ancient Greek *charactēr,* a sharp stylus. *Charactēr* also meant the mark of the stylus' incisions. Recent fashions in literary criticism have reduced "character" in literature to a matter of marks upon a page. But our word "character" also has a very different meaning, matching that of the ancient Greek *ēthos,* "habitual way of life." Shall we say then that literary character is an imitation of human character, or is it just a grouping of marks? The issue is between a critic like Dr. Samuel Johnson, for whom words were as much like people as like things, and a critic like the late Roland Barthes, who told us that "the fact can only exist linguistically, as a term of discourse." Who is closer to our experience of reading literature, Johnson or Barthes? What difference does it make, if we side with one critic rather than the other?

Barthes is famous, like Foucault and other recent French theorists, for having added to Nietzsche's proclamation of the death of God a subsidiary demise, that of the literary author. If there are no authors, then there are no fictional personages, presumably because literature does not refer to a world outside language. Words indeed necessarily refer to other words in the first place, but the impact of words ultimately is drawn from a universe of fact. Stories, poems, and plays are recognizable as such because they are human utterances within traditions of utterances, and traditions, by achieving authority, become a kind of fact, or at least the sense of a fact. Our sense that literary characters, within the context of a fictive cosmos, indeed are fictional personages is also a kind of fact. The meaning and value of every character in a successful work of literary representation depend upon our ideas of persons in the factual reality of our lives.

Literary character is always an invention, and inventions generally are indebted to prior inventions. Shakespeare is the inventor of literary character as we know it; he reformed the universal human expectations for the verbal imitation of personality, and the reformation appears now to be permanent and uncannily inevitable. Remarkable as the Bible and Homer are at representing personages, their characters are relatively unchanging. They age within their stories, but their habitual modes of being do not develop. Jacob and Achilles unfold before us, but without metamorphoses. Lear and Macbeth, Hamlet and Othello severely modify themselves not only by their actions, but by their utterances, and most of all through *overhearing themselves,* whether they speak to themselves or to others. Pondering what they themselves have said, they will to change, and actually do change, sometimes extravagantly yet always persuasively. Or else they suffer change, without willing it, but in reaction not so much to their language as to their relation to that language.

I do not think it useful to say that Shakespeare successfully imitated elements in our characters. Rather, it could be argued that he compelled aspects of character to appear that previously were concealed, or not available to representation. This is not to say that Shakespeare is God, but to remind us that language is not God either. The mimesis of character in Shakespeare's dramas now seems to us normative, and indeed became the accepted mode almost immediately, as Ben Jonson shrewdly and somewhat grudgingly implied. And yet, Shakespearean representation has surprisingly little in common with the imitation of reality in Jonson or in Christopher Marlowe. The origins of Shakespeare's originality in the portrayal of men and women are to be found in the *Canterbury Tales* of Geoffrey Chaucer, insofar as they can be located anywhere before Shakespeare himself. Chaucer's savage and superb Pardoner overhears his own tale-telling, as well as his mocking rehearsal of his own spiel, and through this overhearing he is emboldened to forget himself, and enthusiastically urges all his fellow-pilgrims to come forward to be fleeced by him. His self-awareness, and apocalyptically rancid sense of spiritual fall, are preludes to the even grander abysses of the perverted will in Iago and in Edmund. What might be called the character trait of a negative charisma may be Chaucer's invention, but came to its perfection in Shakespearean mimesis.

The analysis of character is as much Shakespeare's invention as the representation of character is, since Iago and Edmund are adepts at analyzing both themselves and their victims. Hamlet, whose overwhelming charisma has many negative components, is certainly the most comprehensive of all literary characters, and so necessarily prophesies the labyrinthine complexities of the will in Iago and Edmund. Charisma, according to Max Weber, its first codifier, is primarily a natural endowment, and implies a primordial and idiosyncratic power over nature, and so finally over death. Hamlet's uncanniness is at its most suggestive in the scene of his long dying, where the audience, through the mediation of Horatio, itself is compelled to meditate upon suicide, if only because outliving the prince of Denmark scarcely seems an option.

Shakespearean representation has usurped not only our sense of literary character, but our sense of ourselves as characters, with Hamlet playing the part of the largest of these usurpations. Insofar as we have an idea of human disinterestedness, we tend to derive it from the Hamlet of Act V, whose quietism has about it a ghostly authority. Oscar Wilde, in his profound and profoundly witty dialogue, "The Decay of Lying," expressed a permanent insight when he insisted that art shaped every era, far more than any age formed art. Life imitates art, we imitate Shakespeare, because without Shakespeare we would perish for lack of images. Wilde's grandest audacity demystifies Shakespearean mimesis with a Shakespearean vivaciousness: "This unfortunate aphorism about art holding the mirror up to Nature is deliberately said by Hamlet in order to convince the bystanders of his absolute insanity in all art-matters." Of *Hamlet's* influence upon the ages Wilde remarked that: "The world has grown sad because a puppet was once melancholy." "Puppet" is Wilde's own deconstruction, a brilliant reminder that Shakespeare's artistry of illusion has so mastered reality as to have changed reality, evidently forever.

The analysis of character, as a critical pursuit, seems to me as much a Shakespearean invention as literary character was, since much of what we know about how to analyze character necessarily follows Shakespearean procedures. His hero-villains, from Richard III through Iago, Edmund, and Macbeth, are shrewd and endless questers into their own self-motivations. If we could bear to see Hamlet, in his unwearied negations, as another hero-villain, then we would judge him the supreme analyst of the darker recalcitrances in the selfhood. Freud followed the pre-Socratic Empedocles, in arguing that character is fate, a frightening doctrine that maintains the fear that there are no accidents, that overdetermination rules us all of our lives. Hamlet assumes the same, yet adds to this argument the terrible passivity he manifests in Act V. Throughout Shakespeare's tragedies, the most interesting personages seem doom-eager, reminding us again that a Shakespearean reading of Freud would be more illuminating than a Freudian exegesis of Shakespeare. We learn more when we discover Hamlet in the Freudian Death Drive, than when we read *Beyond the Pleasure Principle* into *Hamlet.*

In Shakespearean comedy, character achieves its true literary apotheosis, which is the representation of the inner freedom that can be created by great wit alone. Rosalind and Falstaff, perhaps alone among Shakespeare's personages, match Hamlet in wit, though hardly in the metaphysics of consciousness. Whether in the comic or the modern mode, Shakespeare has set the standard of measurement in the balance between character and passion.

In Shakespeare the self is more dramatized than theatricalized, which is why a Shakespearean reading of Freud works out so well. Character-formation after the passing of the Oedipal stage takes the place of fetishistic fragmentings of the self. Critics who now call literary character into question, and who proclaim also the death of the author, invariably also regard all notions, literary and human, of a stable character as being mere reductions of deeper pre-Oedipal desires. It becomes clear that the fortunes of literary character rise and fall with the prestige of normative conceptions of the ego. Shakespeare's Iago, who wars against being, may be the first deconstructionist of the self, with his proclamation of "I am not what I am." This constitutes the necessary prologue to any view that would regard a fixed ego as a virtual abnormality. But deconstructions of the self are no more modern than Modernism is. Like literary modernism, the decentered ego came out of the Hellenistic culture of ancient Alexandria. The Gnostic heretics believed that the psyche, like the body, was a fallen entity, mechanically fashioned by the Demiurge or false creator. They held however that each of us possessed also a spark or pneuma, which was a fragment of the original Abyss or true, alien God. The soul or psyche within every one of us was thus at war with the self or pneuma, and only that sparklike self could be saved.

Shakespeare, following after Chaucer in this respect, was the first and remains still the greatest master of representing character both as a stable soul and a wavering self. There is a substance that endures in Shakespeare's figures, and there is also a quicksilver rendition of the unsettling sparks. Racine and Tolstoy, Balzac and Dickens, follow in Shakespeare's wake by giving us some sense of pre-Oedipal sparks or drives, and considerably more sense of post-Oedipal character and personality, stabilizations or sublimations of the fetish-seeking drives. Critics like Leo Bersani and René Girard argue eloquently against our taking this mimesis as the only proper work of literature. I would suggest that strong fictions of the self, from the Bible through Samuel Beckett, necessarily participate in both modes, the sublimation of desire, and the persistence of a primordial desire. The mystery of Hamlet or of Lear is intimately invested in the tangled mixture of the two modes of representation.

Psychic mobility is proposed by Bersani as the ideal to which deconstructions of the literary self may yet guide us. The ideal has its pathos, but the realities of literary representation seem to me very different, perhaps destructively so. When a novelist like D. H. Lawrence sought to reduce his characters to Eros and the Death Drive, he still had to persuade us of his authority at mimesis by lavishing upon the figures of *The Rainbow* and *Women in Love* all of the vivid stigmata of normative personality. Birkin and Ursula may represent antithetical and uncanny drives, but they develop and change as characters pondering their own pronouncements and reactions to self and others. The cost of a non-Shakespearean representation is enormous. Pynchon, in *The Crying of Lot 49* and *Gravity's Rainbow*, evades the burden of the normative by resorting to something like Christopher Marlowe's art of caricature in *The Jew of Malta*. Marlowe's Barabas is a marvelous rhetorician, yet he is a cartoon alongside the troublingly equivocal Shylock. Pynchon's personages are deliberate cartoons also, as flat as comic strips. Marlowe's achievement, and Pynchon's, are beyond dispute, yet they are like the prelude and the postlude to Shakespearean reality. They do not wish to engage with our hunger for the empirical world and so they enter the problematic cosmos of literary fantasy.

No writer, not even Shakespeare or Proust, alters the available stock that we agree to call reality, but Shakespeare, more than any other, does show us how much of reality we could encounter if only we retained adequate desire. The strong literary representation of character is already an analysis of character, and is part of the healing work of a literary culture, which implicitly seeks to cure violence through a normative mimesis of ego, *as if it were stable,* whether in actuality it is or is not. I do not believe that this is a social quest taken on by literary culture, but rather that we confront here the aesthetic essence of what makes a culture *literary,* rather than metaphysical or ethical or religious. A culture becomes literary when its conceptual modes have failed it, which means when religion, philosophy, and science have begun to lose their authority. If they cannot heal violence, then literature attempts to do so, which may be only a turning inside out of the critical arguments of Girard and Bersani.

I conclude by offering a particular instance or special case as a paradigm for the healing enterprise that is at once the representation and the analysis of literary character. Let us call it the aesthetics of being outraged, or rather of successfully representing the state of being outraged. W. C. Fields was one modern master of such representation, and Nathanael West was another, as was Faulkner before him. Here also the greatest master remains Shakespeare, whose Macbeth, himself a bloody outrage, yet retains our imaginative sympathy precisely because he grows increasingly outraged as he experiences the equivocation of the fiend that lies like truth. The double natured promises and the prophecies of the weird sisters finally induce in Macbeth an apocalyptic version of the stage actor's anxiety at missing cues, the horror of a phantasmagoric stage fright of missing one's time, of always reacting too late. Macbeth, a veritable monster of solipsistic inwardness but no intellectual, counters his dilemma by fresh murders, that prolong him in time yet provoke him only to a perpetually freshened sense of being outraged, as all his expectations become still worse confounded. We are moved by Macbeth, however estrangedly, because his terrible inwardness is a paradigm for our own solipsism, but also because none of us can resist a strong and successful representation of the human in a state of being outraged.

The ultimate outrage is the necessity of dying, an outrage concealed in a multitude of masks, including the tyrannical ambitions of Macbeth. I suspect that our outrage at being outraged is the most difficult of all our affects for us to represent to ourselves, which is why we are so inclined to imaginative sympathy for a character who strongly conveys that affect to us. The Shrike of West's *Miss Lonelyhearts* or Faulkner's Joe Christmas of *Light in August* are crucial modern instances, but such figures can be located in many other works, since the ability to represent this extreme emotion is one of the tests that strong writers are driven to set for themselves.

However a reader seeks to reduce literary character to a question of marks on a page, she will come at last to the impasse constituted by the thought of death, her death, and before that to all the stations of being outraged that memorialize her own drive towards death. In reading, she quests for evidences that are strong representations, whether of her desire or her despair. Such questings constitute the necessary basis for the analysis of literary character, an enterprise that always will survive every vagary of critical fashion.

EDITOR'S NOTE

This book brings together a representative selection of the best criticism devoted to the analysis of Caddy Compson, the dominant female image and, in some sense, character in William Faulkner's *The Sound and the Fury,* which the novelist considered his masterwork. I am grateful to Steve Mirassou for his skill as a researcher.

My introduction tests Caddy as a representation by the principles set forth in my series essay on "The Analysis of Character" and finds her to be a remarkable triumph of nuance and figurative suggestiveness.

The volume begins with a chronological series of critical extracts, the first being by Faulkner himself, in reflecting belatedly upon his creation of Caddy. Lawrance Thompson studies the mirror imagery associated with Caddy, and Faulkner himself is interviewed upon his favorite fictional child, while Barbara M. Cross sees Caddy as a sacrificial figure. The excerpts from Olga W. Vickery, John W. Hunt, Jackson J. Benson, and John L. Longley, Jr., all focus upon different aspects of Caddy's vexed relations with her brothers, while Mimi Reisel Gladstein emphasizes the enduring strength of Faulkner's heroine. A note by Michael J. Auer speculates upon a New Testament source for Caddy.

The remaining extracts reflect the sharpening of critical perspectives upon Caddy's doomed qualities, even as earlier critics sought to delineate how her brothers provided the context for that doom.

Fuller-scale studies of Caddy begin here with Catherine B. Baum's consideration of the heroine's status, and continue with Sally R. Page's analysis of how obsessiveness distorts her image. John T. Irwin, the most speculative of Faulknerians, relates Caddy to patterns of incestuous doubling and repetition, after which Gladys Milliner reflects upon the heroine as a descendant of Eve. The image of Eurydice is involved as Caddy's archetype by André Bleikasten, while feminist perspectives are employed by Douglas B. Hill, Jr. A Jungian reading by Steve Carter is followed by Linda W. Wagner's language-centered exegesis. A moral emphasis dominates the interpretation of the celebrated Southern literary critic, Cleanth Brooks. The final essay in this volume, by Max Putzel, surprisingly (and interestingly) traces an aspect of Caddy's sacrificial imagery to the Belgian dramatist Maeterlinck.

INTRODUCTION

3 brothers

If one attempts to think of an overwhelmingly memorable woman who is a character in a modern American novel, one is quite likely to come up with Faulkner's Caddy, the central representation in *The Sound and the Fury*. Yet then a critical bewilderment begins, since Caddy is anything but an achieved literary character, in any traditional sense whatsoever. Both as an absence and as a presence, she is wholly mediated by four other characters: her three brothers, and Faulkner's narrative voice in the novel's final section, which counts as a representation of the author himself. Through Benjy, Quentin, Jason, and Faulkner we come to know a single Candace Compson, but only as a heap of broken images. Caddy is an extraordinary composite of personifications, symbols, attributes, associations, comparisons, and connections. The entire range of tropes is evoked by her figurative richness, which recalls the rhetorical splendor of Milton's Eve. If the baroque Faulkner can be regarded as the belated epic bard of the American South, composing the confederate *Paradise Lost,* then Caddy can be judged his vision of the universal female, more the sister than the mother of us all. *The Sound and the Fury* indeed is Faulkner's audacious attempt to match Milton, Melville, and Joyce in the epic dimension, and the endlessly mediated Caddy is therefore the farthest projection of Faulkner's strongest aesthetic longings.

Caddy, as David Minter surmises, is partly Faulkner's answer to the outrageous question: how can you lust incestuously after the sister you never had? The reader, by the time she has finished *The Sound and the Fury,* will be unable to forget an imagistic cluster in association with Caddy: fire, the color red, pear trees, the odor of honeysuckle, the river, twilight. This enchantment (it cannot be regarded as less) in turn evokes a complex of ideas: Southern womanhood, virginity and death, the presence of the past, and above all nostalgia and loss. Equivocal and doubtless chauvinistic, the complex sums up the total image of male desire of the female, as Faulkner powerfully conceives it. Such an image has an immense career in Western literature, from Provençal poetry (at the latest) through W. B. Yeats. Faulkner was one of the last of this old, high line, which the movement of our ideologies now has discredited socially, as it were, but hardly aesthetically. Our current scholars of what I have so amiably termed the School of Resentment are justified in seeing Faulkner as a final citadel of male exploitation of the classical and biblical visions of the female. I myself, being as I am a disciple of Walter Pater, am not much concerned with the dialectics of gender and power, but rather with the problematics of experiential loss and imaginative gain. In that spirit, I will analyze Caddy as a late Romantic vision of desire and its limits, very much in the mode of Pater's Mona Lisa and Yeats's Maud Gonne, and of Joyce's intense nostalgias for an Irish Eve. Moral judgment seems to me redundant in relation to Faulkner's quite Jacobean misogyny, which follows Webster, Tourneur, and Ford in exploiting not so much the social degradation of women as the dramatic (and melodramatic) possibilities made available by that indubitable degradation.

Faulkner himself began the critical tradition (to which I adhere) of seeing *The Sound and the Fury* as a masterpiece of Oedipal ambivalences rather than as a monument, partly involuntary, to the South's social concerns: the shadow of mis-cegenation, and the guilt of African-American slavery and sexual exploitation. It is clear that the Oedipal guilt and the shame of bondage inextricably intersect in *Absalom, Absalom!* and *Light in August.* But *The Sound and the Fury* has more in common with *As I Lay Dying,* Faulkner's masterpiece, which is wholly an Oedipal nightmare, than it does with the sagas of Sutpen and of Joe Christmas. Caddy is the emblem not only of Faulkner's personal family romance, but of his aesthetic romance as a strong novelist, his quest to establish himself as his own father, displacing Conrad and Joyce. That quest, as Hugh Kenner and Eric Sundquist have argued, partly fails, if only because, unlike Conrad and Joyce, Faulkner had little genius for symbol, the trope of synecdoche, of condensing much in little. Faulkner's characteristic trope is expansion or hyperbole, the Sublime mode of seeking em-phasis through protraction and nuance. The success, however qualified, of *The Sound and the Fury* is centered upon Caddy, as she is a grand hyperbole of the enigmas of traditional male desire for the forbidden female, the literary image of incest.

John Irwin, the speculative seer of Faulknerian incest, observes of Caddy that she represents Quentin's longing for death. As such, she becomes Faulkner's met-aphor for Freud's strangest figuration, the Death Drive beyond the Pleasure Prin-ciple, or the dialectical reverse of Eros. That ought to be an impossible complex of ambivalences for any single literary character to embody, and Faulkner's success in conveying Caddy's nuances and overtones is surely one of his most incontro-vertible aesthetic achievements. The Celtic Twilight of Yeats survives in the great image of Maud Gonne as mediated by Yeats's lyrics and autobiographical reveries. Even so the Southern Twilight of Faulkner endures in the marvelous expansions of Caddy in the consciousness of Benjy, Quentin, and Jason, and in the narrative consciousness of Faulkner himself.

For the idiot Benjy, Caddy is loss itself, imageless abyss of pure absence. For the incestuous Quentin, she is obsession itself, the fantasy of fantasy, as it were. For Jason, himself a superb, almost Dickensian grotesque, Caddy is the image of whoredom, of the female conceived as grotesquerie. The most interesting of these versions of Caddy is Faulkner's own, both in and out of the novel. In the Appendix that he wrote for Malcolm Cowley's *Portable Faulkner,* we are given a complex new sense of Caddy as a force that transcends her brothers' various partial portraits. It is as though Faulkner's post–World War II sense of impending doom had found its perfect representation in Caddy's dispassionate love for her doomed brother, Quentin:

> Doomed and knew it; accepted the doom without either seeking or fleeing it. Loved her brother despite him . . . she loved him in spite of but because of the fact that he himself was incapable of love . . .

This Caddy is fatalistic without being doom-eager; she is not in love with death but with what is incapable of loving, and so with what chooses death in consequence. What is it to love the loveless? That is the reduction of Faulkner's deeper question, which might be phrased as: what is it to write what cannot be written? Caddy's character is totally a mediated one in the same way in which *The Sound and the Fury* is a wholly mediated novel, mediated by the precursors, Conrad and Joyce, and by Faulkner's astonishingly oppressive sense of the cultural and familial past. Conrad employed Marlow to mediate Kurtz and Jim for the reader, even as Joyce mediates Poldy and Stephen by way of an arsenal of mythological parallels. Faulkner's swerve from his novelistic fathers is the radical one of making himself into a Compson, into the storytelling, invisible brother of Benjy, Quentin, and Jason, and so of Caddy also. Conrad saw himself as Jim's brother, but had Marlow as defense. Joyce identified both with Poldy and Stephen, yet had language itself as defense. Faulkner, in making himself Caddy's brother, gave himself no defense from her, even as he gave Quentin no defense. It is because the fourfold narrative has no defenses against Candace that we come to know her so well, even while we do not come to know her at all.

—H. B.

CRITICAL EXTRACTS

WILLIAM FAULKNER

When I began the book, I had no plan at all. I wasn't even writing a book. Previous to it I had written three novels, with progressively decreasing ease and pleasure, and reward or emolument. The third one was shopped about for three years during which I sent it from publisher to publisher with a kind of stubborn and fading hope of at least justifying the paper I had used and the time I had spent writing it. This hope must have died at last, because one day it suddenly seemed as if a door had clapped silently and forever to between me and all publishers' addresses and booklists and I said to myself, Now I can write. Now I can just write. Whereupon I, who had three brothers and no sisters and was destined to lose my first daughter in infancy, began to write about a little girl.

I did not realise then that I was trying to manufacture the sister which I did not have and the daughter which I was to lose, though the former might have been apparent from the fact that Caddy had three brothers almost before I wrote her name on paper. I just began to write about a brother and a sister splashing one another in the brook and the sister fell and wet her clothing and the smallest brother cried, thinking that the sister was conquered or perhaps hurt. Or perhaps he knew that he was the baby and that she would quit whatever water battles to comfort him. When she did so, when she quit the water fight and stooped in her wet garments above him, the entire story, which is all told by the same little brother in the first section, seemed to explode on the paper before me.

I saw that peaceful glinting of that branch was to become the dark, harsh flowing of time sweeping her to where she could not return to comfort him, but that just separation, division, would not be enough, not far enough. It must sweep her into dishonor and shame too. And that Benjy must never grow beyond this moment; that for him all knowing must begin and end with that fierce, panting, paused and stooping wet figure which smelled like trees. That he must never grow up to where the grief of bereavement could be leavened with understanding and hence the alleviation of rage as in the case of Jason, and of oblivion as in the case of Quentin.

I saw that they had been sent to the pasture to spend the afternoon to get them away from the house during the grandmother's funeral in order that the three brothers and the nigger children could look up at the muddy seat of Caddy's drawers as she climbed the tree to look in the window at the funeral, without then realising the symbology of the soiled drawers, for here again hers was the courage which was to face later with honor the shame which she was to engender, which Quentin and Jason could not face: the one taking refuge in suicide, the other in vindictive rage which drove him to rob his bastard niece of the meagre sums which Caddy could send her. For I had already gone on to night and the bedroom and Dilsey with the mudstained drawers scrubbing the naked backside of that doomed little girl—trying to cleanse with the sorry byblow of its soiling that body, flesh, whose shame they symbolised and prophesied, as though she already saw the dark future and the part she was to play in it trying to hold that crumbling household together.

—WILLIAM FAULKNER, "An Introduction to The Sound and the Fury" [1933],
Mississippi Quarterly 26, No. 3 (Summer 1973): 412–14

LAWRANCE THOMPSON

(There) is ample evidence that Caddy, motivated by her compassion for her younger brother, has eagerly given Ben the kind of motherly attention previously denied to him because of his own mother's inadequacies. Tenderly, solicitously, Caddy has discovered ways of appealing to Ben's limited responses, to satisfy his instinctive and unreasoning hunger for orderliness, peacefulness, serenity. The fire, the red-yellow cushion, the smooth satin slipper are only a few of the objects used by Caddy to provide him with values which are positive to him because they are somehow sustaining. Then Caddy has also taught Ben the pleasure of multiplying these positive values through their reflections in the mirror. Because she has heightened his awareness of all those symmetrical visions of "bright, smooth shapes" which comfort him, it might be said that Caddy herself has become for Ben a kind of mirror of all his positive values, framed in love: her love for him and his love for her.

Ben's seemingly chaotic reverie in Part One of The Sound and the Fury is so contrived by Faulkner as to focus attention, not merely on fragments of the entire Compson story, but particularly on Ben's all-absorbing love for the Caddy who was and (like the mirror) is now gone. Her presence was Ben's joy; her absence his grief; her possible return his hope. The arrangement of these fragments in Part One enables Faulkner to withhold conclusive information as to how it happened that the finely sensitive and mothering child Caddy has so completely disappeared. The reader's tension of interest concerning that question is gradually resolved through various later uses of mirror analogues which disclose related aspects of Faulkner's complex theme.

Throughout The Sound and the Fury Faulkner employs the convention of using some of his characters to serve as mirrors of other characters; mirrors set at different angles so that they provide contrasting angles of vision. For example, (there are) two contrasting images of Ben: the image reflected in the articulated consciousness of Caddy, as differing from the image reflected in the articulated consciousness of Mrs. Compson. Although various characters in the narrative reflect various images of Ben, all these images may be reduced to two roughly antithetical categories: most of the characters view Ben as a disgrace, a menace, or at least as a slobbering idiot. By contrast, those who genuinely love Ben (particularly Caddy and the Negro servant Dilsey) insist that Ben has certain peculiar and extraordinary powers of perception. As Roskus phrases it, "He know lot more than folks thinks." Repeatedly Ben is represented as having the instinctive and intuitive power to differentiate between objects or actions which are life-encouraging and others which are life-injuring, and these are used by Faulkner to symbolize the antithesis between good and evil. In this limited sense, then, Ben serves as a kind of moral mirror, in which the members of his own family may contemplate reflections of their own potentialities, their own moral strengths and weaknesses. Most of them naturally refuse to acknowledge this power in Ben, because they do not wish to see themselves in any light other than that of self-justification.

Appropriately, Caddy is represented as having the greatest sensitivity to her brother's power of serving as a kind of moral mirror, and her sensitivity is heightened by her unselfish love for him. Faulkner develops this aspect of Ben's significance in four episodes which illuminate the progressive phases of Caddy's growth. When she is old enough to be interested in adolescent courtship, she discovers that Ben's unreasoning reaction against the smell of perfume gives her a sense of guilt and prompts her to wash herself clean—a primitive ritual repeatedly correlated with Ben's potential for serving as moral agent and moral conscience in his family. Later, when Ben escapes from the house one night, to find Caddy and Charlie kissing in the swing on the lawn, Caddy leaves Charlie, ostensibly to quiet Ben, but also because Ben has again evoked in her a sense of guilt.

> We ran out into the moonlight, toward the kitchen. . . . Caddy and I ran. We ran up the kitchen steps, onto the porch, and Caddy knelt down in the dark and held me. I could hear her and feel her chest. "I wont." she said. "I wont anymore, ever. Benjy. Benjy." Then she was crying, and I cried, and we held each other. "Hush." she said. "Hush. I wont anymore." So I hushed and Caddy took the kitchen soap and washed her mouth at the sink, hard.

The third time when Ben is represented as a moral mirror occurs as Caddy returns home immediately after her first complete sexual experience. In that scene Faulkner correlates two implicit analogues which complement each other: first, the analogue of Ben as a moral mirror; secondly, the analogue between simple physical vision and conscious moral vision, suggested by the persistent recurrence of the word "eyes" and the cognate words, "looking" and "seeing," as Ben again evokes in Caddy a deeper sense of guilt.

Caddy came to the door and stood there, looking at Father and Mother. Her eyes flew at me, and away. I began to cry. It went loud and I got up. Caddy came in and stood with her back to the wall, looking at me. I went toward her, crying, and she shrank against the wall and I saw her eyes and I cried louder and pulled at her dress. She put her hands out but I pulled at her dress. Her eyes ran.... We were in the hall, Caddy was still looking at me. Her hand was against her mouth and I saw her eyes and I cried. We went up the stairs. She stopped again, against the wall, looking at me and I cried and she went on and I came on, crying, and she shrank against the wall looking at me. She opened the door to her room, but I pulled at her dress and we went to the bathroom and she stood against the door, looking at me. Then she put her arm across her face and I pushed at her, crying.

Each of these three closely related episodes (involving Ben as moral mirror and also involving the symbolic and penitent ritual of washing away guilt with water) are associated in Ben's recollection with his ultimate reaction, at the time of Caddy's fake wedding, where the sense of guilt was ironically washed away with champagne until the celebration was terminated by Ben's unreasoning and bellowing protest. This fourth episode represents the end of the period in Ben's life when Caddy had been able to help him by bringing relative order out of his relatively chaotic experience, and the end of the period when Ben had served as moral mirror for Caddy. Notice that these two endings are obliquely suggested by reiterative mirror imagery in Quentin's recollection of that incident which broke up the wedding celebration.

She ran right out of the mirror, out of the banked scent. Roses. Roses.... Only she was running already when I heard it. In the mirror she was running before I knew what it was. That quick, her train caught up over her arm she ran out of the mirror like a cloud, her veil swirling in long glints her heels brittle and fast clutching her dress onto her shoulder with the other hand, running out of the mirror the smells roses roses the voice that breathed o'er Eden. Then she was across the porch I couldn't hear her heels then in the moonlight like a cloud, the floating shadow of the veil running across the grass, into the bellowing.

Caddy goes away after the fake wedding ceremony, leaving a double image of herself as reflected in the consciousness of her family. The reader's initial image of Caddy has been that reflected repeatedly in the consciousness of Ben: the sensitive and mothering Caddy whose love for Ben evoked his love for her and gave meaning to his life. That image remains. Antithetically, the second image of Caddy is that soon reflected (with only minor variations) in the consciousness of Mrs. Compson, Quentin, and Jason: the image of the member of the family whose fall from innocence is said to have brought a peculiar disgrace on the entire family; a disgrace considered equal to, or even greater than, that of Ben's idiocy. Gradually, however, the reader appreciates that Mrs. Compson, Quentin, and Jason, each motivated by different kinds of need for self-justification, have first made a scapegoat of Ben and have then made a scapegoat of Caddy, so that they may heap on these two scapegoats the ultimate blame for the disintegration within the Compson family.

—LAWRANCE THOMPSON, "Mirror Analogues in *The Sound and the Fury*," *English Institute Essays 1952* (New York: Columbia University Press, 1954), pp. 87–92

WILLIAM FAULKNER

⟨FEBRUARY 15, 1957:⟩

Q. Mr. Faulkner, in *The Sound and the Fury* the first three sections of that book are narrated by one of the four Compson children, and in view of the fact that Caddy figures so prominently, is there any particular reason why you didn't have a section with—giving her views or impressions of what went on?

A. That's a good question. That—the explanation of that whole book is in that. It began with the picture of the little girl's muddy drawers, climbing that tree to look in the parlor window with her brothers that didn't have the courage to climb the tree waiting to see what she saw. And I tried first to tell it with one brother, and that wasn't enough. That was Section One. I tried with another brother, and that wasn't enough. That was Section Two. I tried the third brother, because Caddy was still to me too beautiful and too moving to reduce her to telling what was going on, that it would be more passionate to see her through somebody else's eyes, I thought. And that failed and I tried myself—the fourth section—to tell what happened, and I still failed.

. . .

Q. Speaking of Caddy, is there any way of getting her back from the clutches of the Nazis, where she ends up in the Appendix?

A. I think that that would be a betrayal of Caddy, that it is best to leave her where she is. If she were resurrected there'd be something a little shabby, a little anti-climactic about it, about this. Her tragedy to me is the best I could do with it—unless, as I said, I could start over and write the book again and that can't be.

. . .

Q. Mr. Faulkner, I've been very much interested in what it seems to me you did—maybe you didn't—in *The Sound and the Fury,* in the character of Caddy. To me she is a very sympathetic character, perhaps the most sympathetic white woman in the book, and yet we get pictures of her only through someone else's comments and most of these comments are quite [?] and wouldn't lead you to admire her on the surface, and yet I do. Did you mean for us to have this feeling for Caddy, and if so, how did you go about reducing her to the negative picture we get of her?

A. To me she was the beautiful one, she was my heart's darling. That's what I wrote the book about and I used the tools which seemed to me the proper tools to try to tell, try to draw the picture of Caddy.

(FEBRUARY 20, 1957)

Q. In connection with the character of Christ, did you make any conscious attempts in *The Sound and the Fury* to use Christian references, as a number of critics have suggested?

A. No. I was just trying to tell a story of Caddy, the little girl who had muddied her drawers and was climbing up to look in the window where her grandmother lay dead.

(MARCH 7, 1957)

Q. You had said previously that *The Sound and the Fury* came from the impression of a little girl up in a tree, and I wondered how you built it from that, and whether you just, as you said, let the story develop itself?

A. Well, impression is the wrong word. It's more an image, a very moving image to me was of the children. 'Course, we didn't know at that time that one was an idiot, but they were three boys, one was a girl and the girl was the only one that was brave enough to climb that tree to look in the forbidden window to see what was going on. And that's what the book—and it took the rest of the four hundred pages to explain why she was brave enough to climb the tree to look in the window. It was an image, a picture to me, a very moving one, which was symbolized by the muddy bottom of her drawers as her brothers looked up into the apple tree that she had climbed to look in the window. And the symbolism of the muddy bottom of the drawers became the lost Caddy, which had caused one brother to commit suicide and the other brother had misused her money that she'd send back to the child, the daughter. It was, I thought, a short story, something that could be done in about two pages, a thousand words, I found out it couldn't. I finished it the first time, and it wasn't right, so I wrote it again, and that was Quentin, that wasn't right. I wrote it again, that was Jason, that wasn't right, then I tried to let Faulkner do it, that was still wrong.

(MAY 15, 1957)

Q. Does it give the author as much pain as it does the reader to produce scenes such as when Caddy wanted to see her baby and Jason just drove by?

A. Yes, it does, but that's—the writer is not simply dragging that in to pull a few tears, he is—he puts that down as an instance of man's injustice to man. That man will always be unjust to man, yet there must always be people, men and women who are capable of the compassion toward that injustice and the hatred of that injustice, and the will to risk public opprobrium, to stand up and say, This is rotten, this stinks, I won't have it.

(MAY 2, 1958)

Q. Did Quentin before actually have that conversation with his father about sleeping with his sister, or was that part of his—?

A. He never did. He said, If I were brave, I would—I might say this to my father, whether it was a lie or not, or if I were—if I would say this to my father, maybe he would answer me back the magic word which would relieve me of this anguish and agony which I live with. No, they were imaginary. He just said, Suppose I say this to my father, would it help me, would it clarify, would I see clearer what it is that I anguish over?

Q. The feeling between him and his sister is pretty strong though, isn't it?

A. Yes, yes. But in Caddy's opinion he was such a weakling that even if they had been no kin, she would never have chosen him for her sweetheart. She would have chosen one like the ex-soldier she did. But never anybody like Quentin.

Q. Is Candace a common name in Mississippi, or—?

A. No. No, Caddy seemed a nice name for her and I had to think of something to justify it.

—WILLIAM FAULKNER, *Faulkner in the University: Class Conferences at the University of Virginia 1957–1958*, ed. Frederick L. Gwynn and Joseph L. Blotner (Charlottesville: University Press of Virginia, 1959), pp. 1–2, 6, 17, 31–32, 148, 262–63

BARBARA M. CROSS

Caddy, who endures the death of sexual love, who "smells like trees" and seems at home climbing them, is the most ambiguous character in the book. Capable of love and departure from the ingrown family, she is the vehicle for the force of life, and because she actually enters the full cycle of life, her career is closest to tragedy. Yet though she "runs out of the mirror," she is damned. Dalton Ames, the efficient cause of her damnation, remains to the reader as to Quentin a papier-mâché hero, chivalric, foot-loose, a Sartoris never trapped by death. Caddy is more realized, but she too remains on the wings of the stage, and the vagueness about her is a weakness in the book. Yet her damnation makes sense within the moral context of the novel. For Caddy with child is "sick," she lacks the placid union with the processes of life through which Lena Grove is rendered invincible. After the birth of her baby, Caddy consigns her child to the death-dealing household.

—BARBARA M. CROSS, "*The Sound and the Fury:* The Pattern of Sacrifice," *Arizona Quarterly* 16, No. 1 (Spring 1960): 13

OLGA W. VICKERY

Within the novel as a whole it is Caddy's surrender to Dalton Ames which serves both as the source of dramatic tension and as the focal point for the various perspectives. This is evident in the fact that the sequence of events is not caused by her act—which could be responded to in very different ways—but by the significance which each of her brothers actually attributes to it. [As a result, the four sections appear quite unrelated even though they repeat certain incidents and are concerned with the same problem, namely Caddy and her loss of virginity.]

Although there is a progressive revelation or rather clarification of the plot, each of the sections is itself static. The consciousness of each character becomes the actual agent illuminating and being illuminated by the central situation. Everything is immobilized in this pattern; there is no development of either character or plot in the traditional manner. This impression is reinforced not only by the shortness of time directly involved in each section but by the absence of any shifts in style of the kind that, for example, accompany the growing maturity of Cash Bundren in *As I Lay Dying.* ⟨...⟩

Within this rigid world Caddy is at once the focus of order and the instrument of its destruction. The pasture, the fire, and sleep, the three things Benjy loves most, are associated with her, as is illustrated by the recurrent phrase "Caddy smelled like trees," his refusal to go to sleep without her, and his memory of her during the rainy evening when for a brief moment everything in his world was in its proper place. Caddy both realizes and respects his fear of change: while playing at the Branch she is quick to reassure him that she is not really going to run away; later, she washes off her perfume and gives the rest of it to Dilsey in order to reassure him. Even when she has accepted the inevitability of change for herself and is preparing to marry Herbert, she tries to bind Quentin to a promise of seeing that Benjy's life is not further disordered by his being committed to a mental institution. Yet what Benjy most expects of Caddy is the one thing she cannot give him, for his expectation is based on his complete indifference to or rather ignorance of time. As long as Caddy is in time, she cannot free either herself or his world from change. His dependence on her physical presence, her scent of trees, is subject to constant threats which he fends off to the best of his ability. The intensity of his reaction is caused by the fact that any alteration in Caddy makes her not-Caddy. Thus, Caddy, as in the Quentin section, is at once identified with the rigid order of Benjy's private world and with the disorder of actual experience. Depending on which of the two is dominant at the moment, Benjy moans or smiles serenely. ⟨...⟩

The order which Quentin had once built around Caddy is as rigid and inflexible as Benjy's and it shares Benjy's fear of change and his expectation that all experience should conform to his pattern. The cause of his ineffectuality and his ultimate destruction is the fact that his system antecedes his experience and eventually is held in defiance of experience. His is an ethical order based on words, on "fine, dead sounds," the meaning of which he has yet to learn. He has, in short, separated ethics from the total context of humanity. Insofar as virginity is a concept, associated with virtue and honor, it becomes the center of Quentin's world, and since it is also physically present in Caddy, it forms a precarious link between his world and that of experience. Mr. Compson remarks that virginity is merely a transient physical state which has been given its ethical significance by men. What they have chosen to make it mean is something which is a defiance of nature, an artificial isolation of the woman. Caddy, who seems almost a symbol of the blind forces of nature, is an unstable guardian for that "concept of Compson honor precariously and ... only temporarily supported by the minute fragile membrane of her maidenhead."

⟨. . .⟩ Both Benjy and Caddy are tests of the family's humanity, he simply because he is not fully human and she because her conduct creates a socio-moral hiatus between the family and Jefferson. Benjy's behavior is a constant trial to the family and to this extent counterpoints Caddy's lone disgracing act. Both challenge the family's capacity for understanding and forgiveness and the family fails both.

—OLGA W. VICKERY, "Worlds in Counterpoint: *The Sound and the Fury,*"
The Novels of William Faulkner: A Critical Interpretation (Baton Rouge:
Louisiana State University Press, 1959; rev. ed. 1964),
pp. 28–29, 35–37, 48

JOHN W. HUNT

Caddy's failure is not from sheer perversity; she fails in Quentin's terms, not her own. Her experiments in sex are "natural," if foolish. She is capable of compassion and love, as her relationship with Benjy and her love for Dalton Ames illustrate. The pathetic irony of Quentin's situation comes from his incapacity, not hers. She is capable—or was before he corrupted her—of the natural power and fertility of the matriarch. Caddy actually functions as a mother to Benjy. When, during Quentin's second phase, she succumbs to his rationalistic moralism, she divests herself of that sovereignty essential to the matriarch—the sovereignty above the rules. Quentin's agony, arising from his myopic moralism, is heightened by the fact that he has not only a promiscuous sister, but also a sister who will not admit, does not know, and cannot believe that her promiscuity involves anything more than a private and personal doom.

Although only with reference to Caddy can he bring his inherited and present worlds together, Caddy is constitutionally incapable of helping him. Only in the second phase of his private struggle does she begin to share his horror of sex and admit to being sick in a fairly deep sense: *"There was something terrible in me sometimes at night I could see it grinning at me I could see it through them grinning at me,"* and *"But now I know I'm dead I tell you."* Prior to his moralistic taunting, she is innocent; she really loves Dalton Ames: "yes I hate him I would die for him I've already died for him I die for him over and over again." Initially, she is only disquieted in the presence of Quentin because she does love in him even that "inflexible corruptless judge of what he considered the family's honor and its doom," and pities his incapacity to enjoy sexual experience: "poor Quentin . . . youve never done that have you . . . that what I have what I did." In the presence of Benjy, however, she feels judged by what in his blundering way is a forgiving love.

—JOHN W. HUNT, "The Locus and Status of Meaning," *William Faulkner:
Art in Theological Tension* (Syracuse: Syracuse University Press,
1965), pp. 57–58

JACKSON J. BENSON

The crucial relationship between Caddy and Quentin in Faulkner's *The Sound and the Fury* has been commonly misinterpreted. Most conspicuously, both Lawrance Thompson ("Mirror Analogues in *The Sound and the Fury*," *William Faulkner: Three Decades of Criticism,* ed. Frederick J. Hoffman and Olga Vickery, New York, 1963, p. 221) and Peter Swiggart (*The Art of Faulkner's Novels,* Austin, 1962, p. 93) hold Quentin "largely responsible" for Caddy's destruction. In this, I think they misread rather badly several major aspects of the novel, namely, Caddy's and Quentin's characters, and the relationship between the two. Faulkner makes it quite clear that Caddy was "doomed and knew it, accepted the doom without either seeking or fleeing it" (p. 412, the new Vintage edition). What causes Caddy's damnation is not nearly so clear as the fact that her doom is Quentin's undoing. Caddy's destruction is pictured throughout the novel as a compulsive self-destruction, and the scenes in which Quentin is pictured censuring his sister for her behavior (which both Thompson and Swiggart cite) prove nothing if they do not prove Caddy's will to persist in her behavior regardless of anything that Quentin can say or do. "That bitter prophet," as Faulkner calls Quentin, can only suffer in response to events that he can foretell, but never change or alter. The charge that Quentin's puritanism, acting to inflict his sense of guilt on his sister, changes her behavior and makes her feel guilty and thus self-destructive is not supported by the text. As a matter of fact, the major instances wherein Caddy displays guilt are in response to *Benjy's* reactions to her change of "smell"; her reactions to Quentin, on the other hand, vary from indulgence to a little brother (who is actually older), to indifference, to anger—she tells him at one point to go to hell.

The charge of Quentin's responsibility also fails to take into account the obvious differences in their personalities. The picture in the story book (p. 215) of "a dark place into which a single weak ray of light came slanting upon two faces lifted out of the shadow" and the reactions of Caddy and Quentin to this "thematic apperception test" tells as well as anything the difference between the two. Indicative of her personality, Caddy's reaction is strong, assertive, and masculine—she was "never a queen or a fairy she was always a king or a giant or a general." In response to the picture, she would "break that place open and drag them out and . . . whip them good." Whereas Quentin's reaction is a kind of prophetic epiphany (he is a small child when he first notices the picture), an exercise of poetic imagination, passive and brooding: he would turn back again and again to the picture until "the dungeon was Mother herself she and Father upward into the weak light holding hands and us lost somewhere below them without even a ray of light." The passage suggests that both children are lost by lacking the parents who are locked away forever in the prison of their self-concern: the mother, in her status-seeking self-ishness, and the father, in his cynical and verbose pessimism, and both in their self-pity. Caddy characteristically acts, both in her reaction to the picture and in her actual relationships to Quentin and Benjy, by assuming the role of parent. Quentin characteristically reacts, assuming, with a mind and emotions already structured by

Calvinism, Southern legends, and Romantic literature, an hereditary guilt implied in the family's condition. Even as a small child, Quentin accurately predicts the family's doom, but it is too much to say that, in light of the personalities involved, he causes it to happen.

—JACKSON J. BENSON, "Quentin's Responsibility for Caddy's Downfall in Faulkner's *The Sound and the Fury*," *Notes on Mississippi Writers* 5, No. 2 (Fall 1972): 63–64

MIMI REISEL GLADSTEIN

In *The Sound and the Fury* it is the cynical Mr. Compson who voices the connection between women and nature. He tries to explain to Quentin that the loss of Caddy's virginity is inevitable. "Father said 'Women are never virgins. Purity is a negative state and therefore contrary to nature.'" Caddy's sexuality is not contrary to nature. It is the rigidity, the "unnatural" standards of the Compson family that drive Caddy away and deprive the family of her loving and giving character. Caddy is a natural woman, responding to her sexual urges, doing her part in the procreation of the species. When the Compson inability to accept Caddy's actions drives her away, the family is left in the hands of two "unnatural" characters, Mrs. Compson and Jason. Mrs. Compson is the antithesis of a "natural" mother for she cannot or does not love her children; Jason is the "unnatural" man, one who does not propagate. In the hands of these unnatural creatures, the line would die out. Only through Caddy and then her daughter can nature assure the continuation of the line.

Whereas Mr. Compson's connection of women and nature is a philosophical one, Benjy must rely on his sense of smell to fuse Caddy with nature. For Benjy, Caddy's natural smell is like leaves and trees. His reactions are not complicated; his perception of her connection to nature is straightforward. "Caddy knelt and put her arms around me and her cold bright face against mine. She smelled like trees." The tree motif is an interesting one. Sally R. Page suggests that "Since Caddy is primarily 'mother' to Benjy, it is probable that the 'tree' motif in *The Sound and the Fury* is meant to suggest that Caddy is a 'mother of life' figure." Walter Brylowski notes Faulkner's connection of trees with virginal girls, not with mother figures. Such a connection would be more in keeping with a number of traditional myths in which chaste young nymphs are turned into trees, or flowers, or springs rather than be seduced by some lustful god, such as the story of the independent, love-and-marriage-hating young huntress Daphne, who turns into a laurel rather than submit to Apollo. In *The Sound and the Fury* Caddy is associated with tree smells as long as she is virginal. When she puts on perfume to attract the boys, when she is in the swing with Charlie, and when she has had her first complete sexual experience, Benjy immediately notices the difference in her smell. She no longer smells like trees.

The tree as a symbol for Caddy is reinforced by the fact that the two dominant images of the novel have to do with trees. Faulkner stated that the book "began with the picture of the little girl's muddy drawers, climbing that tree to look in the parlor window with her brothers that didn't have the courage to climb the tree waiting to see what she saw." In most of the critical discussion which is part of what Eric Sundquist calls "The Myth of *The Sound and the Fury,*" attention has been focused on the muddy drawers, which are very important, but to the exclusion of the tree. The tree, however, is a crucial component of this image. In that scene, which Faulkner saw as his impetus for writing the book, the tree serves as Caddy's passageway to an encounter with the realities of existence, one of which is death. Caddy is courageous enough to accept this reality as well as its opposite, which is her sexuality. A tree (the cedar) is also associated with her first exploration of the male/female relationship. In that situation, and quite appropriately, the smell of honeysuckle is intermingled with the smell of trees. In his imagery Faulkner is moving from the chaste connections of tree symbolism to the erotic connotations of flower symbolism. Quentin's perceptions of Caddy are infused with flower and tree smells. In his attempt to substitute himself for Caddy's male companions he says, "It was me you thought I was in the house where that damn honey suckle trying not to think the swing the cedars the secret surges the breathing locked drinking the wild breath tHE YES YES YES YES."

Another important tree that is used as a passage to experience is the tree that Caddy's daughter, Quentin II, uses to escape from Jason. The tree is also Quentin II's vehicle for the fulfillment of her sexuality as it is used for all her rendezvous. When Luster is asked about her beaux, he replies, "They comes every night she can climb down that tree." Significantly, the tree that Quentin II uses for her escape from the Compsons is a blossoming pear tree: "The window was open. A pear tree grew there, close against the house. It was in bloom and the branches scraped and rasped against the house and the myriad air, driving in the window, brought into the room the forlorn scent of the blossoms." The suggestion of fruitfulness is implicit and the scent of the blossoms suggests Quentin II's sexuality. The tree also suggests continuity and female cycles as it is quite possibly the same pear tree Caddy, her mother, used to witness the death of her grandmother.

Besides the tree imagery that is associated with Caddy, both Quentin and Benjy also relate her to water. The association of woman with water is an ancient one and basic in female symbology. Another characteristic of this same symbology is the identification of woman as vessel. She is the vessel man goes "into," the vessel for carrying and bringing forth the child, the vessel for milk to feed the child. The natural elements that are essentially connected with vessel symbolism include both earth and water. The water is of various types: one is the containing water which is the primordial womb of life from which in innumerable myths life is born. But the waters of the female are not only the maternal waters that contain (amniotic fluid), but also the waters of nourishment (milk), since all living things build up or preserve their existence with the water or milk of the earth. Thus water can be symbolically related to the breast as well as the womb and the rain and the earth waters (springs, lakes, ponds) are as the milk of the earth body. The association of woman with milk-producing animals, especially the cow, is one that Faulkner uses frequently. As Lederer explains: "In the mythological apperception of early man, breast and milk and rain; and woman and cow and earth and spring and stream belong together: the ground water belonged to the belly-womb region, the heavenly rain to the breast region of the Feminine." Faulkner uses these connections when he describes Dilsey, who is surrogate mother and nourisher of the Compson family. He says that she "stood like a cow in the rain."

But to return to the association of Caddy with water, just the suggestion of water is enough to make Benjy's mind immediately travel to memories of Caddy splashing in the branch. After much splashing and playing, and Caddy teasing with threats to run away, she reassures Benjy that she will not. Caddy in this role, both virginal and nurturant, smells a special way to Benjy: "Caddy smelled like trees in the rain."

Quentin's association of Caddy with water is more complex. One of Quentin's problems is that he feels that he has had no mother. Mrs. Compson has abdicated her maternal role. He is very conscious of this loss. "If I could say Mother. Mother," and "if I'd just had a mother so I could say Mother Mother" are his cries. Since he has been rejected by his mother, he fastens his needs onto the person of his sister, who attempts to be surrogate mother to all the boys because "Mother's sick. She and Damuddy are both sick." Mother's "sickness" is passed on to the family and Quentin must attempt a "sick" method of replacing his mother. His desire to isolate his sister from the natural processes of life takes the form of an invented incest. He does not want to mature and he does not want her to. He wants to regress, in effect, to return to the womb. By his suicide he does just that; he returns to the water. Jung has described the desire for drowning as a desire to be reabsorbed into the mother, a death which is "a deep personal longing for quiet and for the profound peace of non-existence, for dreamless sleep in the ebb and flow of the sea of life." By the act of drowning himself, Quentin can metaphorically have both the mother he never had and the sister he wanted. 〈. . .〉

The association of primitive sexuality with both women and Negroes is present in *The Sound and the Fury* as well as in *Light in August.* Quentin connects Caddy's sexual habits with dark woods, ditches, and pastures. Interestingly enough, most of the natural or indestructible females in Faulkner who have not kept to their chaste and cold marble pedestals give in to their natural appetites in the out-of-doors. Lena Grove climbs out a window to meet Lucas Burch; Caddy and Quentin II both climb out of windows to meet their beaux; Eula Varner and Hoake McCarron mate in the middle of a road in a thicket by a creek bridge; Dewey Dell and Addie Bundren also choose the woods for their illicit relationships. This lends to the relationships a more natural or primitive flavor; it is also more animalistic. Quentin makes the connection between race and sexuality when he asks Caddy, "Why dont you bring him to the house, Caddy? Why must you do like nigger women do in the pasture the ditches the dark woods hot hidden furious in the dark woods." Though he is Quentin's psychological opposite, Jason uses similar terms to describe Caddy's daughter Quentin's sexual behavior. Jason accuses her of "going on like a nigger wench." He threatens her: "When people act like niggers, no matter who they are the only thing to do is treat them like a nigger." 〈. . .〉

"Mongrelization" is a word used by racists to conjure up the horrors of integration. Properly applied the word refers to dogs and other animals, and this is precisely the image the racist has of Negro women. They are found sexually attractive and repugnant, but not in terms of human females, but as she-dogs. Faulkner's characters use similar imagery to describe natural women. Both Caddy and Quentin II are called "bitches" by Jason; their canine qualities are emphasized in their descriptions. Quentin II is described as having "eyes hard as a fice dog's." Caddy's face is described in terms that suggest a cur baring its teeth. When she gets angry, her upper lip begins to jump. "Everytime it jumped it would leave a little more of her teeth showing, and all the time she'd be as still as a post, not a muscle moving except her lip jerking higher and higher up her teeth." Like the Negro of the myth, Caddy and Quentin II respond openly and hungrily to their natural urges, a response neither Jason nor Quentin can affect. Their carnal qualities differentiate them from the white males.

Many of Faulkner's indestructible females follow in the same pattern as the mythical Negro woman, who according to the myth of Negro sexhood "is endowed with irresistible sexual attraction and enjoys the sex act more than any creature on earth." Temple Drake ⟨in *Sanctuary*⟩ is pictured, after being raped, as sexually insatiable. She leans her thighs against Popeye's shoulder, caressing his arm with her flanks, rubbing against him and pleading, "Give it to me. Daddy. Daddy. Give it to me, Daddy." A few minutes later with Red, she writhes her loins against him, making a whimpering sound. Her description of her sexual state as she begs Red to have intercourse with her are a direct reference to "heat," like a dog in the estrus cycle. She says, "Please. Please. Please. Dont make me wait. I'm burning up. I'm on fire, I tell you." In *The Sound and the Fury* Caddy's description of her reaction to her sexual relationships shows her passionate nature. Quentin asks her, "Did you love them Caddy did you love them" and her answer is, "When they touched me I died." Quentin tries to believe that Caddy was forced, especially by Dalton Ames, her first sexual partner, but Caddy's answer to his questions of "do you love him" and then "you hate him dont you" is to take Quentin's hand and press it against her chest where her heart is thudding and then against her throat where her heart is hammering in her throat. When Quentin says the name Dalton Ames, he can feel Caddy's blood react; "her blood surged steadily beating and beating against my hand." The image of Caddy is that of a woman at the mercy of her physical urges.

—MIMI REISEL GLADSTEIN, "Faulkner," *The Indestructible Woman in Faulkner, Hemingway, and Steinbeck* [1973] (Ann Arbor, MI: UMI Research Press, 1986), pp. 13–16, 19–21

JOHN L. LONGLEY, JR.

A large body of commentary on *The Sound and the Fury* is in print; some of it very helpful; some not. My own feeling is that the reader should bypass most of it in favor of the novel itself. How can this be done? How much must one know to begin with before he can proceed? Minimally, the reader should know the what and how—what the novel is about and how it works. The subject-matter is the death of a family and the corresponding decay of a society. More narrowly, the novel is about the various Compsons—parents and children, brothers and sisters— and how they are able or not able to love each other, and how the failure of love destroys them all. The central focus is the beautiful and doomed Candace Compson. We never see her full-face or hear her speak in her own *persona*. She lives for us only in the tortured and highly subjective recollection of her three brothers: Benjy, the congenital idiot; Quentin, the moral abstractionist and suicide; Jason, the sociopath who lives only for money ("who to me represented pure evil. He's the most vicious character in my opinion I ever thought of.") ⟨. . .⟩

At the point in her life when she is old enough to turn away from father and brother, and begin courtship, she finds she has nowhere to turn. There is literally no one to help her, certainly not among the jellybeans and town squirts of her adolescence. When she meets a man in Dalton Ames, she does not know how to resist him. Ames is the ultimate *macho:* handsome, powerful, violent, and totally amoral. When Quentin confronts him, and orders him to leave town, Ames is able to subdue him literally with one hand.

Foreshadowing the fate of her daughter, Caddy is driven to nymphomania by the hysterical posturings of her mother and the increasing pressure from Quentin. When Caddy was about fourteen, she was caught kissing a town boy. For three days Caroline Compson walks around the house wearing a black veil and declaring her daughter is dead. She attempts to spy on Caddy's movements, until Mr. Compson forbids it.

Already pregnant, Caddy accompanies her mother to the spa at French Lick. She returns, engaged to marry Herbert Head. One may only imagine the emotional process she has gone through; the forces that have pushed her into marriage with someone like Head, a man who has been expelled from Harvard for cheating at cards and on examinations. He is vulgar, loud, and falsely hearty. On Caddy's wedding day, T.P. finds the champagne for the reception stored in the basement, begins drinking it and giving it to Benjy. Benjy begins to bellow, and the result is pandemonium.

When Head discovers Caddy is pregnant, he divorces her. When her daughter is born, Caddy names her Quentin, for the brother who is now dead by his own hand. Mrs. Compson agrees that the family will take the child and raise it. With the weight of community mores heavily on her side, together with her own hysterics, she is able to impose these conditions: 1) Caddy shall never enter the house again; 2) never see her child again; 3) her name shall never be mentioned to the child.

Occasionally, Mr. Compson will violate this heartless pact by letting Caddy into the house to see her baby. After he is dead, Jason is the remaining competent male Compson, and he enforces the pact even more brutally, including the episode of the hundred dollars and the momentary look at the baby. After Quentin reaches adolescence, takes Jason's accumulated money, and runs away with the showman,

Caddy's last viable link with the Compson house is gone. We have one more glimpse of her in a picture magazine, as the mistress of a Nazi *Stabsgeneral*. The librarian believes the woman in the picture is Caddy; Jason does not. Dilsey will not say. Perhaps it is; perhaps not.

This, in brief, is the life of Candace Compson. Whatever else, that life is the central definitive presence in the lives of her brothers. She is an obsession with each of them, but in different ways. ⟨. . .⟩

Benjy loved three things: firelight, his sister Caddy, and the pasture that was sold to pay for Quentin's year at Harvard and Caddy's fancy wedding. His mental retardation is severe; he cannot speak at all. Yet, he is sensitive to color, light and dark, heat and cold, and above all, smells. He has emotions, and responds to the slightest shift in what he is used to. He hates and fears change, and bellows with outrage and terror at any upset in his routines. He whimpers when he is unhappy. Chronology is beyond him; he cannot distinguish *then* from *now*. All time is the same to him; a sort of continuous present in which he does not know his memories are only memories. Thus he cannot ". . . remember his sister but only the loss of her, and firelight was the same bright shape as going to sleep, and the pasture was even better sold than before because now he and TP could not only follow timeless along the fence the motions which it did not even matter to him were humanbeings swinging golfsticks."

Dilsey takes care of him, and Caddy is his champion and defender when they are little. It is to Caddy and only Caddy that he looks for emotional support ("You're not a poor baby. Are you"). He relies on her to bring him the physical objects that have a quieting effect on him—the paper dolls and the box of tinsel stars. As Caddy grows up, many things become disturbing to Benjy: her interest in boys, her use of perfume, the change to long dresses.

"Benjy." she said, "What is it, Benjy. What has Caddy done."

"He dont like that prissy dress." Jason said. "You think you're grown up, dont you. You think you're better than anybody else, dont you. Prissy."

"You shut your mouth." Caddy said, "You dirty little beast. Benjy . . . Hush, Benjy. You'll disturb Mother. Hush."

But I didn't hush, and when she went away I followed, and she stopped on the stairs and waited and I stopped too . . .

I listened to the water.

I couldn't hear the water, and Caddy opened the door.

"Why, Benjy." she said. She looked at me and I went and she put her arms around me. "Did you find Caddy again." she said. "Did you think Caddy had run away." Caddy smelled like trees.

We went to Caddy's room. She sat down at the mirror. She stopped her hands and looked at me.

"Why, Benjy. What is it." she said. "You mustn't cry. Caddy's not going away. See here." she said. She took up the bottle and took the stopper out and held it to my nose. "Sweet. Smell. Good."

I went away and I didn't hush, and she held the bottle in her hand, looking at me.

"Oh." she said. She put the bottle down and came and put her arms around me. "So that was it. And you were trying to tell Caddy and you couldn't tell her. You wanted to, but you couldn't, could you. Of course Caddy wont. Of course Caddy wont. Just wait till I dress."

Caddy dressed and took up the bottle again and we went down to the kitchen.

"Dilsey." Caddy said, "Benjy's got a present for you." She stooped down and put the bottle in my hand. "Hold it out to Dilsey now." Caddy held my hand out and Dilsey took the bottle.

"Well I'll declare." Dilsey said, "If my baby aint give Dilsey a bottle of perfume. Just look here, Roskus."

Caddy smelled like trees. "We dont like perfume ourselves." Caddy said.
She smelled like trees.

In one highly symbolic scene (which will be repeated many years later with Caddy's daughter), Caddy is sitting in the swing in the yard with one of the town jellybeans. We can only speculate how far Caddy's sexual experimentation has gone at this point, nor do we know what sensory means Benjy used to know of it, but know he does.

It was two now, and then one in the swing. Caddy came fast, white in the darkness.

"Benjy," she said. "How did you slip out. Where's Versh."

She put her arms around me and I hushed and held to her dress and tried to pull her away.

"Why, Benjy." she said. "What is it. T.P." she called.

The one in the swing got up and came, and I cried and pulled Caddy's dress.

"Benjy." Caddy said. "It's just Charlie. Dont you know Charlie."

"Where's his nigger." Charlie said. "What do they let him runaround loose for."

"Hush, Benjy." Caddy said. "Go away, Charlie. He doesn't like you." Charlie went away and I hushed. I pulled at Caddy's dress . . .

Caddy and I ran. We ran up the kitchen steps, onto the porch, and Caddy knelt down in the dark and held me. I could hear her and feel her chest. "I wont." she said. "I wont anymore, ever. Benjy. Benjy." The she was crying, and I cried, and we held each other. "Hush." she said. "Hush. I wont anymore." So I hushed and Caddy got up and we went into the kitchen and turned the light on and Caddy took the kitchen soap and washed her mouth at the sink, hard. Caddy smelled like trees.

But the day comes when Caddy can no longer simply wash off her lipstick or perfume, or a jellybean's kisses. On her wedding day, Benjy is deeply distressed by the furious activity he cannot understand. He telescopes what is happening back into the night of Damuddy's funeral, when Caddy in her muddy drawers climbed the tree to look in the window. Now he is big enough to see into the window for himself. *I saw them. Then I saw Caddy, with flowers in her hair, and a long veil like shining wind. Caddy Caddy.* Then it is night and the reception is being held. No doubt T.P. has been ordered to keep Benjy away from the festivities. They creep into the cellar, where T.P. has found the cases of champagne. He drinks and Benjy drinks. They both are soon very drunk. T.P. yells and Benjy bellows his grief and loneliness. He tries to climb out of the cellar and onto the box to see in the window again. They are both too drunk to stand up.

> "Hush up." T.P. said, trying not to laugh, "Lawd, they'll all hear us. Get up." T.P. said, "Get up, Benjy, quick." He was thrashing about and laughing and I tried to get up . . . T.P. ran behind me saying "Hush up hush up" Then he fell into the flowers, laughing, and I ran into the box. But when I tried to climb onto it it jumped away and hit me on the back of the head and my throat made a sound. It made the sound again and I stopped trying to get up, and it made the sound again and I began to cry. But my throat kept on making the sound while T.P. was pulling me. It kept on making it and I couldn't tell if I was crying or not, and T.P. fell down on top of me, laughing, and it kept on making the sound and Quentin kicked T.P. and Cad put her arms around me, and her shining veil, and I couldn't smell trees anymore and I began to cry.

Sometime after that, we may assume, Caddy goes away on her honeymoon. From here on, Benjy will not have a sister; only the loss of her to remember. What can we say of him; his child-like nature, his man's body, and his eyes empty and blue and serene? Benjy is, as Ratliff once said of another unfortunate, ". . . something that dont want nothing but to walk and feel the sun and wouldn't know how to hurt no man even if it would and wouldn't want to even if it could . . ."

—JOHN L. LONGLEY, JR., " 'Who Never Had a Sister': A Reading of *The Sound and the Fury*," *The Novels of William Faulkner*, ed. R. G. Collins and Kenneth McRobbie (Winnipeg: University of Manitoba Press, 1973), pp. 36–37, 39–42

DOUGLAS MESSERLI

I see Caddy as motivator of the action in the novel, but more importantly, I see her as dynamism itself. As Faulkner stresses time and again, *The Sound and the Fury* "began with the picture of the little girl's muddy drawers, climbing that tree to look in the parlor window with her brothers that didn't have the courage to climb the tree waiting to see what she saw"; "It is a tragedy of two lost women: Caddy and her daughter"; "I was just trying to tell a story of Caddy, the little girl who had muddied her drawers and was climbing up to look in the window where her grandmother lay dead."

What Caddy sees in that tree, of course, is death, and she recognizes through it that evil exists in the world. But the important thing here is not just that she recognizes the evil, but that she reacts to it. As Faulkner says of her in the appendix, she was "doomed and knew it, accepted the doom without either seeking it or fleeing." I believe that what Faulkner means by doom is suggested in the etymology of Ikketumbe's name: l'Homme, de l'homme, The Man, doom. In other words, doom is everyman's doom, death. As ⟨Eugène⟩ Minkowski says, "It is not in being born but in dying that one becomes a whole, a man." What I am saying is that Caddy in seeing death recognized her doom; as in the garden of Eden she gained the knowledge of herself, recognized that if that grandmother lying rigid on the bed was death, and that she who was still living was doomed to die, to become rigid, then life was not rigid, living was dynamic as opposed to this stasis of death.

The tragedy of the novel lies in the fact that her three brothers who did not have the courage to see what she saw, cannot understand Caddy's dynamism, her dynamic living and loving which is inevitably separated from them. It is not Dilsey who can stop Benjy's tears, but only Caddy's slipper which is for him the same as Caddy which is the same as love. Quentin tries to stop time in order to get back to his childhood with Caddy before her sexual maturity. It is not that Quentin is a Calvinist, but that Caddy's sexual maturing caused a rupture between him and Caddy; he could no longer be a child with her as the child-mother, loving him with what Faulkner implies in the appendix is an unconditional mother-type of love. As Aswell Duncan points out, Jason can no more free himself from his obsession with Caddy than Quentin and Benjy. Jason's ties with his real mother who is incapable of giving love put him in opposition to Caddy who is the only one who could have loved him. Thus, Jason grew up without love. As a result he can only hate; he is jealous of Quentin even in death, in a sense jealous of Benjy who cannot even understand love. His jealousy and hatred are vented simultaneously upon Quentin, Candace's daughter. Jason's meaningless chase after his niece is, perhaps, really a quest for love which can only be expressed in hatred. But since he does not really believe in love and has never known it; the search for love always becomes what Jason has replaced love with, a search for money. These motifs are inextricably combined when Quentin steals his money, and Jason's hatred is vindicated.

In other words, Caddy is the real force of the Compson decline. As Michel Gresset perceives, "Caddy works evil within the family because she objectively starts a process that will eventually prevent all members from living together on good terms ever again." The evil, however, is not in Caddy alone, but in the world, in change, in the fact that being alive is opposed to being dead. It is because of her brothers' inability to recognize or accept this that chaos is loosed upon them.

I am not at all concerned with viewing Caddy's later sexual exploits as a moral decline. In fact, one's condemnation of her relationships may only reinforce Faulkner's point. In pure dynamism, in becoming there is no morality. Only with the idea of death as perceived in the lived future can a morality exist, can ethical action have meaning. Caddy is without a future; she is total becoming moving further and further from its source. To demonstrate this more clearly Faulkner has Quentin repeat Caddy's action; the becoming is perpetuated.

But how does this relate to Dilsey? In the appendix Faulkner relates a later incident concerning Caddy. Melissa Meek, the town librarian, discovers a picture in a magazine of Caddy, "ageless and beautiful, cold, serene and damned," standing beside a German staff general. She takes the picture to Memphis to show Dilsey. Dilsey claims that her eyes are not good anymore, but Melissa believes, ". . . she didn't want to see it know whether it was Caddy or not because she knows Caddy doesn't want to be saved hasn't anything anymore worth being saved for nothing worth being lost that she can lose[.]"

One can interpret this event in two ways: either one can disbelieve Melissa's opinion and see Dilsey as a nearly blind old woman, her eyes closed to life because they are upon death; or one can accept Melissa's statement and see in Dilsey's refusal to see Caddy a recognition of the tragedy of the human condition. What I am suggesting in the second interpretation is that Dilsey recognizes Caddy as the force of life, forever changing and flowing toward the doom which is the individual's death. For Dilsey it is painful as is all expectation. Dilsey's life has been a life of work to make that becoming, that raw and dynamic force, into something meaningful. The need for this she has recognized in the lived future. But upon the force of life itself her ethical acts can have no meaning; they are important only as they make life stable, make life able to be endured; but they cannot stop becoming. To Dilsey pure becoming is an almost Satanic force, a force she has recognized in Caddy from the night Caddy climbed into the tree. It is because of that force and its effects upon Caddy's brothers that Dilsey's love and sacrifice have had no visible effect. This is not to say that ethical actions have no effect on other men. All actions, ethical or not, affect. To Faulkner every act has ramifications throughout the world because man is fused with humanity whether he comes to recognize it or not.

But no act can stop life. Man can transcend it through lived experience, through the lived future; he can even carry within him the idea of "after death," but becoming and its inevitable end, death, cannot be stayed. Essentially, this is what Caddy perceived or saw that night of her grandmother's death. And seeing it she gave herself totally up to a life which *ends* with death.

Caddy has nothing "worth being saved . . . nothing she can lose" because becoming can have no possessive quality; it only persists. It is only in the lived future that the idea of being saved can have any meaning. Caddy is not good; Dilsey is good. But Caddy is beautiful; she is terrifyingly beautiful.

Dilsey's life does have meaning: she is Faulkner's moral order, representative of all the potentialities of man, of man's capacity to endure and prevail. Caddy in her pure dynamism, in pure becoming is life itself without human order. She is the link between all of the characters who struggle in all of their various attempts to order. *The Sound and the Fury* is, then, a novel about time and the way four people experience it.

—DOUGLAS MESSERLI, "The Problem of Time in *The Sound and the Fury:* A Critical Reassessment and Reinterpretation," *Southern Literary Journal* 6, No. 2 (Spring 1974): 37–41

MICHAEL J. AUER

To date, the only published speculation on the source and meaning of the name "Candace" in *The Sound and the Fury* is that of Joseph M. Backus in "Names of Characters in Faulkner's *The Sound and the Fury*" (*Names,* 6 [1958], 226–33). In this article, Backus suggests that the name has a deeper significance for the novel than that of merely providing the nickname "Caddy" (a nickname highly useful, of course, in Benjy's section of the novel), for the combination of the name "Candace" and the incestuous relationship between brother and sister in this work, according to Backus, "recalls specifically Ovid's *Heroides* (Epistle XI) and the incestuous relationship there involving a sister named 'Canace'" (p. 228).

To the obvious objection that "Canace" is not "Candace," the author answers that "in literature, the two similar names have been used interchangeably at least since the time of Chaucer; and Chaucer's annotators have not neglected to call this confusion to the attention of modern readers" (p. 228). And the author concludes his remarks on the subject by saying that "thus Faulkner, through even a casual acquaintance with Chaucer, could have become aware of the significance of 'Canace' and the historic misapplication of 'Candace.' In any case, his choice of a name that is only suggestive of incest, rather than one that is obviously associated with it, is consistent with his usual subtlety—particularly in the introduction of an incestuous relationship into *The Sound and the Fury*" (p. 228).

While it is not impossible that the sources Backus cites for the name of the "heroine" in *The Sound and the Fury*—Ovid and Chaucer—did occur to Faulkner when he created the figure of Caddy Compson, I would like to suggest a much more direct and accessible source, a source which bears unexpected significance for Benjy as well as for Candace, namely, the Acts of the Apostles, 8:26–40. The passage relates the story of Philip and the Ethiopian eunuch. Verses 26–33 are especially interesting to the reader of *The Sound and the Fury:*

> And the angel of the Lord spake unto Philip, saying, Arise, and go toward the south, unto the way that goeth down from Jerusalem unto Gaza, which is desert. And he arose and went: and, behold, a man of Ethiopia, a eunuch of great authority under Candace queen of the Ethiopians, who had the charge of all her treasure, and had come to Jerusalem for to worship, Was returning, and sitting in his chariot read Esaias the prophet. Then the Spirit said unto Philip, Go near, and join thyself to this chariot. And Philip ran thither to him, and heard him read the prophet Esaias, and said, Understandest thou what thou readest? And he said, How can I, except some man should guide me?

And he desired Philip that he would come up and sit with him. The place of the scripture which he read was this, He was led as a sheep to the slaughter; and like a lamb dumb before his shearer, so opened he not his mouth: In his humiliation his judgment was taken away: and who shall declare his generation? for his life is taken from the earth (King James Version).

The claim for this passage to be the direct source of the name "Candace" is, assuredly, much stronger than those of Ovid and Chaucer, though these latter may well be indirect sources which add new reverberations of meaning, and especially the overtones of incest, as Backus contends.

Relevant though the passage certainly is to Candace, it is more significant yet in regard to Benjy. Like the Ethiopian official, Benjy is a eunuch. Like the Ethiopian who "had the charge of all [the Queen's] treasure," Benjy in some mysterious way has charge of all Caddy's treasure; he knows instinctively, for example, when she loses her virginity. A final insight which this passage from Acts affords us is the applicability of the text from Isaiah which the Ethiopian is reading to Benjy himself, and thus the strengthening of the association of Christ imagery with Benjy which critics of the novel have found in past years; like Christ (to whom Philip applies the quotation in his discourse with the eunuch), Benjy "was led as a sheep to the slaughter; and like a lamb dumb before his shearer, so opened he not his mouth."

Over forty years of criticism have overlooked this scriptural passage and the obvious importance it bears to *The Sound and the Fury*. Perhaps other, equally meaningful though heretofore ignored, biblical allusions can be found in this masterpiece.

—MICHAEL J. AUER, "Caddy, Benjy, and the Acts of the Apostles:
A Note on *The Sound and the Fury*," *Studies in the Novel* 6, No. 4
(Winter 1974): 475–76

BOYD DAVIS

The Demeter-Persephone/Proserpine motif is ⟨. . .⟩ a key element in *Sanctuary*, according to Thomas L. McHaney, whose close reading also offers parallels between motifs and scenes from the novel and Sir James Frazer's compendium of myth, *The Golden Bough*. McHaney adds that *The Sound and the Fury* uses the Demeter-Persephone material as well as elements of the myths about Isis-Osiris.

One element of the story of the abduction of Proserpine is the desire of Pluto to possess her, thereby perhaps to control her fecundity according to his rules in dark Hades. *The Sound and the Fury* charts various desires to possess Caddy Compson, a brave, doomed, muddied little girl who once climbed a tree and whose daughter, forsaken and victimized, climbed down it.

In *Faulkner's Olympian Laugh*, Walter Brylowski draws on Faulkner's use of the tree image from the context of classical mythology, adding that in *The Sound and the Fury*, the image expands to focus on and reveal "the mythic approach to the problem of evil." Brylowski interprets Faulkner's comments about Caddy to mean that the work was to focus on Caddy and Eden. However, adds Brylowski, "The image which ostensibly gave impetus to the story does not dominate it." While Caddy's tree may not be the dominant image, what happens in and with the tree is one of the key structural and symbolic elements of the novel. The single image of a girl in a tree gradually accrues different perspectives throughout the four sections of the novel. The impact of the image is felt most at the beginning and at the ending; it is one of the unifying elements of the novel.

In Benjy's section, two separate images, each of a girl in a tree, are blended both literally and symbolically. When Caddy and later her daughter Quentin are in the tree, the movements of each cause the tree to shake. This shaking is imprinted on Benjy's consciousness. Even though the two events occur over two decades apart, Benjy associates them and reports them together. For the one event complements the other: Quentin's flight down the tree completes the doom prefigured by her mother's ascent. In section four, we are returned to the tree, framed now by the open window through which Quentin has escaped.

Images of Caddy and her daughter circle toward each other and coalesce in Benjy's section; their images flicker like the fire Quentin seeks and Benjy loves. Benjy reports movement; the reader "sees" Versh push Caddy up "to the first limb. We watched the muddy bottom of her drawers. Then we couldn't see her." With the children, we hear the tree thrash, then quiet down: "We looked up into the still branches." Images of separation and change intervene: Benjy sees Caddy at the wedding, cries out against her perfume, bellows at efforts to keep them apart at bedtime. Then he returns to Caddy in the tree. Our first glimpse of her ends and the second begins with the children looking up at the tree, and Frony's whispers: " 'What you seeing' "; " 'What she seeing, Versh.' " The branches thrash again, her legs appear, and Dilsey lifts her down. Benjy shifts to report on another scene of motion, Quentin in the swing with a man. Crying, Benjy sees the swingers blend and shifts to a previous time when Caddy was in the swing: "It was two now, and then one in the swing. Caddy came fast, white in the darkness." The image of Caddy washing her mouth fades back into that of her daughter's love-making in the swing; Benjy reports Luster's comment that Quentin sees other men: " 'They comes every night she can climb down that tree.' "

The movement of one girl triggers Benjy's memories of similar motion by the other. At the end of his section, Benjy and Luster look out the window: *"It came out of Quentin's window and climbed across into the tree. We watched the tree shaking. The shaking went down the tree, then it came out and we watched it go away across the grass."* As Quentin escapes—and they must be observing her from the rear—Benjy "sees" Dilsey scrubbing Caddy's bottom with the muddy drawers.

Throughout the Benjy section, Benjy reacts according to whether Caddy does, or does not, smell like trees. Scent plays an important role in the Quentin section, but this time, the odor is that of honeysuckle, which pervades his memories of Caddy in the water and the woods. He associates the smell of apple trees with Caddy's wedding and the song, "The voice that breathed o'er Eden"; he is an anguished Adonis unable to have the white Aphrodite for a consort, a king of

Hades incapable of taking Proserpine down to the dark kingdoms with him in person. Honeysuckle clings to his memories of his aborted effort to kill Caddy and his "sight" of her muddy drawers; it comes "up in damp waves" when he recalls Caddy's meeting with Dalton Ames and his subsequent fight in the woods with Ames. Reliving those moments, he finds the honeysuckle keeps getting into it; calling it "the saddest odour of all," he makes his final preparations for suicide. The tree around which he, like the honeysuckle, could twine is gone. ⟨...⟩

Unlike Chaucer's May, Caddy Compson does not climb up a tree in order to deceive. Caddy climbs up her tree to seek the knowledge of human relationships and experiences which her family tries to deny her any part in: love, death, sexuality, suffering and growth. Her climb, however, is seen negatively by her family; even Dilsey says "You, Satan . . . Come down from there" when she looks up into the tree and sees the branches shaking. The efforts at repression by the Compson family are rooted in a possessiveness which makes this Eden barren. For Faulkner's tree stands in an inverted paradise. Here, the waters are of death, not life, as they foreshadow Quentin's suicide; wet mud on Caddy's pants prefigures her courageous, if doomed, efforts to replace the negation of possession by the affirmation of love. Caddy's daughter Quentin is the final victim of Compson possessiveness. Rejected by her grandmother and uncle, she is unable to respond to Dilsey or to care for Benjy; she has no way to learn that love can be anything other than a physical act. Quentin does not climb up a tree of knowledge or of life; she can only climb down, reversing May's journey: first to meet men ("They comes every night she can climb down that tree") and then to carry away the gold Jason has fleeced from her in her final escape down the tree.

A lovely frozen moment occurs in the final section of the novel, as Jason realizes that the broken window in his room, and Quentin's absence from breakfast, are connected. Climbing the stairs to Quentin's room, he finds the window open: "A pear tree grew there, close against the house. It was in bloom and the branches scraped and rasped against the house and the myriad air, driving in the window, brought into the room the forlorn scent of the blossoms." With this tree, Dilsey's beginning becomes the ending; the coalescence of Caddy and Quentin, that Benjy unwittingly recorded earlier, is completed.

The falseness of the Compson Eden is ironically underscored by the final action of the novel. The tree-goddess has been dispossessed; prevented from growing to her role as Demeter, her association with the tree is now a negation. Caddy and her daughter are outside the barren garden, doomed to wander forever.

—BOYD DAVIS , "Caddy Compson's Eden," Mississippi Quarterly 30, No. 3
(Summer 1977): 388–91, 393–94

M. D. FABER

Faulkner lends structural emphasis to the all-determining role of the mother substitute. Caddy, sister of the Compson men, each of whom receives a "section" of the novel, does not receive a section of her own, for Caddy, in the deepest psychological sense, is *in* the men, in them as a structural link to the disastrous introjection of the mother. Caddy's role in the Compson family, Faulkner's structural design informs us, can only be grasped from the *inside,* from *within* the male characters. In this way, the novel's form gives dynamic support to theoretical notions concerning the formation and quality of the internal world, or the endopsychic *structure.* The novel is a formal, aesthetic *model* of object relations theory. To read of Benjy is to read of Caddy because Benjy and Caddy are, at one deep level, indistinguishable; and this, of course, applies as dramatically to Quentin. Jason is the psychological "brother" of his brothers in that his life is also bound up overwhelmingly with the maternal influence; but with Jason, it is the actual *mother* who remains at the center. True, Jason accomplishes fantasy transference to related female characters, the second Quentin, for example, constituting in Jason's mind both a split-off version of the forbidden object—the mother as seducer—and a link to Caddy through whom the original splitting of the maternal figure was furthered. Nevertheless, Jason remains bound in a fundamental way to the actual mother while Benjy and Quentin transfer their regressive questing to the maternal substitute, the sister. Among many other things, this means that Benjy and Quentin will relate to their inner presences in one dynamic fashion and Jason in another. ⟨. . .⟩

In his room at Harvard, and with his roommate, Shreve, Quentin, on the day during which his suicide will be accomplished, allows his thoughts to run on as follows:

> If it had been cloudy I could have looked at the window, thinking what he said about idle habits. Thinking it would be nice for them down at New London if the weather held up like this. Why shouldn't it? The month of brides, the voice that breathed *She ran right out of the mirror, out of the banked scent. Roses. Roses. Mr. and Mrs. Jason Richmond Compson announce the marriage of.* Roses. Not virgins like dogwood, milkweed. I said I have committed incest, Father I said. Roses. Cunning and serene. If you attend Harvard one year, but don't see the boat-race, there should be a refund.

The "she" who is "running right out of the mirror," is, of course, Caddy, and the fact that she does so immediately after the notion of "bride" has crossed Quentin's mind focuses what might be termed the "objective correlative" or the efficient cause of the reactivation Quentin experiences during the course of this section. Caddy's marriage he apprehends in an emotive context of loss and betrayal, an emotive context that engages deeply buried affect from the early time. As for the reference to "incest," and the implied confession of incest to father, a confession that is, incidentally, false, it focuses not only the intensity of the hero's cathexis to Caddy, but his need to expiate his incestuous proclivity through specious confession. For if Caddy is a link to *mother,* then Quentin, in his incestuous bent, is ultimately the betrayer of *father and mother.* To confess incestuous contact with Caddy *as if* it were not, at the deepest level, contact with mother is to anticipate and finally *to obviate* retaliation from the conscience by *denying* the central object of the drive. That Quentin tells his father a similar story on a number of occasions supports this, of course; but there are further perspectives from which to grasp the young man's strategy. Briefly, if father were to punish Quentin for this incest, he would dispel the terrible retaliation Quentin fantasizes for the other incest. Nothing father might actually do in reality can equal what father is already doing in Quentin's unconscious. Again, were father to absolve the hero for his oedipal aim, Quentin would be able to employ such absolution as a placation of the paternal superego which stands in large measure behind the anticipation of punishment. At the level of secondary processes, he could stop worrying.

When we consider the hero's confessional strategy from the standpoint of unconscious processes, however, we recognize its essential futility. Even if father were to forgive, or punish, the hero would still be obliged to cope with the destructive internalizations of his inner world, particularly the maternal superego in its rejective, annihilative capacity. But father neither believes nor absolves. In fact, father does not appear especially *concerned* with what Quentin tells him, which reminds us that Quentin's confession is motivated to some degree by a desire simply to get a genuine fatherly (oedipal) response out of a father who has withdrawn from genuine emotive participation in the lives of his children. Quentin needs Mr. Compson to be father, to take control of a familial situation that grows ever more primitive and desperate.

When Quentin reiterates his confession of incest on a later page we gain further insight into the conflict. The "Ames" to whom he refers in this quotation is Caddy's first lover:

> If we could just have done something so dreadful that they would have fled hell except us. *I have committed incest I said Father it was not Dalton Ames.* And when he put Dalton Ames. Dalton Ames. Dalton Ames. When he put the pistol in my hand I didn't. That's why I didn't. He would be there and she would and I would. Dalton Ames. Dalton Ames. Dalton Ames. If we could have just done something so dreadful at all they cannot even remember tomorrow what seemed dreadful today and I said, You can shirk all things and he said, Ah can you.

Quentin, by claiming to be Caddy's lover—"It was I not Dalton Ames"—is simply denying the reality of what he takes to be the sister-mother's defection and betrayal and, in the process of making this denial, revealing his inability to apprehend Caddy's personal involvements outside the incestuous maternal context. In this way, Quentin announces, from the standpoint of his unconscious mentation, not only that it is better to confess incest with sister than to love under the threat of castration for incest with mother, but that it is better to confess incest and face retaliation than to *lose* the maternal object upon whom he depends. Again we recognize the fundamental problem that invariably stands behind incestuous proclivity, the problem of maternal betrayal and loss, the problem of unsatisfactory object relations between the mother and the child. In one deep sense, however, it *is* Quentin, along with Ames, who has intercourse with Caddy. So close, so psychically close, is the young man's relationship with his sister that he is able to participate, at the emotive, fantasy level, in her sexual encounters with others. Paradoxically, and to some extent homoerotically, when Ames penetrates Caddy he penetrates Quentin as well. And in addition to that, he allows Quentin to penetrate Caddy. Thus Quentin, in his unconscious, has not only committed incest with sister-mother, he has been violated by the powerful male. Of course such dynamic patterns or meanings "sound idiotic," or "don't make sense;" but that only calls Faulkner's title to mind, a title that reflects the author's recognition of the degree to which the "idiot" unconscious governs our behavior.

To stress Quentin's emotive, fantasy participation in Caddy's life is to stress Quentin's inability to see or to comprehend himself apart from the sister-mother. The hero is bound to the maternal substitute totally; her loss is apprehended as betrayal, annihilation, just as the infant apprehends annihilation and betrayal upon the loss of the mother. Which brings us to the analytic significance of Caddy "running out of the mirror." I mean that Quentin's fantasy measures, finally, *his inability to differentiate himself from the object. The symbolic mirror of his mind offers him the representation of another whose psychic presence in the hero's mentation is so real that he is precariously close to an objectification of mental entities.* It is as if Quentin and Caddy comprise, for Quentin, a single psychological unit, a unit which recalls the very early symbiotic relationship of mother and infant where *lack of differentiation* on the infant's part is the rule. We know, of course, that the ability to internalize the world, to form a symbolic world of external objects, depends largely upon a satisfactory mother-infant interaction. The breakdown of that ability is marked by an emotive regression to the early oral stage, and that is what we are witnessing here. In a very curious way that is captured in the mirror reference, Caddy has become a kind of *numinous double* of Quentin.

The traumatic reactivation that Quentin undergoes upon Caddy's "defection" to Ames and subsequent marriage to Herbert Head is dissimilar analytically to the powerful, traumatic reactivation that Hamlet undergoes upon Gertrude's "defection" and marriage, for Caddy's actions do not, as Gertrude's, catalyze the swift unrepressing of forbidden, incestuous urges toward the bad object. Indeed, Quentin has experienced those urges for some time. Her actions catalyze, rather, a sudden, stunning reawareness of emptiness, of the absence of narcissistic supplies, and an anxiety over the loss of one through whom such supplies are to be attained. The incestuous urges of Quentin *themselves* constitute at one deep-level—the deepest—his futile, impossible method of achieving symbiotic union with the longed-for good object. Which calls to mind one of the novel's principal ironies, one that can be characterized as an irony of the unconscious: The method by which Quentin would achieve union with the good object destroys the goodness of that object. This is, of course, but another way of saying that when Caddy succeeds to the role of mother substitute for Quentin she is fated to become in his unconscious, as mother is, *both* the succoring object and the alluring object. Because of the damage done him during his early interaction with the schizoid mother, there is no way for Quentin to successfully negotiate this paradox at the emotive level.

Caddy must be all things to all men, or better, all children. She must be Quentin's good object and Quentin's bad object; she must nourish and support him, and at the same time permit him to act-out, or attempt to work through, his incestuous fixation. And she must be Benjy's mother substitute, Benjy's good object, as well.

> —M. D. FABER, "Faulkner's *The Sound and the Fury:* Object Relations and Narrative Structure," *American Imago* 34, No. 4 (Winter 1977): 327–32

SUSAN GALLAGHER

The commitment that love implies often results in a struggle over priorities, involving questions of whether to put individuals or ideals first in one's actions. The brother/ sister pairs of Quentin and Caddy Compson and Henry and Judith Sutpen face this dilemma. Judith and Caddy evidence a selfless love of individuals despite traditional concepts of honor and ideals. Henry and Quentin both choose ideals, their concepts of honor, over concerns for individuals in a kind of love that is ultimately selfish. Quentin and Caddy each carry their personal decisions to an extreme. Their misuse of a potential quality results in self-destruction of each, and an evil is made out of an element of proper love. The story of Henry and Judith shows a more gradual progression. Over the course of events and through differing narrations we see them slowly developing toward their final decision of priority. The selfless love of Caddy and Judith is admirable to a point, but Caddy's story shows how destruction can result from a total disregard for ideals. These brother/ sister pairs demonstrate that it is never morally right to assert ideals of honor without a concern for individuals, but that those concepts are vital to human life and relationships.

Caddy Compson exhibits both the admirable aspects of selfless love and its potential for damnation if it is not properly curbed. Her character was frequently misunderstood by the critics of the 1950s and '60s, who overlooked both her giving love and her central role in the novel. Recent criticism has taken to glamorizing Caddy as a brave heroine who does no wrong, but deliberately rebels against a stifling society. Gladys Milliner's comment is representative of this approach: "Caddy, the unconventional Southern Woman, defies that tradition by becoming a mother, not through love or temptation, but deliberately to assert her sexual freedom and to escape conformity and eventually to escape the isolation of the Compson garden." Caddy is seen as a more tragic heroine by (Sally R.) Page and (David L.) Williams, who accuse the Compson family and its false codes of honor of destroying Caddy's natural capacity for love. These conceptions of Caddy as rebel and victim are shown to be fallacious by her own recognition of guilt and confession of responsibility: *"There was something terrible in me sometimes at night I could see it . . . through them grinning at me through their faces it's gone now and I'm sick."* As Catherine Baum points out, Caddy's admirable quality of selflessness manifests itself in her indifference to her virginity, and the world takes advantage of such selflessness.

The progression of Caddy's life reveals how easily selfless love can be distorted when it is not held in check by a moral concept. Her love took appropriate forms within the confines of her family, especially in her concern and care for Benjy. But when Caddy freely offered herself to Dalton Ames she violated a moral ideal in order to please an individual. When Dalton leaves town, she turns to many nameless faces in an attempt to blot out the anguish of her love for him. Even when the pregnant Caddy is packing to go to the salt licks to look for her husband, she apparently is still obsessed with Dalton; if she forgets him then all the talk will die away, Mrs. Compson believes. Caddy marries for the sake of her family, her love for them overpowering her knowledge that the marriage is morally wrong. She and Herbert are neither in love nor compatible, and have the disadvantage that she is pregnant with another man's child. She puts her love for her father and Benjy before the proper concept of marriage. This last act of selfless love completes her doom by relegating her to a socially bereft condition. Her family denies her, placing undue emphasis on conventions rather than personal love, and Caddy is left to shift for herself in an uncaring world, probably by unselfishly selling her body. By placing individual love over a moral code, Caddy has lost everything.

—SUSAN GALLAGHER, "Brothers and Sisters in Yoknapatawpha County,"
Essays in Literature 7, No. 2 (Fall 1980): 217–18

DAVID L. MINTER

To the end of his life, Faulkner spoke of Caddy with deep devotion. She was, he suggested, both the sister of his imagination and "the daughter of his mind." Born of his own discontent, she was for him "the beautiful one," his "heart's darling." It was Caddy, or more precisely, Faulkner's feelings for Caddy, that turned a story called "Twilight" into a novel called *The Sound and the Fury:* "I loved her so much," he said, that "I couldn't decide to give her life just for the duration of a short story. She deserved more than that. So my novel was created, almost in spite of myself." 〈...〉

Given the novel's technical brilliance, it is easy to forget how simple and moving its basic story is. In it we observe four children come of age amid the decay and dissolution of their family. His sense of it began, Faulkner recalled, with "a brother and a sister splashing one another in the brook" where they have been sent to play during the funeral of a grandmother they call Damuddy. From this scene came one of the central images of the novel—Caddy's muddy drawers. As she clambers up a tree outside the Compson home to observe the funeral inside, we and her brothers see her drawers from below. From this sequence, Faulkner got several things: his sense of the brook as "the dark, harsh flowing of time" that was sweeping Caddy away from her brothers; his sense that the girl who had the courage to climb the tree would also find the courage to face change and loss; and his sense that her brothers, who had waited below, would respond very differently—that Benjy would fail to understand his loss; that Quentin would seek oblivion rather than face his; and that Jason would meet his with terrible rage and ambition. The novel thus focuses not only on the three brothers Faulkner possessed when he began but also on Caddy, the figure he added to memory—which is to say, on the only child whose story he never directly told as well as on those whose stories he directly tells. His decision to approach Caddy only by indirection, through the eyes and needs and demands of her brothers, was in part technical; by the time he came to the fourth telling, he wanted a more public voice. In addition, he thought indirection more "passionate." It was, he said, more moving to present "the shadow of the branch, and let the mind create the tree."

But in fact Caddy grew as she is presented, by indirection—in response to needs and strategies shared by Faulkner and his characters. Having discovered Benjy, in whom he saw "the blind, self-centeredness of innocence, typified by children," Faulkner became "interested in the relationship of the idiot to the world that he was in but would never be able to cope with." What particularly agitated him was whether and where such a one as Benjy could "get the tenderness, the help, to shield him." The answer he hit upon had nothing to do with Mr. and Mrs. Compson, and only a little to do with Dilsey. Mr. Compson is a weak, nihilistic alcoholic who toys with the emotions and needs of his children. Even when he feels sympathy and compassion, he fails to show it effectively. Mrs. Compson is a cold, self-involved woman who expends her energies worrying about her ailments, complaining about her life, and clinging to her notions of respectability. "If I could say Mother. Mother," Quentin says to himself. Dilsey, who recalls Mammy Callie, epitomizes the kind of Christian Faulkner most admired. She is saved by a minimum of theology. Though her understanding is small, her wisdom and love are large. Living in the world of the Compsons, she commits herself to the immediate; she "does de bes" she can to fill the vacancies left in the lives of the children around her by their loveless and faithless parents. Since by virtue of her faith she is part of a larger world, she is able "to stand above the fallen ruins of the family." She has seen, she says, the first and the last. But Dilsey's life combines a measure of effective action with a measure of pathetic resignation. Most of Benjy's needs for tenderness and comfort, if not help and protection, he takes to his sister. And it was thus, Faulkner said, that "the character of his sister began to emerge." Like Benjy, Quentin and Jason also turn toward Caddy, seeking to find in her some way of meeting needs frustrated by their parents. Treasuring some concept of family honor his parents seem to him to have forfeited, Quentin seeks to turn his fair and beautiful sister into a fair, unravished, and unravishable maiden. Believing that his parents have sold his birthright when they sold their land, yet still lusting after an inheritance, Jason tries to use Caddy's marriage to secure a substitute fortune.

The parental generation thus plays a crucial, destructive role in *The Sound and the Fury.* Several readers have felt that Faulkner's sympathies as a fictionist lie more with men than with women. But his fathers, at least, rarely fare better than his mothers, the decisive direction of his sympathy being toward children, as we see not only in *The Sound and the Fury* but also in works that followed it. Jewel Bundren must live without a visible father, while Darl discovers that in some fundamental sense he "never had a mother." Thomas and Ellen Sutpen's children live and die without having either an adequate father or an adequate mother. Rosa Coldfield lives a long life only to discover that she had lost childhood before she possessed it. Held fast yet held without gentleness, these characters find repetition easy, independence and innovation almost impossible.

Although he is aggressive in expressing the hostility he feels for his parents, Jason is never able satisfactorily to avenge himself on them. Accordingly, he takes his victims where he finds them, his preference being for those who are most helpless, like Benjy and Luster, or most desperate, like Caddy. Enlarged, the contempt he feels for his family enables him to reject the past and embrace the New South, which he does without recognizing in himself vulgar versions of the materialism and self-pity that we associate with his mother. Left without sufficient tenderness and love, Quentin, Caddy, and Benjy turn toward Dilsey and each other. Without becoming aggressive, Benjy feels the vacancies his parents create in his life, and so tries to hold fast to those moments in which Caddy has met his need for tenderness. In Quentin we observe a very different desire: repulsed by the world around him, he determines to possess moments only in idealized form. Like the hero of Pound's *Cantos,* he lives wondering whether any sight can be worth the beauty of his thought. His dis-ease with the immediate, which becomes a desire to escape time itself, accounts for the strange convolutions of his mind and the strange transformations of his emotions. In the end it leads him to a still harbor where he fastidiously completes the logic of his father's life. Unlike her brothers, Caddy establishes her independence and achieves freedom. But her flight severs ties, making it impossible for her to help Quentin, comfort Benjy, or protect her daughter. Finally, freedom sweeps "her into dishonor and shame." Deserted by her mother, Miss Quentin is left no one with whom to learn love, and so repeats her mother's dishonor and flight without knowing her tenderness. If in the story of Jason we observe the near-triumph of all that is repugnant, in the stories of Caddy and Miss Quentin we observe the degradation of all that is beautiful. No modern story has done more than theirs to explore Yeats's terrible vision of modernity in "The Second Coming," where the "best lack all conviction" while the "worst are full of passionate intensity."

Faulkner thus seems to have discovered Caddy in essentially the way he presents her—through the felt needs of her brothers. Only later did he realize that he had also been trying to meet needs of his own: that in Caddy he had created the sister he had wanted but never had and the daughter he was fated to lose, "though the former might have been apparent," he added, "from the fact that Caddy had three brothers almost before I wrote her name on paper." Taken together, then, the Compson brothers may be seen as manifesting the needs Faulkner expressed through his creation of Caddy. In Benjy's need for tenderness we see signs of the emotional confluence that preceded the writing of *The Sound and the Fury.* The ecstasy and relief Faulkner associated with the writing of the novel as a whole, he associated particularly with "the writing of Benjy's section." In Jason's preoccupation with making a fortune, we see a vulgar version of the hope Faulkner was trying to relinquish. In Quentin's almost Manichaean revulsion toward all things material and physical, we see both a version of the imagination Allen Tate has called "angelic" and a version of the moral sensibility that Faulkner associated with the fastidious aesthete. It is more than accident of imagery that Quentin, another of Faulkner's poets manqués, seeks refuge, first, in the frail "vessel" he calls Caddy, and then, in something very like the "still harbor" in which Faulkner had imagined Hergesheimer submerging himself—"where the age cannot hurt him and where rumor of the world reaches him only as a far faint sound of rain."

In one of his more elaborate as well as more suggestive descriptions of what the creation of Caddy meant to him, Faulkner associated her with one of his favorite images. "I said to myself, Now I can write. Now I can make myself a vase like that which the old Roman kept at his bedside and wore the rim slowly away with kissing it. So I, who had never had a sister and was fated to lose my daughter in infancy, set out to make myself a beautiful and tragic little girl." The image of the urn or vase had turned up in the Hergesheimer review, "Elmer," *Mosquitoes,* and *Flags in the Dust;* it had appeared recently in the letter to Aunt Bama describing his new love; and it would make several later appearances. It was an image, we may fairly assume, that possessed special force for Faulkner, and several connotations, including at least three of crucial significance.

The simplest of these connotations—stressing a desire for escape—Faulkner had earlier associated with Hergesheimer's "still harbor" and later associated with "the classic and serene vase" that shelters Gail Hightower "from the harsh gale of living." In *The Sound and the Fury* Benjy comes to us as a wholly dependent creature seeking shelter. Sentenced to a truncated life of pain—"like something eyeless and voiceless which . . . existed merely because of its ability to suffer"—he is all need and all helplessness. What loss of Caddy means to him is a life of unrelieved and meaningless suffering. For Quentin, on the other hand, loss of Caddy means despair. In him we observe a desire, first for relief and shelter, then for escape. In one of the New Orleans sketches, Faulkner introduces a girl who presents herself to her lover as "Little Sister Death." In the allegory he wrote for Helen Baird, a maiden of the same name turns up in the company of a courtly knight and lover—which is, of course, the role Quentin seeks to play. At first all Quentin's desire seems to focus on Caddy as the maiden of his dreams. But as his desire becomes associated with "night and unrest," Caddy begins to merge with "Little Sister Death"—that is, with an incestuous love forbidden on threat of death. Rendered impotent by that threat, Quentin comes to love, not the body of his sister, nor even some concept of Compson honor, but death itself. In the end, he ceremoniously gives himself, not to Caddy but to the river. "The saddest thing about love," says a character in *Soldiers' Pay,* "is that not only the love cannot last forever, but even the heartbreak is soon forgotten." Quentin kills himself in part as punishment for his forbidden desires; in part because Caddy proves corruptible;

in part, perhaps, because he decides "that even she was not quite worth despair." But he also kills himself because he fears his own inconstancy. What he discovers in himself is deep psychological impotence that manifests itself in his inability to play either of the heroic roles—seducer or avenger—that he deems appropriate to his fiction of himself as a gallant, chivalric lover. But beyond the failure he experiences lies the failure he anticipates, a moment when Caddy's corruption no longer matters to him. Suicide thus completes his commitment to the only role left him, that of the despairing lover.

> —DAVID L. MINTER, "The Self's Own Lamp," *William Faulkner: His Life and Work* (Baltimore: Johns Hopkins University Press, 1980), pp. 95–100

GAIL L. MORTIMER

Caddy Compson is the apotheosis of the images that Faulkner brought together in speaking of his art. She is unattainable, being both "the sister he never had and . . . the daughter he was fated to lose" ⟨David L. Minter, *William Faulkner: His Life and Work*⟩. Because her portrayal is done obliquely, she can retain the imaginative shape Faulkner is reaching toward. She is his "heart's darling." Minter writes: "In a figure like Caddy Compson he had brought many of his loves together. Creating for 'himself a maid that life had not had time to create,' he had 'laid upon her frail and unbowed shoulders the whole burden of man's history of his impossible heart's desire.' "

Caddy, in turn, is linked to an image we noted earlier, the vase or urn, an image for Faulkner of the work of art. Minter writes: "the vase becomes both Caddy and *The Sound and the Fury*; both 'the beautiful one' for whom he created the novel as a commodious space and the novel in which she found protection and privacy as well as expression. In its basic doubleness the vase is many things: a haven or shelter into which the artist may retreat; a feminine ideal to which he can give his devotion; a work of art that he can leave behind when he is dead; and a burial urn that will contain at least one expression of his self as an artist. If it is a mouth he may freely kiss, it is also a world in which he may find shelter . . ." Minter recognizes the overdetermined quality of this favorite Faulknerian image; in the language of my own study, he has seen the vase as a container in which precious things may be preserved, a place in which he can rest and be safe, a womblike place, and a trace of himself as an artist. The urn, the object of art, the novel in which she appears, and Caddy herself all become associated with the bright shape that is their source: "it takes only one book to do it. It's not the sum of a lot of scribbling, it's one perfect book, you see. It's one single urn or shape that you want to do."

In his art, then, Faulkner makes a choice very like that of his protagonists who feel incestuous longings for their sisters. It is precisely their unattainability that constitutes their value. Forbidden love is desirable because it will survive as passion, not end in decay or disappointment or shabbiness. Faulkner associated his "heart's darling" Caddy "with Keats's urn, which he in turn associated with life and with art—with life because it depicted love that was dreamed yet denied, felt yet deferred; and with art because it epitomized form." To feel something yet defer it is to sustain passion and not risk loss. It is also a masterful solution to an ambivalence toward physical closeness with the object of your love.

—GAIL L. MORTIMER, "The Terror of History," *Faulkner's Rhetoric of Loss: A Study in Perception and Meaning* (Austin: University of Texas Press, 1983), pp. 127–28

CRITICAL ESSAYS

Catherine B. Baum

"THE BEAUTIFUL ONE"

William Faulkner's statement that *The Sound and the Fury* is "a tragedy of two lost women: Caddy and her daughter"[1] indicates that he intended Caddy Compson to be both a central and a tragic figure in the novel. None of the critics, however, emphasizes the role of Caddy as much as Faulkner does, and even those who do consider her life a unifying force in the novel have not thought of the novel as her tragedy. Lawrence Bowling points out that Caddy is "the essential center of the main action . . . the primary obsession with Benjy and Quentin and Jason throughout the first three sections of the book,"[2] yet he treats her life as but one aspect of the "theme of innocence"[3] he finds in the novel, thus ignoring her role as tragic heroine. Similarly, Olga Vickery sees Caddy as a center of action, but she thinks Caddy's importance is primarily technical, rather than thematic: "Within the novel as a whole it is Caddy's surrender to Dalton Ames which serves both as the source of dramatic tension and as the focal point for the various perspectives."[4] Caddy's function, Miss Vickery believes, is to provide an opportunity for each of the brothers to react to her and thereby to reveal his own character. In view of Faulkner's remarks, however, it seems just as likely that the reverse is true—that the main function of the other characters is to reveal something about Caddy.

Because no one of the Compsons has a complete and unbiased view of Caddy, there is an obscurity surrounding her character, but it is not an impenetrable obscurity. In fact, a main aim of the novel is to allow the reader to piece together information and derive for himself a true picture of Caddy. Faulkner's technique in *The Sound and the Fury* is very much like that he used in *Absalom, Absalom!*, of which he said: "It was . . . thirteen ways of looking at a blackbird. But . . . when the reader has read all these thirteen different ways of looking at the blackbird, the reader has his own fourteenth image of that blackbird which I would like to think is the truth."[5] Similarly, the reader can see several distorted ways of looking at Caddy, but through careful reading and discernment, he will be able to derive that fourteenth image, the truest picture of Caddy.

From *Modern Fiction Studies* 13, No. 1 (Spring 1967): 33–44.

That Caddy's life is a cohesive force in the novel can easily be seen. She is the central concern of each brother, and the telling of her story is the common purpose of each section. She causes the other characters to speak out. She is the only human factor in Benjy's life which gives it meaning, for the other things he loves are inanimate objects—the fire, the pasture, the red and yellow cushion, the blue bottle, and the jimson weed. Caddy is also the main interest of her brother Quentin. His thoughts turn ceaselessly from the present—his trip on the bus, his walk on the bridge, his adventure with the Italian girl—to the past, and the past for Quentin *is* Caddy. His thoughts revolve around her pregnancy, her wedding, and the question of honor, which to him is inextricably bound up with Caddy. She likewise is important to Jason, her antagonist, as the ruination of his plans for the future.

Many explanations have been offered for the arrangement of the four sections of the novel, but no one has noticed the most simple and probable one: a logical and traditional ordering based on the chronology of Caddy's life, her childhood, adolescence, and maturity. Because the past is as immediate to Benjy as the present, he reveals Caddy's personality as a child, and his section logically comes first. With an ever-present concern about chastity and honor, Quentin is best suited to tell of Caddy's adolescence and loss of innocence. His section therefore follows Benjy's. Since Jason is interested not in morals, but in money, he is concerned about Caddy only as she affects his financial welfare; for this reason, she impinges on his consciousness only after her divorce from Herbert, which costs Jason his promised job. She is again of interest to him when he can appropriate to himself the money she sends Quentin. Jason then, fittingly enough, tells the story of Caddy's adulthood, her divorce and her relationship with her daughter. The climax of the novel is Caddy's defeat at the hands of Jason, who leaves her stammering, helpless, and broken, as she acknowledges, "'I have nothing at stake.... Nuh-nuh-nothing....'"[6]

The final section of the novel comments on life without Caddy and the love she represents. As Dilsey says, "'I seed de beginnin, en now I sees de endin'" (p. 313). The events of this day, as Quentin, "the extension of Caddy,"[7] runs away, mark the disintegration and the "endin" of the Compson family. Without the warmth of Caddy's love, everything seems cold and dying. The house is "decaying" (p. 301) and "rotting" (p. 313), and the word "cold" is used repeatedly to describe the weather, the house, the meals, Jason, and Mrs. Compson. Benjy's sorrowful moans have the effect of a Greek chorus crying "woe." As "the grave hopeless sound of all voiceless misery under the sun" (p. 332), these cries furnish an appropriate dirge for the loss of Caddy.

All that remains of Caddy is her "white satin slipper ... yellow now, and cracked and soiled" (p. 332). This slipper is a touching and effective symbol of Caddy's life, which once was clean and shining too, but now is spoiled and dirty like the slipper.

In addition to its structural significance, Caddy's life also thematically represents love, compassion, pity, and sacrifice in a family which is destroying itself through its lack of these qualities. This most important role is also the most neglected by the critics. Before one can understand Caddy's unselfish love, he must understand her character, and it is here that many critics seem to have gone astray, apparently accepting at face value Jason's and Quentin's evaluations. To Charles Anderson, Caddy is only a promiscuous nymphomaniac;[8] to Carvel Collins, she represents the libido, and "...her development as charted in the novel is a twisting of the libido's normal development toward full sexuality";[9] to Bowling, "...Caddy is essentially like Jason in that she is a naturalist and never rises above her natural state."[10] Powell speaks of "the darkness of her soul,"[11] and Foster describes her as "a sensitive, beautiful girl, but given to bitchery from her early teens."[12] Certainly there is some basis for these feelings. Caddy has affairs with several men, becomes pregnant and marries a man she does not love in order to give her unborn child a father.

To judge her solely on the basis of these facts, however, is to distort her character completely. Faulkner in 1957 remembered her as "the beautiful one, she was my heart's darling. That's what I wrote the book about and I used the tools which seemed to me the proper tools to try to tell, try to draw the picture of Caddy."[13] And he adds, " '...Caddy was still to me too beautiful and too moving to reduce her to telling what was going on...' "[14] Thus to Faulkner, Caddy is not only central, but also beautiful and moving.

Caddy's most important and distinctive quality is unselfish love. She is the only Compson who loves without thought for self and with a genuine desire for the happiness of others, especially for her two innocent brothers, Benjy and Quentin. Caddy offers the care that Benjy needs, "the tenderness," Faulkner says, "to shield him in his innocence."[15] She gets into bed with him to help him go to sleep, she is concerned about him when his hands are cold, and she tries to make him happy by telling him about Christmas: " 'Santy Claus, Benjy. Santy Claus' " (p. 27). She has the ability to sense what he wants and the initiative to get it for him: " 'You want to carry the letter.' Caddy said. 'You can carry it' " (p. 32); " 'He wants your lightning bugs, T. P. Let him hold it a while' " (p. 55). She knows that Benjy likes the red and yellow cushion and that " 'if you'll hold him, he'll stop [crying]' " (p. 82). These are things the other members of the family either do not know or do not care about.

The beauty of Caddy's love becomes especially prominent when seen against the background of the other characters' lack of concern for Benjy's happiness. Quentin never hurts Benjy, but neither does he show any affection for him. Jason pesters and teases Benjy by cutting up his paper dolls; Luster impishly whispers "Caddy" in his ear to make him cry (p. 74); Mrs. Compson's words to Benjy are usually sharp and chilled—" 'You, Benjamin' " (p. 60)—or they are admonitions to the rest of the household to keep him quiet. Mr. Compson and Dilsey both seem to care about Benjy, but they are either too busy or too preoccupied to do anything for him. Mr. Compson's " 'Well, Benjy.... Have you been a good boy today' " (p. 83) shows some distracted interest, but he does not play an active role in Benjy's life. Dilsey tries to protect Benjy from Luster's teasings (p. 74), but she is kept too busy by her work around the house and the whining demands of Mrs. Compson. Only Caddy is actively interested in his welfare.

The reaction of Caddy's daughter, Quentin, to Benjy heightens the effect of Caddy's tenderness by contrast. Quentin feels only disgust and repugnance for Benjy and his repulsive table manners (p. 89), whereas Caddy had solicitously and patiently fed him. When Benjy was distressed at finding Caddy and Charlie in the swing, Caddy ran to comfort Benjy and gave up Charlie (p. 67). On the other hand, when Benjy finds Quentin with her boyfriend in the swing, Quentin calls him an *"old crazy loon"* (p. 67) and runs to the house, not to comfort Benjy, but to complain to Dilsey.

Caddy has other qualities as admirable as her selfless love. In the first section of the novel she is an active and curious little girl. She is the one who asks many questions about Damuddy's funeral and who finds an ingenious way of getting around her father's orders that the children go to bed immediately after supper:

> 'Your pa say for you to come right on up stairs when you et supper. You heard him.'
> 'He said to mind me.' Caddy said. (p. 46)

While Jason tags along saying " 'I'm going to tell ...' " (p. 46) and while Quentin obediently stays behind on the kitchen steps (p. 47), Caddy leads the way to the tree outside the parlor window so that she can see what's going on inside. She is the one, as Faulkner put it, "brave enough to climb that tree to look in the forbidden window."[16] Although Caddy disobeys her father's instructions, still her behavior is better than Quentin's excessive obedience which keeps him from participating in life, and it is an indication of her independence and spirit.

Only Caddy knows her brother Jason for what he is. When he makes one of his numerous threats to "tell," Caddy defies him: " 'Let him tell. ... I don't give a cuss' " (p. 39). When Jason destroys Benjy's dolls, Caddy's fierce protectiveness reveals the intensity of her love:

> 'He cut up all Benjy's dolls.' Caddy said. 'I'll slit his gizzle.'
> 'Candace.' Father said.
> 'I will.' Caddy said. 'I will.' She fought. Father held her. She kicked at Jason. He rolled into the corner, out of the mirror. (p. 84)

Caddy's tone here suggests her youthful confidence that she can handle anything. The poignancy of the scene, however, is that Jason cannot be destroyed so easily.

The qualities Caddy evinces before her loss of innocence—her self-reliance, courage, independence, and especially her love—are attributes that certainly make her "beautiful and moving,"[17] and Benjy's section of the novel serves largely to reveal these traits. That Caddy loses these qualities is her tragedy, and the remainder of the novel depicts the tragic changes as the world finally destroys her courage and her love.

Caddy is doomed, Lawrence Bowling points out, by "the general state of lovelessness into which all the Compson children were born without any choice on their part."[18] The lack of guidance from her father, the coldness of her mother, the vengefulness of Jason—all contribute to her downfall. More than this, she is doomed by society itself for violating its mores and by the attitude of men like Dalton who consider women only "bitches" (p. 179).

One cannot, however, place all the blame on circumstances or the Compson family. A large part of the reason for Caddy's damnation is found in herself. Ironically enough, those qualities in her character that are admirable are the ones which lead to her fall: her complete selflessness, which leads her to be indifferent to her virginity and to what happens to her; her willingness to put the other person's interests first; and her great desire to communicate love. She is too selfless for the world she is in, because all that the world, in the form of Jason and Dalton, knows how to do is take advantage of that selflessness. What Cash said of Darl in *As I Lay Dying* is applicable also to Caddy: "this world is not his world; this life his life."[19] This world is not "the right place for love"[20] for Caddy. In a family which needs tenderness and compassion as urgently as do the Compsons, the destruction of such a capacity for love is a terrifying waste.

By the end of *The Sound and the Fury*, Caddy has changed from a loving, innocent girl to a feverish, anxious woman who, as Jason said, looked "like some kind of a toy that's wound up too tight and about to burst all to pieces" (p. 227). In the novel's appendix, published in 1946, it is evident that she has changed even more: she has become the mistress of a German staff general, and she has become "ageless and beautiful, cold serene and damned" (p. 12). Now, as the librarian Melissa Meek believes, "... *Caddy doesn't want to be saved hasn't anything anymore worth being saved for nothing worth being lost that she can lose*" (p. 16). If the older Caddy is impervious now to harm from the world, she is also completely and irrevocably damned. Quentin believes "temporary" is the saddest word (p. 197), but for Caddy the saddest thing is the permanence of her doom.

Caddy's constant and selfless love for others makes it momentarily difficult to understand her coldness when she is with the Nazi. Yet the change has been prepared for in the novel, and her coldness years later is only the logical culmination of forces working against her earlier. The dramatic alteration of her character can be traced in stages through her relationships with the seven men important in her life: Benjy, Charlie, Dalton, Quentin, Herbert, Jason, and the Nazi general. Mr. Compson can be omitted because he does not delineate any particular segment of her life; his influence on her is a more general one.

In her childhood relations with Benjy, Caddy is self-confident, warm, and innocent. Then the beginning of Caddy's sexual experience and her loss of innocence is marked by the episode with Charlie in the swing. But she is still in control of her feelings and is able to give up Charlie for Benjy's sake. When she meets Dalton, however, she loses her mastery over herself:

> he's crossed all the oceans all around the world
> then she talked about him clasping her wet knees her face tilted back in
> the grey light the smell of honeysuckle.... (p. 169)

She is a childlike Desdemona in her wonder at knowing someone who has seen "all the oceans." She seems still innocent mentally and spiritually, if not physically.

When Quentin asks Caddy if she loves Dalton, she does not declare her love in words:

> ...Caddy you hate him dont you dont you
> she held my hand against her chest her heart thudding I turned and caught her arm
> Caddy you hate him dont you
> she moved my hand up against her throat her heart was hammering there. (p. 169)

Her pounding heart should prove her love more than words could, but Quentin cannot understand. "Incapable of love" (p. 10), he must hear the word to comprehend it. To Quentin, love is just a word, as Addie Bundren puts it, "a shape to fill a lack."[21] To Caddy, who knows the meaning of love and who has loved, the word is not necessary.

Caddy's interest in men is a natural part of growing up, like her playing with the perfume and the hat. Since she should not remain as much a child as Benjy, it is wrong to condemn her interest in Dalton. What one could censure her for, however, and what the world *does* censure her for, is that she gives herself completely and without reserve to Dalton. She loves Dalton and wishes to communicate her love, and the lack of love in the Compson household drives her to seek it outside the family. Robert Penn Warren writes that the only real villains in Faulkner are "those who deny the human bond"[22]—like Jason, Quentin, and Mrs. Compson. Caddy fights to assert the human bond. Her love for Dalton is not passive, but active; she did not *"let"* him kiss her, she *"made"* him. (p. 152).

Caddy's giving herself to Dalton reveals not only her love, but also her selflessness. Love to her is more important than morality, and she has been taught no good reason for preserving her chastity. All her mother cares about is the appearance of virtue and Caddy places no value on her maidenhood, which means "no more than a hangnail" (p. 10) to her. What does matter to her is the communication of love. Mr. Compson perhaps best expresses Caddy's attitude toward virginity when he says it is "'contrary to nature" (p. 135), or, as Olga Vickery says, it is "an artificial isolation of the woman."[23] Virginity, therefore, is just one of the "high dead words."[24]

Caddy's loss of mental and spiritual innocence comes towards the end of her affair with Dalton. Thinking Dalton has hurt Quentin, she tells him to go away. Then she realizes Quentin is not hurt, and she is anxious to go to Dalton. Her words indicate her growing awareness of his true feeling toward her:

> let me go Ive got to catch him and ask his let me go Quentin please let me go let me go

all at once she quit her wrists went lax

yes I can tell him I can make him believe anytime I can make him...anytime he will believe me. (pp. 181–2)

The repetition of "let me go" and "anytime I can make him believe me" seems to indicate an increasing desperation on Caddy's part and a fearful realization that she might not be able to make Dalton believe her. Caddy does not say what it is she can make him believe, but a probable answer is that she is afraid she is pregnant and is apprehensive about whether or not he will believe he is the father. She seems to know that Dalton is not as close to her as she would like to think.

In her relationship to Quentin after her affair with Dalton, Caddy's sense of despair is evident in her willingness for Quentin to kill her or commit incest with her (pp. 170–171). It makes no difference to her which alternative he chooses: "yes Ill do anything you want me to anything yes" (p. 175). Her own well-being is a matter of no concern to her, and her independence seems to have disappeared. Her affair with Dalton, she knows, hurts both Quentin and Benjy. Quentin she pities because he cannot understand what it is to love: "poor Quentin...youve never done that have you" (p. 170). The sad thing for Quentin is that he has never done anything. As T. S. Eliot has pointed out, "...it is better, in a paradoxical way, to do evil than to do nothing; at least we exist."[25] In these terms, Caddy's fall is better than Quentin's innocence.

That Benjy is hurt by Caddy's actions is evident in his bellowings and pulling at her dress when she comes in after having been with Dalton (pp. 87–88). Quentin notices that when Caddy is near Benjy now, her eyes are "like cornered rats" (p. 168). Torn as she is between her love for Benjy and her new love for Dalton, she has good cause to feel despair.

The men in Caddy's life after Dalton appear only vaguely in *The Sound and the Fury,* and one can only speculate about Caddy's motives in going with them. There is no evidence that she loved them as she had Dalton, but her indifferent attitude toward virginity and her need to give and receive love may explain her giving herself to them.

Just before her marriage to Herbert, Caddy tells Quentin, "... *I died last year I told you I had but I didnt know then what I meant I didnt know what I was saying...But now I know I'm dead I tell you*" (pp. 142–143). Even with Dalton she had half suspected that he would not "believe" her and might betray her. Since then, she has evidently learned that she can trust no one. When she becomes pregnant and is forced to face the consequences of her actions, she knows that she is dead.

In her marriage to Herbert, Caddy is willing to assume responsibility for her actions. She cares nothing for Herbert, but her concern for Benjy and her father has convinced her that marrying Herbert is the only thing she can do. When Quentin says, "...*we can go away you and Benjy and me where nobody knows us where...,*" Caddy's answer shows both her realism and her ever-present concern for Benjy: *"On what on your school money the money they sold the pasture for so you could go to Harvard dont you see you've got to finish now if you dont finish he'll have nothing"* (p. 143). When Quentin tells Caddy to think of Benjy and her father and not to marry Herbert, Caddy's interest in the welfare of others is still predominant: *"What else can I think about what else have I thought about... Father will be dead in a year they say if he doesnt stop drinking and he wont stop he cant stop since I since last summer and then they'll send Benjy to Jackson I cant cry I cant even cry..."* (pp. 142–143). Her love for her father is also revealed in the broken, rushed way she speaks of him. By marrying Herbert, Caddy hopes she will enable her father to stop worrying about her and to stop drinking. Then he will not die in a year, and Benjy will not have to be sent to Jackson. So, although Slatoff castigates Caddy for "abandon[ing] Benjy,"[26] the marriage is really one of her most selfless acts; it will, she hopes, benefit Benjy in the long run.

Caddy's compassion for Benjy and reluctance to leave him are seen on her wedding day. When she hears Benjy crying, she rushes out to him and hugs him (pp. 59, 101). She has not stopped loving Quentin either, for as Herbert tells Quentin, "... Candace talked about you all the time up there at the Licks... she couldnt have talked about you any more if you'd been the only man in the world..." (pp. 126–127). In her eagerness to have Quentin promise to take care of Benjy and Mr. Compson, she not only expresses her heart-felt concern for them but also seeks to divert Quentin's mind from the shattering fact of her pregnancy. Although he tenaciously tries to find out about her pregnancy, her own situation is of such slight importance to her and the well-being of Benjy and her father are of such major importance that she brushes off his questions in order to extract his promise:

> *Have there been very many Caddy*
> *I dont know too many will you look after Benjy and Father*
> *You dont know whose it is then does he know*
> *Dont touch me will you look after Benjy and Father.* (p. 134)

After her marriage and subsequent divorce from Herbert, Caddy sends her daughter back to Jefferson with Mr. Compson. At first, this act seems heartless, but it is almost the only thing she could do. In entrusting Quentin to her father, Caddy probably hoped that things would turn out well for her, and at any rate, as Jason pointed out later to her, Caddy had no way to provide for her. When Mrs. Compson coldly refused to let Caddy come home in spite of Mr. Compson's pleas that she be allowed to do so (p. 228), she practically determined Caddy's fate. Thrown entirely on her own, Caddy could do little but become a mistress or a prostitute, and she did not want her daughter to become part of such a life.

Caddy did not forget her daughter, however, and Jason remarks that she would come back once or twice a year to see her (p. 228). The first time she came back, Jason allowed her only a passing glimpse of Quentin, and he noticed that "... Caddy saw her and sort of jumped forward" (p. 223). The involuntary movement shows love for Quentin and eagerness to have her back. The only way Jason can keep her from going out to see Quentin is by attacking her in her most vulnerable spot, her love for Benjy: "So the next time I told her that if she tried Dilsey again, Mother was going to fire Dilsey and send Ben to Jackson and take Quentin and go away" (pp. 225–226). This threat seems to have been effective, for there is no evidence of Caddy's again trying to go to the house.

Slatoff criticizes Caddy for her attitude toward Quentin: "We learn that she is concerned about her daughter Quentin's welfare, but not concerned enough to do anything serious about it."[27] What Slatoff ignores is that Caddy is so hamstrung by the maneuverings of Jason and the unforgivingness of Mrs. Compson that she is powerless to do anything more for Quentin than send her money. Caddy is cut off almost entirely from communication with the Compson household: Jason censors her letters to Quentin (p. 208), she learns of her father's death only by accident (p. 220), and Jason tells her, " 'We dont even know your name at that house' " (p. 221).

The most important reason for Caddy's not taking Quentin away is again her love. She does not want Quentin to become a mistress or a prostitute, and Jason knows it. When she offers Jason a thousand dollars to let her have Quentin back, he mocks her:

> 'And I know how you'll get it,' I says, 'You'll get it the same way you got her. And when she gets big enough—' Then I thought she really was going to hit at me. . . .
>
> 'Oh, I'm crazy,' she says, 'I'm insane. I can't take her. Keep her. What am I thinking of.' (p. 227)

Now like a wound-up toy (p. 227), Caddy is completely frustrated and broken down by her lifelong antagonist, Jason. He notes that "her hands were hot as fever" and that she is making a strange noise: ". . . she begun to laugh and to try to hold it back all at the same time. 'No. I have nothing at stake,' she says, making that noise, putting her hands to her mouth, 'Nuh-nuh-nothing,' she says" (p. 227). This is a terrifying picture of the collapse of her spirit.

Still, Caddy is anxious about Quentin; even though she realizes that Jason has not " 'a drop of warm blood' " in him (p. 226), she pleads with him to take care of Quentin. Her broken and incoherent sentences indicate her highly emotional state and her sense of helplessness: " 'Just promise that she'll—that she—You can do that. Things for her. Be kind to her. Little things that I cant, they wont let . . .' " (p. 226). By this time Caddy has lost her self-confidence and her innocence; she is reduced to pleading with the brother she knows will not help her. The only quality Caddy has not lost is her love, for she still cares about Quentin.

But in Faulkner's appendix to the novel, when Caddy is seen with the Nazi, even the love is gone, and destruction is complete. Yet even though Caddy's final position with the Nazi represents spiritual damnation, it seems to be, ironically enough, one of worldly success. The picture of Caddy which the librarian finds is "filled with luxury and money and sunlight—a Cannebière backdrop of mountains and palms and cypresses and the sea, an open powerful expensive chromium-trimmed sports car, the woman's face hatless between a rich scarf and a seal coat, ageless and beautiful, cold serene and damned…" (p. 12).

The description of Caddy here resembles that of Eula Varner riding out of Frenchman's Bend with her impotent bridegroom: "The beautiful face did not even turn as the surrey drew abreast of the store. It passed in profile, calm, oblivious, incurious. It was not a tragic face: it was just damned."[28] The coldness and serenity isolate and protect the two women from the world. Yet there is an important difference between Caddy and Eula. Eula's face is not tragic, just damned: she had had nothing to lose; Caddy had much to lose, and her face is both tragic and damned. Although she gains the "luxury and money and sunlight" (p. 12), she loses *"anything… worth being saved for,"* as the librarian Melissa Meek pointed out, and she now has *"nothing worth being lost that she can lose"* (p. 16). Caddy is damned because she has become cold, empty-eyed, and passionless like Eula Varner. She has lost her capacity for love, and Dilsey's comment "What a sinful waste…" (p. 109) is the most apt summary of her tragedy. Even selfless love can result in the destruction of the person who practices it. The wasteful loss of Caddy's great capacity for compassion and sacrifice makes her fate the most unbearable and tragic doom in *The Sound and the Fury.*

NOTES

[1]Jean Stein, "William Faulkner," *Writers at Work: The* Paris Review *Interviews,* ed. Malcolm Cowley (New York, 1958), p. 130.
[2]Lawrence Bowling, "Faulkner and the Theme of Innocence," *Kenyon Review,* XX (1958), 475.
[3]Bowling, p. 466.
[4]Olga Vickery, *"The Sound and the Fury:* A Study in Perspective," *Publications of the Modern Language Association,* LXIX (1954), 1017.
[5]Frederick L. Gwynn and Joseph L. Blotner, eds., *Faulkner in the University* (Charlottesville, Virginia, 1959), p. 274.
[6]William Faulkner, *The Sound and the Fury* (New York, 1946), p. 227. Subsequent references, which appear in the text, are to this edition.
[7]Bowling, p. 475.
[8]Charles Anderson, "Faulkner's Moral Center," *Etudes Anglaises,* VII (1954), 57.
[9]Carvel Collins, "A Conscious Literary Use of Freud?," *Literature and Psychology,* III, iii (1953), 3.
[10]Bowling, p. 476.
[11]Sumner C. Powell, "William Faulkner Celebrates Easter, 1928," *Perspective,* II (1949), 208.
[12]Ruel E. Foster, "Dream as Symbolic Act in Faulkner," *Perspective,* II (1949), 181.
[13]Gwynn and Blotner, p. 6.
[14]Gwynn and Blotner, p. 1.
[15]Robert A. Jellife, *Faulkner at Nagano* (Tokyo, 1956), p. 104.
[16]Gwynn and Blotner, p. 31.
[17]Gwynn and Blotner, p. 1.
[18]Bowling, p. 479.
[19]William Faulkner, *As I Lay Dying* (New York, 1946), p. 532.
[20]Robert Frost, "Birches," *The Poems of Robert Frost* (New York, 1946), p. 128.
[21]Faulkner, *As I Lay Dying,* p. 464.
[22]Robert Penn Warren, *William Faulkner and His South,* The First Peter Rushton Seminar in Contem-

porary Prose and Poetry, No. 16 (unpublished essay, Univ. of Virginia, Charlottesville, Virginia, 1951), p. 14.

[23]Vickery, p. 1026.

[24]Faulkner, *As I Lay Dying,* p. 467.

[25]T. S. Eliot, "Baudelaire" (1930), *Selected Essays 1917–1932* (New York, 1932), p. 344.

[26]Walter J. Slatoff, *Quest for Failure: A Study of William Faulkner* (New York, 1960), p. 151.

[27]Slatoff, p. 151.

[28]William Faulkner, *The Hamlet* (New York, 1940), p. 270.

Sally R. Page

THE IDEAL OF MOTHERHOOD

The thematic meaning of *The Sound and the Fury* is grounded in man's need of the emotional and moral order which is created by motherly devotion. The importance of the theme of motherhood in the novel is indicated by the centrality of the role played by the major women characters, Mrs. Compson, Caddy, Quentin, and Dilsey. Mrs. Compson, Caddy, and Quentin are the driving forces behind every thought and action of the Compson brothers, who narrate the first three sections of the novel. Dilsey is the subject of its fourth section. The Compson family is dying because Mrs. Compson is incapable of loving or caring for her children; she is a total failure as a mother. As a result, the affectionate child Caddy assumes the false role of playing "mother" to her brothers.

Caddy's mothering love fulfills the need of her idiot brother Benjy. Since Benjy remains a perpetual three-year-old, the potential problems created by Caddy's assumed role are limited; only her absence can hurt him. However, Caddy's false role of motherhood tragically complicates her relation to Quentin and results in confusion and frustration for herself and a disastrous incestuous love on the part of her brother. When Caddy is destroyed, the full burden of motherhood in the Compson family falls upon the Negro servant Dilsey. Sections one and two present Mrs. Compson's rejection of Benjy and Quentin and their need of Caddy as a substitute mother. Section three depicts the chaos and decay of the Compson household without a mother. Section four focuses on Dilseys' heroic effort to hold together the family's last remnants by her sacrificial assumption of the responsibilities of motherhood to a family that is not her own.

The Sound and the Fury is a novel of extreme technical complexity and thematic multiplicity. However, Faulkner asserted on numerous occasions that this masterpiece was created from a single stirring image—Caddy with her muddy drawers climbing the pear tree to peek in at Damuddy's funeral. Faulkner repeatedly emphasized the importance of Caddy's character to the novel.

From *Faulkner's Women: Characterization and Meaning* (DeLand, FL: Everett/Edwards, 1972), pp. 47–54, 62–66.

One day I seemed to shut a door between me and all publishers' addresses and book lists. I said to myself, Now I can write. Now I can make myself a vase like that which the Old Roman kept at his bedside and wore the rim slowly away with kissing it. So I, who had never had a sister and was fated to lose my daughter in infancy, set out to make myself a beautiful and tragic little girl.[1]

To me she was the beautiful one, she was my heart's darling. That's what I wrote the book about and I used the tools which seemed to me the proper tools to try to tell it, try to draw the picture of Caddy.[2]

In the light of the importance of woman in Faulkner's apprentice fiction, it is not surprising that a character like Caddy should emerge as the focus of interest and emotional attachment in his fourth novel. Indeed, its central characters, its imagery, and its themes relate *The Sound and the Fury* very closely to Faulkner's earlier fiction. Caddy is a symbol of man's "heart's desire," the image of the woman whose mysterious beauty provokes man's yearning for the ideal. However, *The Sound and the Fury,* unlike Faulkner's earlier fiction, is a powerful indictment of the idealization of virgin purity and a moving portrayal of the destructiveness this idealism precipitates. Quentin's effort to limit Caddy's existence to symbolic ideality destroys her. Caddy's character is much more compelling than the ideal "heart's desire" of Faulkner's earlier works, for she is tragically human. That Faulkner should imagine his "heart's darling" as a very fallible and human woman indicates the shift in his attitude that makes *The Sound and the Fury* a contrast to his earlier works. Man's need of woman remains the primary theme; however, man does not need virgin purity, a Caddy of perpetual childish innocence, but in the midst of the chaos of reality man needs the ordering power of committed human love. Caddy is a central character in *The Sound and the Fury* because the Compson family desperately needs her feminine qualities of warmth and responsiveness, her aggressive courage, and her ability to assess realistically life's possibilities and limitations.

Though she is always seen through the "haze" of her brothers' attitudes toward her, the striking descriptions of Caddy's appearance and gestures, which accompany their recollections of her, serve to make her physical presence felt throughout the novel. Out of the unchronological disorder of the brothers' individual recollections of their sister, there emerge a number of powerfully dramatic pictures of Caddy in which she assumes some significant pose that captures the essence of her character at the different stages of its development. Caddy in her muddy drawers climbing the pear tree and Caddy with her arms about Benjy are memorable representations of the nature of her childhood character. In Quentin's section the picture of Caddy enraptured by love, her clothes soaked with the branch water, her arms hugging her knees, and her face looking skyward and the picture of Caddy in her bridal gown running to the bellowing Benjy are unforgettable. The tragedy of Caddy's life is made acutely visual by Jason's recollection of her in the black cloak standing over her father's grave in a drenching rain.

These pictures of Caddy make her a convincingly life-like and individual fictional creation. At the same time they render in a manner which is almost symbolic the nature and significance of her character. However, the full importance and complexity of Caddy's character are revealed completely only by an examination of her relationship to the two brothers who love her. Faulkner indicates the intensity and the complexity of man's need of woman through his portrayal of Benjy's and Quentin's need of Caddy and their devotion to her.

The opening pages of *The Sound and the Fury* make it immediately apparent that Benjy's mother has rejected her idiot child, while Caddy's whole childhood has focused on her mothering love and care for her idiot brother. Benjy recalls a cold day shortly before Christmas when he eagerly awaited Caddy's arrival from school. His frantic effort to communicate to someone his desire to get outside to meet Caddy is countered by his mother's cruel verbal attacks which are framed in the language of "motherly" discipline but are grounded in her desire to be rid of Benjy or to use him as an excuse for her privilege of always evading the responsibilities of motherhood. His moaning provokes only threats, "If you don't be good, you'll have to go to the kitchen." She insists that he wear his overshoes outside because she does not want him ill at Christmas time "with the house full of company." When at the end of the sequence she draws Benjy to her and laments, "My poor baby," it is obvious that her pity is not for Benjy but for herself. Caddy's beautiful and moving response is, "You're not a poor baby. Are you. You've got your Caddy. Haven't you got your Caddy?"[3]

The scene superbly demonstrates that Benjy is not a "poor baby" because he does possess the complete devotion and love of his sister. When Caddy returns from school and sees Benjy at the gate, her walking changes to running. She joyfully greets him, thrilled that he has come to meet her. Caddy's presence creates the overpowering joy of love in Benjy, an emotion which he compares to "bright rustling leaves." Mrs. Compson's rebuke of Caddy that closes the sequence is painfully ironic. "You must think. . . . Someday I'll be gone, and you'll have to think for him" (*SF*, p. 8). It is tragic that Benjy's mother has never thought "for" him, and that it is not she he loses, but Caddy.

The pattern of this opening scene is repeated at the end of section one in another dramatic presentation of the contrast between Caddy's and Mrs. Compson's treatment of Benjy. The scene demonstrates Caddy's competence as Benjy's "mother" by portraying her thorough understanding of his needs and her skill at preserving his sense of security. On the other hand, Mrs. Compson's ineptness as a mother is indicated by her unrealistic insistence that Benjy be disciplined as if he were a normal child and by her cruel and unreasonable scolding of Caddy which reveals her blindness to the fact that Caddy's attitudes should be her own. The fire and the soft red and yellow cushion symbolize love, comfort, and security to Benjy. When Mrs. Compson orders Caddy to bring Benjy to her, Caddy wisely recommends that she wait until he "finishes looking at the fire." Mrs. Compson refuses, and Caddy lifts Benjy to take him to his mother. The love and understanding of Benjy's needs which provoke Caddy's action are incomprehensible to Mrs. Compson, who rebukes her daugher for ruining her carriage. Caddy skillfully smooths over Benjy's loss of the fire by giving him the cushion, but she is immediately scolded for "humor[ing] him too much." Mrs. Compson takes the cushion away because "He must learn to mind," but she collapses in tears at the onslaught of Benjy's bellowing. Caddy must take command, pacify Benjy, and usher her mother off to bed. Caddy is not only a willing mother to Benjy; she is also a skillful and intelligent one.

Numerous other scenes in section one depict Caddy's love for Benjy, her loyalty to him, and her skill in caring for him. She tries to communicate with him and to teach him. By outwitting the other children, she procures for him whatever he desires. She fights Jason in order to protect him. She directs Versh in caring for him, feeds him herself, and sleeps with him. Caddy's assumption of the role of mother to Benjy makes it natural that she should play the same role with her other brothers. She is their natural leader; her personality is more aggressive than theirs, and she possesses the feminine self-confidence and sense of personal fulfillment that are the consequence of being needed as a mother. She has a meaningful role to perform, and her outgoing personality makes it inevitable that she will beg that her brothers be made to "mind her," and that her father and Dilsey will not only acquiesce to her childish demand but also rely upon her for Benjy's comfort and care.

Since Caddy performs the task of mother to Benjy, it is apparent that he would regard her as his real and only mother. Benjy's painful "present" depicts his childish longing not so much for the absent sister as for the lost mother. In *The Marble Faun* and *Soldiers' Pay* Faulkner relied quite heavily on "'tree" imagery to depict the graceful physical beauty of young virgins. Benjy's repeated "Caddy smells like trees" suggests that she possesses this attractiveness. However, the imagery in the earlier works is extensive and picturesque, emphasizing the physical appearance of girls, whereas the physical descriptions of Caddy are much less elaborate. Since Caddy is primarily "mother" to Benjy, it is probable that the "tree" motif in *The Sound and the Fury* is meant to suggest that Caddy is a "mother of life" figure. The "tree" smell of Caddy is Benjy's reassurance of the presence of the security of a mother's love. When Caddy dons her cheap perfume, when she is embraced by Charlie, and when she engages in illicit sexual relations, Benjy weeps not so much because he is an "innocent" who senses his sister's immorality, as because he is a child who senses that the new odors signify the severing of the bonds of Caddy's motherhood. He is wholly comforted on the first occasion, for Caddy immediately washes herself and gives her perfume to Dilsey. On the second occasion Caddy is overcome by confusion, flees Charlie, and clings to Benjy, weeping. On the third occasion Caddy can no longer comfort Benjy, for the bond between them has been broken.

Caddy's willingness to be a mother to Benjy and his responsive devotion to her are virtually the only acts of natural love in the Compson family. Their relationship, however, cannot be indefinitely sustained. Caddy plays an honorable and worthy role, but one which her own need for growth and fulfillment must eventually nullify. Caddy is not Benjy's mother; she is his sister. As soon as she begins the natural process of seeking love outside her family, she is faced with a frustrating problem of identity—the confusion of her real self with the role she has assumed. It is impossible for Benjy's love to be anything but possessive, for he is as entirely dependent upon Caddy as is any three-year-old child upon its mother. Caddy is torn between her love and loyalty for Benjy and her natural drive to become a real mother. When the inevitable break occurs, Benjy becomes a pathetically lost and motherless child. Luster's search for the lost quarter, whose mandala shape suggests wholeness, coherence, and order, is paralleled by Benjy's wandering search for the security, wholeness, and order wrought by the love of Caddy. Every call of the golfers reminds Benjy of his loss, and he clings to the comforting symbols of that love—the dirty slipper he caresses, the blazing fire that signifies love's warmth and vitality, the grave that offers security, and the progression of the bright shapes in their ordered place.

Quentin Compson's obsession with his sister Caddy, the subject of the second section of The Sound and the Fury, is the most intense and complex of all Faulkner's portrayals of man's need of woman. Like Benjy, Quentin forces Caddy's life into unnatural patterns because of his need of her, but his desire for Caddy is much more subtly expressed than Benjy's and is both more irresponsible and more destructive. Quentin's obsession with Caddy is the result of his devotion to her as a Romantic ideal, but it is also the result of his sexual need of her. Further, it is the expression of his unconscious desire that Caddy fulfill the role of mother to him.

Caddy as the youthful pure virgin represents for Quentin the ideality which he imagines would enable him to transcend spiritually the decadence, lovelessness, and immorality of his family. Caddy's virginity, for Quentin the symbol of innocence, is the one pure thing in his environment. This idealization of Caddy is, however, the most unreal and impossible ideality that any of Faulkner's searching heroes project. Statues of marble purity and sheer glass vases can be "practical" symbols of ideality, but the virginity of human and mutable woman is an ideal inevitably doomed to destruction. From his childhood Quentin struggles to "isolate her out of the loud world," but Caddy's very humanity continually mocks his dream.[4] Quentin's effort to actualize his yearning for ideality by the preservation of Caddy's virginity is self-deceiving, selfish, and evil, for it entails the destruction of Caddy's humanity. The second section of The Sound and the Fury depicts the defeated Romanticist mourning the loss of the ideal. The section elicits from the reader the tense and painful response of juxtaposed sympathy and judgment, sympathy for the yearning idealist, but judgment on Quentin's lack of concern for Caddy as a separate and human person. ⟨...⟩

Quentin's inner struggle reaches climactic and tragic intensity because, unlike Jesus and St. Francis, he has a sister, and upon Caddy is projected all his futile longing. Because she exists, and as a child is willing to love and mother him, it is possible for Quentin to possess momentarily the love his mother has denied him. However, because Caddy's naturalness and the maturing process constantly threaten to break the bonds between them, Quentin clings unnaturally to her affection. He posits her virginity as his ideal because that alone would assure his lifetime possession of her, and when that is lost, he permits himself to speak the hidden and forsaken desire for incest which would make her entirely his own.

Two poignant scenes depict Quentin's dependence on Caddy as a mother figure. The first, Quentin's childish sexual experimentation with Natalie, is significantly accompanied by a drenching rain. Quentin's guilt about his behavior makes him desire that Caddy will fulfill the role of mother by disapproving of his actions, disciplining him, and thus relieving his feelings of shame. When Caddy's response is, "I don't give a damn what you were doing," he violently attacks her to force the blows which he dreadfully needs and to "make" her care.

Caddy's love of Dalton Ames and her illicit relations with him are for Quentin an outright betrayal not only of his vision of ideality but, more crucially, of his son-like love for Caddy. The second branch scene, when Caddy confesses her love for Ames, is an intense portrayal of Quentin's child-like need of Caddy as a mother and of his severe and torturous sexual love for her. Throughout the scene he weeps pathetically, a broken distraught child, and Caddy holds him, hushes him and comforts him as if he were a child: "then I was crying her hand touched me again and I was crying against her damp blouse" (*SF*, p. 188). Quentin does not weep for Caddy, but for himself and his loss of her. The nature and intensity of Quentin's desire for Caddy is powerfully suggested by the repeated descriptions of the water, the dampness, the trees, the shadowy night, and particularly, the omnipresent honeysuckle odor. That his love is the perverted, serpentine longing for the "terrible" mother is indicated by the references to twisted things such as the "matted" vines and briers of the ditch and the "crisscrossed" twig marks on Quentin's palm, as well as by the murderous phallic knife.

Two symbolic phantasies at the end of his inner monologue indicate that Quentin faintly senses the truth of his psychological condition. The first is the picture-book dungeon with "'a single weak ray of light" and "two faces lifted out of the shadow" at which Quentin gazes until "the dungeon was Mother herself she and Father upward into weak light holding hands and us lost somewhere below them without even a ray of light" (*SF*, p. 215). Quentin's unconfessed, repressed longing makes him the victim of the "terrible" mother and dooms him to eternal darkness and isolation.

The second phantasy is the recalled childhood experience of rising at night to get water; the repetition of the word "door" suggests the possibility of escape from darkness and isolation and the achievement of the life-giving waters. In real life Quentin is incapable of reaching the door, of breaking the chains of his repressed desires and achieving rebirth through the normal processes of life. Unlike the symbolic trout which rises like an arrow, plunges into the water, and persistently arises again, Quentin suspects that when he is called to "Rise," the flat irons will hold him in the peaceful idleness of repression and eternal death. His life has not been characterized by sacrifice and renewal and neither will be his death. Quentin's complex need of Caddy shapes the pattern of her life, forcing her at a crucial moment to withdraw from the natural life process and dooming her to a lifetime of the serene deadliness he chooses for himself.

There is a contrast throughout the second section of *The Sound and the Fury* between Quentin's unnatural desire for Caddy and her normal devotion to him. Caddy's openness and responsiveness to her brothers' need for love and affection is well developed by the portrayal of her devotion to Benjy in section one. That she refused to give Quentin this kind of attention during their adolescence is indicative of her very natural adjustment to the realistic demands of maturity. She feels regret at severing the bond of her motherhood to Benjy because he remains in effect a child and his continued need of her is inevitable. Though she is patient with Quentin's demands on her, she is emotionally detached from him. Caddy considers him her equal and expects him to face life and its responsibilities independently.

As a child Caddy defies Quentin's efforts to correct and control her, and she likewise refuses to exercise any power of "parental" authority over him. It is most appropriate that she does not "give a damn" about his relationship with Natalie. It is abnormal and unnatural that Quentin does care intensely about Caddy's relationship with Dalton Ames. In the portrayal of her entrancement with love during the second branch scene, she gazes always up and beyond Quentin, soothing his childish sorrow but well removed from him in emotional attachment. Caddy's realistic acceptance of her fate enables her calmly to "mother" Quentin, who in contrast is child-like in his grief and anger.

> QUENTIN: I wish you were dead
>   CADDY: do you you coming now
>
>   * * *
>
>   Ill kill you do you hear
>   lets go out to the swing they'll hear you here
>   * * *
>
>   Im not crying do you say Im crying
>   no hush now we'll wake Benjy up
>   you go on into the house go on now
>   I am dont cry Im bad anyway you cant help it
>   theres a curse on us its not our fault is it our fault
>   hush come on and go to bed now
>   you cant make me theres a curse on us

(SF, pp. 195–196)

Caddy's response to Dalton Ames is the natural outgrowth of the warm affection she has given her brothers. She acts according to the normal and inevitable process of life; she is born to be both wife and mother. She responds to love when it is given, and it is the abnormal absence of genuine and natural love in her home that makes her submission unrestrained. That Ames's seduction is not altogether irresponsible is suggested by Quentin's recollection of the embracing lovers. "I could see her face a blur against his shoulder he held her in one arm like she was no bigger than a child . . ." (*SF*, p. 192). Quentin's clumsy and furious attack on Caddy's seducer is preceded by Ames's concerned inquiries about Caddy's welfare—"listen save this for a while I want to know if shes all right have they been bothering her up there" (*SF*, p. 198). Ames extended his hand to Quentin; had Quentin urged Ames to fulfill his responsibility to Caddy, to love her and help her escape the Compson decay, her life might not have ended in tragedy. Instead, Quentin attacks Ames verbally, though he is incapable of doing so physically, and drives him away. Caddy's plaintive gasps, "let me go Ive got to catch him and ask his let me go Quentin please let me go . . . yes I can tell him I can make him believe anytime I can make him" (*SF*, p. 202), are her first cries of death, her apprehension that love and the hope of a normal life may be lost.

Because of her family Caddy loses the man she loves; her resulting promiscuity is her despairing cry at the loss of life. The deadly serenity that is born in her is the sign that the naturally responsive and loving child has been sacrificed to the unnatural—sex without love. Her mother's subsequent demand that she submit herself to a hypocritical marriage seals her doom. Quentin and Mrs. Compson succeed in destroying Caddy's humanity; by scorning her grasp at life and depriving her of a normal outlet for creativity, motherhood, love, and freedom, they kill the real Caddy and create a deadly serene lost woman.

After the death of her father Caddy's concern for her daughter Quentin forces her to submit herself to the control of Jason's cruelty and greed. Her several appearances in section three of the novel reveal the pathos of her hopeless condition. She loves Quentin and longs to see her, but Jason responds to every attempt with extortion or threats that he will fire Dilsey, send Benjy to Jackson, and take Quentin and go away. When Caddy grasps the inevitability of Jason's hardness, she begs to have her child back. Jason, however, mocks Caddy's "occupation," and she is immediately forced to recognize that she cannot keep Quentin without destroying her every chance "to be like other girls." Caddy's exasperation with Jason makes her like "a toy that's wound up too tight and about to burst all to pieces." As Jason puts it, Caddy does have nothing at stake and her realization that she has lost everything breaks her. " 'No,' she says, then she began to laugh and to try to hold it back at the same time. 'No. I have nothing at stake,' she says, making that noise, putting her hands to her mouth, 'nuh-nuh-nothing,' she says" (*SF*, p. 260). Had Caddy been allowed to return home to care for Quentin and Benjy and thus to fulfill the destiny of her nature, the Compson history might have been different. Instead, the tragedy of Caddy's life is repeated by her child.

The content of Benjy's and Quentin's sections is based on their obsessed love for Caddy; the content of Jason's section is based on his obsessed agitation with Quentin. His day is spent in attempts to catch her whoring and in designs to swindle away the money her mother sends her. Quentin is trapped by the circumstances of her life; Jason's treatment of her destroys her.

"It's his fault," she says, "He wont let me alone, and I have to. If he doesn't want me here, why wont he let me go back to—."

NOTES

[1] Quoted in Michael Millgate, *The Achievement of William Faulkner* (New York, 1965), p. 26.

[2] Frederick L. Gwynn and Joseph L. Blotner, ed., *Faulkner in the University* (Charlottesville, Va., 1959), p. 6.

[3] *The Sound and the Fury* (New York, 1929), p. 8. Subsequent references are to this edition.

[4] Quentin's Romantic dilemma is well expressed by Robert M. Slabey in "The 'Romanticism' of *The Sound and the Fury*," *Mississippi Quarterly*, XVI (Summer 1963), pp. 153–155: "Quentin's ideal is likewise [like Shelley's ideal, visionary woman, the Epipsyche] embodied in a woman, in Caddy as virgin and as a symbol of family and traditional honor—with unhealthy undertones of eroticism and incest. When the ideal is spoiled and soiled, Quentin is disillusioned and desolate.... His love was a love of childhood, of innocence, an impossible thing in the adult world; Caddy's pregnancy irrevocably removed the possibility of a return to childhood innocence.... Fundamentally, the position of the Romantic is fallacious; his 'philosophy' is inadequate in coping with reality; because of this he cannot bear the human condition, and he is defeated by it...."

John T. Irwin
QUENTIN AND CADDY

If Quentin's determination to drown his shadow represents the substitutive punishment, upon his own person, of the brother seducer (the dark self, the ego
shadowed by the unconscious) by the brother avenger (the bright self, the ego
controlled by the superego), then it is only appropriate that the events from
Quentin's past that obsessively recur during the internal narrative leading up to his
drowning are events that emphasize Quentin's failure as both brother avenger and
brother seducer in relation to his sister Candace—failures which his drowning of
himself is meant to redeem. On the one hand, Quentin is haunted by his inability
to kill Candace's lover Dalton Ames and by his further inability to prevent Candace
from marrying Herbert Head, whom he knows to be a cheat. But on the other
hand, he is equally tormented by his own failure to commit incest with his sister.
In this connection it is significant that one of the obsessive motifs in the narrative
of Quentin's last day is the continual juxtaposition of Quentin's own virginity to his
sister's loss of virginity: "In the South you are ashamed of being a virgin. Boys. Men.
They lie about it. Because it means less to women, Father said. He said it was men
invented virginity not women. Father said it's like death: only a state in which the
others are left and I said, But to believe it doesn't matter and he said, That's what's
so sad about anything: not only virginity, and I said, Why couldn't it have been me
and not her who is unvirgin and he said, That's why that's sad too; nothing is even
worth the changing of it."[1]

In Quentin's world young men lose their virginity as soon as possible, but their
sisters keep their virginity until they are married. The reversal of this situation in
the case of Quentin and Candace makes Quentin feel that his sister has assumed
the masculine role and that he has assumed the feminine role. Quentin's obsessive
concern with Candace's loss of virginity is a displaced concern with his own inability
to lose his virginity, for, as both novels clearly imply, Quentin's virginity is psychological impotence. Approaching manhood, Quentin finds himself unable to assume

From *Doubling and Incest/Repetition and Revenge: A Speculative Reading of Faulkner* (Baltimore: Johns
Hopkins University Press, 1975), pp. 37–49.

the role of a man. Consider his failure as the avenging brother when he encounters Dalton Ames on the bridge—Ames whom Quentin has earlier associated with the figure of the shadow (pp. 173, 174). He tells Ames to leave town by sundown or he will kill him. Ames replies by drawing a pistol and demonstrating his marksmanship. He then offers the pistol to Quentin:

> youll need it from what you said Im giving you this one because youve seen what itll do
> to hell with your gun
> I hit him I was still trying to hit him long after he was holding my wrists but I still tried then it was like I was looking at him through a piece of coloured glass I could hear my blood and then I could see the sky again and branches against it and the sun slanting through them and he holding me on my feet
> did you hit me
> I couldn't hear
> what
> yes how do you feel
> all right let go
> he let me go I leaned against the rail (p. 180)

Later, sick and ashamed, Quentin thinks, "I knew he hadnt hit me that he had lied about that for her sake too and that I had just passed out like a girl..." (p. 181). Quentin, by rejecting the use of the pistol with its phallic significance and thus avoiding the necessity of risking his life to back up his words, relinquishes the masculine role of avenging brother and finds suddenly that in relation to the seducer he has shifted to a feminine role. Struggling in Ames's grasp, Quentin faints "like a girl," and Ames, because he sees the sister in the brother, refuses to hurt Quentin and even lies to keep from humiliating him.

Quentin's failure of potency in the role of avenging brother is a repetition of an earlier failure in the role of brother seducer. On that occasion, Quentin had gone looking for Candace, suspecting that she had slipped away to meet Dalton Ames, and he found her lying on her back in the stream: "...I ran down the hill in that vacuum of crickets like a breath travelling across a mirror she was lying on her back in the water her head on the sand spit the water flowing about her hips there was a little more light in the water her skirt half saturated flopped along her flanks to the waters motion in heavy ripples going nowhere..." (p.168). Forcing Candace to get out of the water, Quentin begins to question her about Ames, only to find that the questioning suddenly turns to the subject of his own virginity:

> Caddy you hate him dont you
> she moved my hand up against her throat her heart was hammering there...
> Yes I hate him I would die for him I've already died for him I die for him over and over again everytime this goes...

poor Quentin
she leaned back on her arms her hands locked about her knees
youve never done that have you
what done what
that what I have what I did
yes yes lots of times with lots of girls
then I was crying her hand touched me again and I was crying against her damp blouse then she lying on her back looking past my head into the sky I could see a rim of white under her irises I opened my knife
do you remember the day damuddy died when you sat down in the water in your drawers
yes
I held the point of the knife at her throat
it wont take but a second just a second then I can do mine I can do mine then
all right can you do yours by yourself
yes the blades long enough benjys in bed by now
yes
it wont take but a second Ill try not to hurt
all right
will you close your eyes
no like this youll have to push it harder
touch your hand to it . . .
but she didnt move her eyes were wide open looking past my head at the sky
Caddy do you remember how Dilsey fussed at you because your drawers were muddy
dont cry
Im not crying Caddy
push it are you going to
do you want me to
yes push it
touch your hand to it
dont cry poor Quentin . . .
what is it what are you doing
her muscles gathered I sat up
its my knife I dropped it
she sat up
what time is it
I dont know
she rose to her feet I fumbled along the ground
Im going let it go
I could feel her standing there I could smell her damp clothes feeling her there

its right here somewhere
let it go you can find it tomorrow come on
wait a minute I'll find it
are you afraid to
here it is it was right here all the time
was it come on . . .
its funny how you can sit down and drop something and have to hunt
all around for it (pp. 169–72)

Candace says that she had died for her lover many times, but for the narcissistic
Quentin the mention of sexual death evokes the threat of real death, the feared
dissolution of the ego through sexual union with another, the swallowing up of the
ego in the instinctual ocean of the unconscious. And Quentin, tormented by his
virginity, by his impotence ("poor Quentin youve never done that have you"), can
only reply to Candace's sexual death by offering a real *liebestod*. He puts his knife
to his sister's throat and proposes that they be joined forever in a murder/suicide—
a double killing that represents the equivalent, on the level of brother/sister incest,
of the suicidal murder of the brother seducer by the brother avenger. For if the
brother-seducer/brother-avenger relationship represents doubling and the brother-
sister relationship incest, then the brother/brother relationship is also a kind of
incest and the brother/sister relationship a kind of doubling. In at least one version
of the Narcissus myth (Pausanias 9.31.6), Narcissus is rendered inconsolable by the
death of his identical twin sister, and when he sees himself reflected in the water
he transfers to his own image the love that he felt for his dead twin. In this light,
consider once again the image that begins the scene: Quentin says, "I ran down
the hill in that vacuum of crickets like a breath travelling across a mirror she was
lying on her back in the water. . . ." The narcissistic implication is that his sister lying
on her back in the stream is like a mirror image of himself, and indeed, one of
the recurring motifs in Quentin's internal narrative is the image of his sister in her
wedding dress running toward him out of a mirror (pp. 96, 100). Further, Quentin
says that Ames was always "looking at me through her like through a piece of
coloured glass . . ." (p. 193).

It would appear that for Quentin the double as a male figure is associated
with the shadow and the double as a female figure is associated with the mirror
image. If so, then his suicide represents the attempt to merge those two images.
During his walk in the country on the afternoon of his death, Quentin senses the
nearness of a river and suddenly the smell of water evokes a memory of his desire
for his sister and his desire for death:

The draft in the door smelled of water, a damp steady breath. Sometimes I
could put myself to sleep saying that over and over until after the honeysuckle
got all mixed up in it the whole thing came to symbolise night and unrest I
seemed to be lying neither asleep nor awake looking down a long corridor
of grey halflight where all stable things had become shadowy paradoxical all
I had done shadows all I had felt suffered taking visible form antic and perverse

mocking without relevance inherent themselves with the denial of the significance they should have affirmed thinking I was I was not who was not was
not who.

I could smell the curves of the river beyond the dusk and I saw the last
light supine and tranquil upon tide-flats like pieces of broken mirror. . . . Benjamin the child of. How he used to sit before that mirror. Refuge
unfailing in which conflict tempered silenced reconciled. (pp. 188–89)

The image of Benjamin, Quentin's idiot younger brother, staring at himself in a
mirror, locked forever in mental childhood, is a forceful evocation of the infantile,
regressive character of narcissism, and it is in light of that infantile, regressive
character that we can understand Quentin's drowning of himself in the river as an
attempt to merge the shadow and the mirror image. Quentin's narcissism is, in
Freudian terms, a fixation in secondary narcissism, a repetition during a later period
of life (usually adolescence) of that primary narcissism that occurs between the
sixth and the eighteenth months, wherein the child first learns to identify with its
image and thus begins the work that will lead to the constitution of the ego as the
image of the self and the object of love. The fixation in secondary narcissism in
which the ego at a later period is recathected as the *sole* object of love condemns
the individual to an endless repetition of an infantile state. This attempt to make
the subject the sole object of its own love, to merge the subject and the object
in an internal love union, reveals the ultimate goal of all infantile, regressive tendencies, narcissism included: it is the attempt to return to a state in which subject
and object did not yet exist, to a time before that division occurred out of which
the ego sprang—in short, to return to the womb, to reenter the waters of birth.
But the desire to return to the womb is the desire for incest. Thus, Quentin's
narcissism is necessarily linked with his incestuous desire for his sister, for as Otto
Rank points out, brother-sister incest is a substitute for child-parent incest—what
the brother seeks in his sister is his mother.[2] And we see that the triangle of sister/
brother avenger/brother seducer is a substitute for the Oedipal triangle of mother/
father/son. Quentin's drowning of his shadow, then, is not only the punishment,
upon his own person, of the brother seducer by the brother avenger, it is as well
the union of the brother seducer with the sister, the union of Quentin's shadow
with his mirror image in the water, the mirror image of himself that evokes his
sister lying on her back in the stream. The punishment of the brother seducer by
the brother avenger is death, but the union of the brother seducer and the sister
is also death, for the attempt to merge the shadow and the mirror image results
in the total immersion of both in the water on which they are reflected, the
immersion of the masculine ego consciousness in the waters of its birth, in the
womb of the feminine unconscious from which it was originally differentiated. By
drowning his shadow, Quentin is able simultaneously to satisfy his incestuous desire
and to punish it, and as we noted earlier it is precisely this simultaneous satisfaction
and punishment of a repressed desire that is at the core of doubling. For Quentin,
the incestuous union and the punishment of that union upon his own person can

be accomplished by a single act because both the union and its punishment are a
liebestod, a dying of the ego into the other.

In the confrontation between Quentin and Candace at the stream, this linking
of sexual desire and death centers for Quentin around the image of Candace's
muddy drawers and the death of their grandmother, "Damuddy." The image recalls
an incident in their childhood when, during their grandmother's funeral, they had
been sent away from the house to play. Candace goes wading in the stream, and
when Quentin and Versh tell her that she'll get a whipping for getting her dress
wet, she says that she'll take it off to let it dry, and she asks the black boy Versh
to unbutton the back:

> "Dont you do it, Versh." Quentin said.
> "Taint none of my dress." Versh said.
> "You unbutton it, Versh." Caddy said, "Or I'll tell Dilsey what you did
> yesterday." So Versh unbuttoned it.
> "You just take your dress off." Quentin said. Caddy took her dress off
> and threw it on the bank. Then she didn't have on anything but her bodice
> and drawers, and Quentin slapped her and she slipped and fell down in the
> water. (pp. 37–38)

Candace splashes water on Quentin, an act that in retrospect is sexually symbolic,
and Quentin's fear that now they will both get a whipping destroys his attempt to
play the role of the protective brother. Shifting from an active to a passive role,
Quentin sees Caddy take charge and lead the children back to the house while
he lags behind, taunted by Caddy. When they reach the house, Caddy climbs the
tree outside the parlor window to see the funeral, and at that point the image of
her muddy drawers seen by the children below is fused with the image of Damuddy's death. It is significant that Quentin's obsessive linking of these two images
(his sexual desire for his sister and death) involves the repetition, in each case, of
the same word—the word "muddy" in Candace's "muddy drawers" and "Damuddy's" funeral, for the threat that sexual union poses to the bright, narcissistic
ego is, in Quentin's mind, associated with the image of mud—soft, dark, corrupt,
enveloping—the image of being swallowed up by the earth. In the scene where
Candace interrupts an abortive sexual encounter in the barn between Quentin
and a girl named Natalie ("a dirty girl like Natalie," as Candace says), Quentin
retaliates by jumping into the hog wallow and then smearing his sister with mud:

> *She had her back turned I went around in front of her. You know what I
> was doing? She turned her back I went around in front of her the rain creeping
> into the mud flatting her bodice through her dress it smelled horrible. I was
> hugging her that's what I was doing. . . .*
>
> *I dont give a damn what you were doing*
>
> *You dont you dont I'll make you I'll make you give a damn. She hit my
> hands away I smeared mud on her with the other hand I couldn't feel the
> wet smacking of her hand I wiped mud from my legs smeared it on her wet*

hard turning body hearing her fingers going into my face but I couldn't feel it even when the rain began to taste sweet on my lips. . . .

    We lay in the wet grass panting the rain like cold shot on my back. Do you care now do you do you

    My Lord we sure are in a mess get up. Where the rain touched my forehead it began to smart my hand came red away streaking of pink in the rain. Does it hurt

    Of course it does what do you reckon

    I tried to scratch your eyes out my Lord we sure do stink we better try to wash it off in the branch . . . (pp. 155–57)

Later, when Quentin identifies with his sister's love Dalton Ames and imagines Ames and Candace making "the beast with two backs" (p. 167), the image of Quentin and Candace smeared with mud from the hog wallow metamorphoses into the image of the swine of Eubuleus—the swine that are swallowed up into the earth when Hades carries Persephone down to be the queen of the dead. And a variant of this image occurs in Quentin's last internal monologue before he drowns himself when he imagines the clump of cedars where Candace used to meet her lovers: "Just by imagining the clump it seemed to me that I could hear whispers secret surges smell the beating of hot blood under wild unsecret flesh watching against red eyelids the swine untethered in pairs rushing coupled into the sea . . ." (p. 195).

    Since Quentin's incestuous desire for his sister is synonymous with death, it is no surprise that in the scene by the branch, where Quentin puts his knife to his sister's throat and offers to kill her and then himself, their conversation parodies that of sexual intercourse:

will you close your eyes
no like this youll have to push it harder
touch your hand to it . . .
push it are you going to
do you want me to
yes push it
touch your hand to it

It is a mark of the brilliance and centrality of this scene that its imagery evokes as well the reason for that fear which continually unmans Quentin whenever he tries to assume the masculine role. When Quentin puts his knife to his sister's throat, he is placing his knife at the throat of someone who is an image of himself, thereby evoking the threat of castration—the traditional punishment for incest. The brother seducer with the phallic knife at his sister's throat is as well the brother avenger with the castrating knife at the brother seducer's throat—the father with the castrating knife at the son's penis. The fear of castration fixes Quentin in secondary narcissism, for by making sexual union with a woman synonymous with death, the castration fear prevents the establishment of a love object outside the ego. Quentin's fear of castration is projected onto the figure of his sister, incest with whom would be punished by castration. Thus in her encounters with Quentin, Candace becomes the castrator. When Candace tells him to go ahead and use the knife, his fear unmans him; he drops the phallic knife and loses it, and when he tells Candace that he will find it in a moment, she asks, "Are you afraid to?" Recall as well that in the scene at the hog wallow Candace says that she tried to scratch Quentin's eyes out. Having failed in the masculine role of brother seducer in relation to Candace, Quentin shifts to a passive, feminine role, and Candace assumes the active, masculine role. It is a shift like the one that Quentin undergoes when he fails in the masculine role of brother avenger in relation to the seducer Dalton Ames; Quentin immediately assumes a feminine role, fainting like a girl in Ames's grasp. Indeed, brooding on that fear of risking his life that caused him to reject Ames's offer of the phallic pistol, Quentin thinks, "'And when he put Dalton Ames. Dalton Ames. Dalton Ames. When he put the pistol in my hand I didn't. . . . Dalton Ames. Dalton Ames. Dalton Ames. If I could have been his mother lying with open body lifted laughing, holding his father with my hand refraining, seeing, watching him die before he lived" (p. 99).

The explanation for this shifting from a masculine to a feminine role is to be found in the son's ambivalence toward his father in the castration complex. On the one hand, there is an aggressive reaction of the son toward the castrating father, a desire for the father's death, a desire to kill him. But on the other hand, there is a tender reaction, a desire to renounce the object that has caused the father's anger, to give up the penis and thus to retain the father's love by assuming a passive, feminine role in relation to him—in short, to become the mother in relation to the father.[3] In this second situation (the tender, passive reaction) the fear of castration turns into a longing for castration, and since, as Freud points out, the fear of death is an analogue of the fear of castration (S.E., 20:130), this transformation of the castration fear into a desire for castration within the incest scenario has as its analogue, within the scenario of narcissistic doubling, that fear of death that becomes a longing for death—the paradox, as Rank says, of a thanatophobia that leads to suicide. What the fear of castration is to incest the fear of death is to doubling, and as the fear of castration and the fear of death are analogues, so too are incest and doubling. We need only recall in this connection that the characteristic doubling scenario of madness leading to suicide often includes incidents of self-mutilation, for self-mutilation is simply a partial form of self-destruction. During the walk in the country that Quentin takes on the day of his suicide, he stops on a bridge and looks down at his shadow in the water and remembers,

> Versh told me about a man mutilated himself. He went into the woods and did it with a razor, sitting in a ditch. A broken razor, flinging them backward over his shoulder the same motion complete the jerked skein of blood backward not looping. But that's not it. It's not not having them. It's never to have had them then I could say O That That's Chinese I dont know Chinese. And Father said it's because you are a virgin: dont you see? Women are never

virgins. Purity is a negative state and therefore contrary to nature. It's nature is hurting you not Caddy and I said That's just words and he said So is virginity and I said you dont know. You cant know and he said Yes. On the instant when we come to realise that tragedy is second-hand.

Where the shadow of the bridge fell I could see down for a long way, but not as far as the bottom. (pp. 134–35)

In a real or imagined conversation with his father, bits of which recur during his internal narrative, Quentin confesses that he and Candace have committed incest, and he seeks a punishment, he says, that will isolate himself and his sister from the loud world. When his father asks him if he tried to force Candace to commit incest, Quentin replies, "i was afraid to i was afraid she might" (p. 195).

NOTES

[1] *The Sound and the Fury* (New York: Random House, 1946), p. 97. All subsequent quotations from *The Sound and the Fury* are taken from this edition.

[2] Otto Rank, *Das Inzest-Motive in Dichtung und Sage* (Leipzig and Vienna: Franz Deuticke, 1912), pp. 443–65.

[3] Sigmund Freud, *The Standard Edition of the Complete Psychological Works of Sigmund Freud*, trans. and ed. James Strachey, et al. (London: Hogarth Press, 1953), 20:106–7. All subsequent quotations from Freud are taken from this edition, which will be cited hereafter as S.E.

Gladys Milliner
THE THIRD EVE

Images of women in literature have been dominated by the two Eves—the First Eve, temptress, sinner, and mother of men; and the Second Eve, Virgin, sinless, and mother of the Redeemer of men. It is difficult to find a woman character who does not conform to some facet of one of these models and insists upon being herself, emerging as an individual human being, especially in the works of male writers. But William Faulkner created such a woman in Caddy Compson, who is many Eves to her brothers, but primarily a courageous woman, who refuses to conform to the stereotype of a lady and asserts her independence as a person, a Third Eve.

There is evidence that it was this quality that attracted Faulkner to her, that made him admire her so greatly, and that inspired him to write *The Sound and the Fury* in an attempt to capture the spirit of this Eve of the "weed-choked" garden of the Fallen Eden of the Old South. Yet, while Faulkner draws the characters of the ineffectual Adams, the three brothers, with sharp perception and deep insight, the portrait of Caddy remains blurred, even though he tried four times in the novel "to tell, try to draw the picture of Caddy." When asked why he did not have a section devoted to Caddy herself, Faulkner explained: "It began with the picture of the little girl's muddy drawers, climbing that tree to look in the parlor window with her brothers that didn't have the courage to climb the tree waiting to see what she saw. And I tried first to tell it with one brother, and that wasn't enough. That was Section One. I tried with another brother, and that wasn't enough. That was Section Two. I tried the third brother, because Caddy was still to me too beautiful and moving to reduce her to telling what was going on ... And that failed and I tried myself—the fourth section—to tell what happened, and I still failed."[1] Consequently, Caddy is seen only through the eyes of men, never from her point of view, as a woman might see herself. Yet by piecing together the various views of Caddy, a portrait of her does emerge—incomplete though it is—as neither the First Eve nor the Second Eve, but a montage of the qualities of both with something more that is herself—the Third Eve.

From *Midwest Quarterly* 16, No. 3 (Spring 1975): 268–75.

Since Faulkner never explained why Caddy is "too beautiful and too moving," the explanation must be found in the qualities that he attributed to the beauty of the human spirit. The first is the courage to prevail, to free the individual spirit from the restrictions put upon it by society. Caddy is the only Compson brave enough to escape from the isolation that shuts in the Compsons as it shuts in the South. She also has compassion, which she shows toward Benjy, Quentin, her father, and Dilsey. Most importantly, Caddy is the only Compson with the desire to know. Faulkner believed that, since "'the child has the capacity to do but it can't know," it must seek knowledge that will bring it maturity and wisdom "'when it is no longer able to do."[2]

In the decay of the Compson place, Faulkner creates the impression of a Fallen Eden, suggestive of the decay of the Compson family and of the South. According to Richard P. Adams' interpretation of Faulkner's South, "that region before the Civil War was an Eden of simplicity and innocence, ruined by the war and Reconstruction," and during the time of *The Sound and the Fury* is "a waste land where the aristocratic virtues of the old order have been abandoned . . . and the meaning and value of human life corrupted by money, mechanization, and moral relativity."[3] Each Compson child in a different way is an innocent of the Fallen Eden: Benjy, forever an innocent because he can never know corruption; Quentin, with his virginity and code of honor; Jason, with his naive belief in materialism and equally naive disbelief in virtue; and Caddy, always an innocent because she retains her childish curiosity about life.

The abandoned garden of the Compson place suggests a Fallen Eden in several respects. Against the house stands an apple tree that the children have been forbidden to climb because it leads to a vision of death through a window, the body of Damuddy, the children's grandmother, representative of the old order that is dying. Like Eve, Caddy is attracted to the forbidden tree in search of knowledge. When the children approach the tree, a snake crawls from under the house, symbolic of the evil that has corrupted the garden. The evil, according to Faulkner, is the old evil within man, but since the decadence of the Old South is involved, the snake must be symbolic of the curse upon the South that Faulkner believed was slavery, saying that "the South has got to work that curse out."[4] The effects of that curse linger in the South and upon the Compson children.

Only Caddy has the curiosity and the courage to defy authority by climbing the tree, while her timid brothers watch her from below in a tableau that is held throughout the novel. To Benjy, the idiot, who records the tableau in his mind, Caddy is the unfallen Eve in a natural Eden. Repeatedly he describes her as he apprehends nature through the sense of smell: "Caddy smelled like trees in the rain."[5] To Benjy, she is part of the tree he sees her climb, a part of nature, an unfallen world. To Quentin, Caddy is a virgin, the Second Eve, in the lost garden of the past. He, too, receives an impression of her through his senses—the scent of rain and honeysuckle, with a suggestion of fertility and life. But he also receives an impression of moral decay in association with the drawers dampened by the branch water and stained by mud, an impression of the fallen First Eve. Mingled with the associations with water is the too-sweet scent of honeysuckle, suggestive of Caddy's sexual promiscuity and the putrefaction of death, the death that comes through sin to Eden. To Jason, the fat, greedy little coward, standing with his grasping fists buried in his pockets, Caddy has about her the scent of money. He is not concerned with her muddy drawers because he is not concerned with sex. He is concerned only with whatever value she can be to him if he tells upon her transgression, the profit he can make from her sin.

As the Compson children grow older, moving in time from 1898 to 1910, the interior monologues of the brothers, always centered upon Caddy, the Eve in the tree, reveal differing views of their world, as well as of Caddy. Of their association of the tree with Caddy, Melvin Backman says, "Paradoxically, Caddy was the tree of life for Benjy, but for Quentin she would prove the fatal tree of knowledge."[6] Benjy's view of the world, formed by his senses, is compounded of an attraction to love and a rejection of corruption. Before Caddy becomes tainted by sexual promiscuity, she embodies for him an innocent world of love. She is not only the unfallen Eve, the clean, life-giving smell of trees, but she is also the mother figure, a kind of virgin mother, who is the warmth and purity of fire, the comfort of an old slipper, and the companionable, rounding form of a pillow. Like the mirror in the living room, she is for him the mirror of life, which he can apprehend only obliquely. In the mirror he can watch "the bright, smooth shapes" and the fire, but he can also see "Caddy, with flowers in her hair, and a long veil like shining wind," going away out of the mirror (p. 47). With Caddy's fall, Benjy makes the discovery of corruption in the world that she represents, of sin in Eden, when the smell of trees is replaced by the scent of perfume, suggestive of sex and Caddy's lovers, which Benjy rejects: "Caddy put her arms around me, and her shining veil, and I couldn't smell the trees anymore and I began to cry" (p. 48). Thus, when Caddy becomes a fallen Eve, a virgin mother who has lost her virginity, a woman who is a human being, she is rejected by the childlike, immature Adam.

Quentin, the Adam concerned with sin, is tormented by thoughts of the innocent Eve in the tree and the fallen Eve with the muddy drawers. For him the world that revolves around Caddy is divided between the decadent garden of the Old South, which he attempts to preserve, as he attempts to preserve Caddy's virginity, and the chaotic life of the present, outside that garden, to which he fears he will be banished. The Calvinistic concept of sin and morality, ingrained in Southern culture, and the Southern code of honor, based upon the preservation of the purity of the white woman, the image of the Second Eve, are associated with Caddy by Quentin, "Who loved not his sister's body but some concept of Compson honor precariously (and he knew well) only temporarily supported by the minute fragile membrane of her maidenhead" (p. 411). But Caddy, a woman, not a myth, rejects Southern tradition by regarding virginity as completely unimportant. According to Mr. Compson, ideals of honor have been imposed upon white women in Southern society by white men to preserve the line of descent. As Quentin recalls on his last day in Cambridge, it is a gentleman's duty "Because it means less to women Father said. He said it was men invented virginity not women" (p. 96). From his father Quentin has inherited the code that demands protection of the white woman as protection of the lines of descent.

But Caddy, the unconventional Southern woman, defies that tradition, by becoming a mother, not through love or temptation, but deliberately to assert her sexual freedom and to escape conformity and eventually to escape from the isolation of the Compson garden. She is the only one of the Compson children to produce a child, because she is the only Compson with the spirit of life within her. Ironically, none of the males has an heir, and Caddy's child is a girl, thus relegating the Compson name and family to the dead world of the garden of the past.

The girl Quentin is the obverse image of her mother. The story that began with the image of the girl Caddy climbing up the tree of knowledge ends with her daughter climbing down to escape with bitter knowledge. Faulkner pointed out the significance of this dual image: "And then I realized the symbolism of the soiled pants, and that image was replaced by the one of the fatherless and motherless girl climbing down the rainpipe to escape from the only home she had, where she had never been offered love or affection or understanding."[7] Aware that Jason is the cause of her fallen character, she tells him, "I'm bad and I'm going to hell, and I don't care. I'd rather be in hell than anywhere you are" (p. 235). Her outburst is an inversion of her uncle Quentin's desire to be damned in hell with Caddy, the Calvinistic Adam's desire to share hell with Eve.

Of the Compson children only Caddy, "the frail doomed vessel" of the Compsons' honor, escapes from the garden of the past into the world of the present. But in the modern world she becomes lost, and Faulkner's vision of her fades. In the last section of the novel, Faulkner's omniscient section, Caddy is an illusory figure outside the Compson garden, whose presence is made known only by the money she sends to Jason for her daughter. Little else is known of Caddy's life after she makes her escape, except what can be gathered from a snapshot of her with a Nazi officer, with the implication that she is his mistress. The novel that began with the vivid picture of the girl in the tree ends with a hazy picture of that girl as a woman wandering aimlessly in a confused world. Yet Faulkner wrote the novel in an effort to portray his vision of the beauty of Caddy's dynamic spirit in a changing world. As he said after the death of his first daughter, "I, who never had a sister and was fated to lose my daughter in infancy, set out to make myself a beautiful and tragic little girl."[8] But even the "beautiful and tragic little girl" of the novel is lost when she becomes a woman.

A central question, then, is why the girl about whom the novel was written is only an unseen presence in the concluding section. The girl who was too beautiful to tell her own story ends that story as the mistress of a Nazi officer. The "voice that breathed o'er Eden" is silenced. If it could have spoken, it might have described a different fate for the woman who had the courage to escape from the mythical Eden of the past to become a free woman in the present. In facing the realities of the modern world, such a woman might have survived in a better, more independent way than as a kept woman, moving from one sordid affair to another. Since Faulkner narrates the last section, it would have been possible for him to tell the story that Caddy could not tell if his vision of her had not been lost in the confusion of the modern world. In that section he creates quite vividly the portrait of another woman, Dilsey, with her love and endurance. Dilsey conforms to the traditional image of the black woman, fulfilling the roles of mother and servant, patiently mothering and serving a white family and taking their abuse, with none of the inner rebellion that might be expected in her because she is both black and female. But Caddy does not conform to the traditional image of the white woman, either as the First Eve or as the Second Eve. Faulkner created a vision of a girl surrounded by a wall of myth, but lost it when that girl became a woman and passed beyond that wall.

Although Caddy is seen only dimly through the mirror of the minds of her brothers, the effect is an impressionistic portrait of a woman as she is visualized by men. As Benjy sees her, she is a woman with the natural innocence of the First Eve and the motherly instincts of the Second Eve. As Quentin sees her, she is a woman with the purity of the Second Eve that is destroyed by the sexual attraction and taint of sin of the First Eve. As Jason sees her, she is the fallen Eve, who must bear the blame for sin, while he profits from the wages of her sin, never admitting that he is equally guilty in his own sterile sexual affair. As Faulkner sees her, she has the beauty of the human spirit, but is doomed as a woman despite her curiosity, courage, and strength. Perhaps that is why he believed her story could never be finished, but that is also why there is a story. Caddy is not a myth but a woman who is also a human being. Faulkner's girl in the tree is a vision of a Third Eve, an image that is rare in literature.

NOTES

[1]See *Faulkner in the University,* ed. Frederick L. Gwynn and Joseph L. Blotner (New York: Vintage Books, 1965) pp. 1, 6.
[2]"William Faulkner: An Interview," *Writers at Work,* ed. Malcom Cowley (New York: Viking Press, 1958), p. 140.
[3]Richard P. Adams, *Faulkner: Myth and Motion* (Princeton: Princeton University Press, 1966), p. 77.
[4]*Faulkner in the University,* p. 79.
[5]William Faulkner, *The Sound and the Fury* (New York: Vintage Books, 1956), p. 22. Subsequent references will occur in the text.
[6]Melvin Backman, *Faulkner: The Major Years* (Bloomington, Ind.: Indiana University Press, 1966), p. 29.
[7]"William Faulkner: An Interview," p. 140.
[8]James B. Meriwether, "An Introduction for *The Sound and the Fury,*" *Southern Review,* VIII, N.S. (Autumn 1972), p. 710.

André Bleikasten

CADDY, OR THE QUEST
FOR EURYDICE

That literature functions as a substitute is an assumption verified by Faulkner's own testimony: "the beautiful and tragic little girl" whom he set out to create through the power of words was manifestly intended to fill a vacancy. In his introduction to the novel, he refers to absence ("I, who had never had a sister") as well as to mourning ("...fated to lose my daughter in infancy"), equating in retrospect the imaginary *lack* with an actual *loss*. It is also interesting to note that the seminal image of the novel is focused on the grandmother's death, and that Faulkner's initial concern was with the Compson children's reactions to this event:

> It struck me that it would be interesting to imagine the thoughts of a group of children who were sent away from the house the day of their grandmother's funeral, their curiosity about the activity in the house, their efforts to find out what was going on, and the notions that would come into their minds.[1]

It is worth recalling, too, that *As I Lay Dying*, whose composition is chronologically close to that of *The Sound and the Fury*, revolves around a mother's death and the behavior of her family during and after the event. Mourning, then, is not only a possible key to the process of Faulkner's creation, but a motif readily traced in the novels themselves, notably those of his early maturity. One would like to know, of course, what its emergence at this point means in psycho-biographical terms; yet, apart from the hints one can find in Faulkner's comments and above all in his fiction, there is unfortunately little to gratify our curiosity. *The Sound and the Fury*, Faulkner told Maurice-Edgar Coindreau, his French translator, was written at a time when he "was beset with personal problems."[2] What these "personal problems" actually were must remain a matter of pure speculation.

What is fairly obvious, however, is that the novels written during those years, especially *The Sound and the Fury* and *As I Lay Dying*, are novels *about* lack and loss, in which desire is always intimately bound up with death. And it is clear too

From *The Most Splendid Failure: Faulkner's* The Sound and the Fury (Bloomington: Indiana University Press, 1976), pp. 52–66.

that they have sprung *out of* a deep sense of lack and loss—texts spun around a primal gap.

In *The Sound and the Fury* this gap is reduplicated and represented in the pathetic and intriguing figure of Caddy Compson, the lost sister. Even when the novel was still a vague project in the author's mind, "the beautiful and tragic little girl" was already there, and we find her again in the basic image which was to inform the whole book:

> . . . perhaps the only thing in literature which would ever move me very much: Caddy climbing the pear tree to look in the window at her grandmother's funeral while Quentin and Jason and Benjy and the negroes looked up at the muddy seat of her drawers.[3]

Out of this emotion-packed image the novel grew. In retrospect, one is tempted to read it as the latter's prefiguration, or at least as a foreshadowing of its dominant themes: an image of innocence confronted with what eludes and threatens it; an image of childhood caught on the brink of forbidden knowledge—evil, sex, death. To Faulkner it must have presented itself as an enigma to be questioned, a secret to be deciphered, and in this respect one should note the emphasis given in the little tableau to the act of seeing and watching: the three brothers looking up at Caddy's muddy drawers; Caddy looking in the window at the funeral preparations. Curiosity about sex and curiosity about death prompt their common desire to see. Yet it is certainly not fortuitous that while the boys' curiosity comes close to sexual voyeurism, their reckless sister is fascinated by the mystery of death. Caddy is the only one to climb the tree of knowledge; her brothers stay timidly below and are content with staring at the stain on her drawers. Caddy occupies in fact an intermediary position, suspended as she is between her brothers and the intriguing scene of death—a symbolic reminder, perhaps, of the mythic mediating function of woman through whom, for man, passes all knowledge about the origins, all knowledge about the twin enigmas of life and death.

One could carry the investigation further and point out the striking parallels between this matricial scene and the "primal fantasies" postulated by psychoanalysis. The symbolic significance of the scene lies first of all in its insistence on perplexed watching: hinging upon the question of origins, as all *ur*-fantasies do,[4] it relates a desire to *know* back to the primitive, infantile wish to *see*. As to the ultimate objects of the children's curiosity, they are clearly designated as death and sex, but the point here is that in the spatial pattern of the scene the brothers are to Caddy as Caddy is to the window, thus suggesting a virtual equation of sex (the muddy drawers) with death (Damuddy's funeral).[5] Equally relevant in this connection is the fact that the boys are peering at a little girl's drawers—that which both conceals and betrays her sexual identity, that is, in psychoanalytic terms, her lack of a penis. Freud writes in his essay on fetishism that "probably no male human being is spared the terrifying shock of threatened castration at the sight of the female genitals."[6] True, there is no such shock in Faulkner's evocation of the scene; yet, curiously enough, when in the same essay Freud accounts for the nature of certain fetishes by "the circumstance that the inquisitive boy used to peer up the woman's legs towards her genitals."[7] he seems to be describing the very position of the Compson brothers in relation to Caddy. Moreover, even though castration is not referred to explicitly, it is suggested by the symbolic intersection of sex and death. Castration—according to Freud the equivalent of death in the language of the unconscious—provides a further link between the two themes.

The whole scene may thus be read as the emblem of a dual revelation: the simultaneous discovery of the difference between the sexes and of death. The working out of the episode of Damuddy's death in the first section of the novel definitely bears out such a reading. Revelation (etymologically the removal of the *velum,* i.e., the veil) becomes there quite literally a denudation, a laying bare: on the day when their grandmother dies, Caddy undresses at the branch—an act to which Quentin responds with violence by slapping her,[8] and the scene is strangely echoed by Caddy's later allusions to the "undressing" of the dead mare Nancy by the buzzards (see 40), and to the possibility of an identical fate for Damuddy's corpse (see 42). Once again, sex and death are brought into resonance through a common motif.

Considered in all its implications, the seminal scene points unmistakably forward to what is at stake in the novel. It also sheds light on the author's deeper motivations, for in a sense these curious children, confronted with the mysteries of sex and death, are the fictive delegates of that supreme voyeur who is none other than the novelist. He too wants to see and know. Just as we, his readers, do.

At the heart of the enigma: Caddy, a turbulent little Eve, rash and defiant, perched on a pear tree,[9] and already significantly associated with the Edenic innocence of trees and with mud, symbol of guilt and sin. It is her story—and that of her daughter Quentin, Caddy's debased copy—that Faulkner wanted to tell in *The Sound and the Fury:* "a tragedy of two lost women."[10] And the privileged place this book held in his affection is inseparable from his abiding tenderness for Caddy:

> To me she was the beautiful one, she was my heart's darling. That's what I wrote the book about and I used the tools which seemed to me the proper tools to try to tell, try to draw the picture of Caddy.[11]

It is hardly surprising that Faulkner should speak of Caddy with the accents of love.[12] Wasn't she from the outset a creation of desire? Before becoming the "real" sister of Benjy, Quentin and Jason in the novel, Caddy had been Faulkner's imaginary one, invented to make up for a lack. Yet fiction here does not play the customary game of illusion; it does not work out as a consoling substitute. For Caddy is exposed as a fiction within the fiction, her presence in the novel being rendered in such a way as to make her appear throughout as a pure figure of *absence.* Caddy, "the beautiful one," is no sooner found than she is lost again. *The Sound and the Fury* does not celebrate the (imaginary) triumph of desire, but reduplicates its necessary defeat. This novel is Faulkner's first descent into Hell, and Caddy remains his ever-elusive Eurydice.

This is why Caddy, the novelist's secret Muse and the very soul of the novel, cannot be considered the heroine of the book in any traditional sense. A chimera to the author, she never ceases to be a chimera in the novel. To deplore that she escapes satisfactory definition is a hardly relevant complaint, for she is both more and less than a "character": she is at once the focal and the vanishing point, the bewitching *image* around which everything revolves. From the writer's mind she has slipped into the narrators'; from being Faulkner's private fantasy she becomes the obsessive memory of the Compson brothers, without ever really assuming shape and substance in the space of fiction.

One might even argue that Caddy is little more than a blank counter, an empty signifier, a name in itself void of meaning and thus apt to receive any meaning. Her function within the novel's semantic structure could be compared to that of a joker in a game of cards: the word "Caddy" assumes meaning only in relation to the contextual network within which it occurs, and since, from one section to another, it is drawn into different verbal environments, woven into different textures, it is invested with ever-renewed significances. Caddy is a sign, with all the arbitrariness of the sign, and Faulkner's keen awareness of the chancy and shifting relationships between word and thing, language and meaning, is attested on the very first page of the novel by his deliberate punning on "caddie" and "Caddy."[13] The homophony is confusing to Benjy, who mistakes "caddie" for the name of his beloved sister, and so it is, ironically enough, to the reader who, at this point, realizes that the setting is a golf course, but is not yet in a position to understand what "caddie" evokes in Benjy's mind and why it makes him moan with grief. As most openings in fiction do, the initial golf course scene in *The Sound and the Fury* serves the purpose of establishing the rules of the game to be played by the readers. By exploiting from the outset the polysemy of words, Faulkner disorients the reader, frustrates his expectations, alerts him to the trickeries and duplicities of language, as if to warn him that the world he is about to enter is not *his* world. The words used in Benjy's monologue may be simple, but their familiar surfaces soon turn out to be extremely deceptive. We must learn the alphabet and grammar of his idiolect before we can begin to discover what his fumbling speech is all about.

Words are an inexhaustible source of ambiguities and confusions, so that the communication they permit is always liable to misapprehensions. Words are signs everyone assembles in transitory patterns and fills with private significances that often make sense for him alone. What "caddie" means for the golfers is different from what it means for Benjy; what it means for Benjy is different from what it means for us. Yet in its active emptiness and its extreme plasticity, language possesses formidable powers, and the random utterance of two syllables is enough to arouse Benjy's anguish and grief.

Caddy is just a name, or the deceptive echo of a name. On the day when the novel begins—April 7, 1928—the person to whom it refers has been missing from the Compson family for many years. Benjy's moaning points at once to an absence, an absence which the perception of anything however remotely related to his lost sister instantly quickens and thickens in his vacant mind. To Benjy, Caddy is the nearest of absences. His memory has no memories. He cannot remember; he cannot forget. For him it is as though Caddy had only departed a few seconds ago: her trace is forever fresh, and the merest sensation—something seen, heard, smelled—recalls her presence with agonizing immediacy. In surprisingly similar ways, Caddy also haunts her brother Quentin, holding him in her spell, leaving him no rest and no escape except in death. And even to Jason, for all his declared indifference and contempt, she will be a festering wound.

Yet at the same time—precisely because she is nothing but a haunting memory—Caddy remains to the end a being out of reach, an elusive figure not unlike Proust's "creatures of flight." She is the presence of what is not there, the imperious call of absence, and it is from her tantalizing remoteness that she holds her uncanny power over those she has left.

All the scenes out of the past which come to beset memory both bring her closer and remove her further away. Of Caddy nothing remains but a series of snapshots, vivid and unreal, in which her fleeting image is forever fixed:

> Only she was running already when I heard it. In the mirror she was running before I knew what it was. That quick, her train caught up over her arm she ran out of the mirror like a cloud, her veil swirling in long glints her heels brittle and fast clutching her dress onto her shoulder with the other hand, running out of the mirror . . . (100).

Barely glimpsed, Caddy the (no longer "unravish'd") bride at once vanishes, and all that a glance could grasp was a silent rush reflected in a mirror. What lingers in the memory is at best the reflection of a reflection.

Or consider this other obsessive image of the lost sister, likewise linked to an event that Quentin cannot forget, the loss of her virginity: Caddy no longer caught running away, but immobilized in the silent suddenness of her appearance: "One minute she was standing by the door" (98).[14] Whether Caddy's silhouette is fleetingly reflected in a mirror or emerges unexpectedly in the doorway, there is each time the same disturbing oscillation between absence and presence, the same paradoxical sense of receding proximity or close remoteness.

It is noteworthy too that Caddy is associated time and again with the immaterial and the impalpable: reflections (79, 95, 100, 186), shadows (100, 192), moonlight (100), a cloud (100), a breath (186), "a long veil like shining wind" (47; see also 48, 100). Caddy's evanescence in space constantly parallels her inaccessibility in time. Not that she is ever etherealized into a conventionally "poetic" creature. But insofar as she must remain the ambiguous and evasive object of desire and memory, she can be approached and apprehended only in oblique ways. Caddy cannot be described; she can only be circumscribed, conjured up through the suggestive powers of metaphor and metonymy. A realistic rendering of the character is out of the question. Only the ruses and indirections of poetic discourse can do justice to the burning absence which Caddy "embodies" in the novel.

To the very extent that Caddy is literally nowhere, she is metaphorically everywhere. Her presence/absence becomes diffused all over the world, pointing, like so many feminine figures of Faulkner's earlier and later work, to an elemental complicity between Woman and the immemorial Earth. Her swiftness and lightness relate her to the wind; her vital warmth to "the bright smooth shapes" of fire;[15] her muddy drawers and treelike odor[16] to the fecundity and foulness of the land. Yet above all Caddy is the most enticing and most pathetic of Faulkner's nymphs. In the entire novel there is scarcely a scene in which Caddy does not appear in close conjunction with *water*. It is in the branch near the Compson house that she wets her dress and drawers on the day of Damuddy's death (19–22); it is in the same branch that Quentin and Caddy wash off the stinking mud of the pig trough after the Natalie incident (172);[17] and it is there again that Quentin finds his sister, sitting in the water, one summer evening, after the family has discovered her affair with Dalton Ames (186). Lastly, in the third section, Jason remembers her standing over her father's grave in a drenching rain (251). Throughout the novel, water is Caddy's element, and like Caddy herself, it is drawn into an extremely ambiguous symbolic pattern. In the branch scenes it is primarily the lustral water of purification rituals, and it would be easy to supply further illustrations of its cleansing function: Caddy, at fourteen, washing off the perfume to quiet Benjy (50); Caddy, washing her mouth after kissing Charlie in the swing (58); and, finally, Benjy pulling at his sister's dress, dragging her into the bathroom after the loss of her virginity (84–85). After these ritual ablutions, Caddy "smells like trees" again, except in the last scene where Benjy keeps on crying even after Caddy has bathed herself.

Water, however, is not only a symbol of purity. If it possesses a restorative power, at least in the eyes of the novel's characters, and if Faulkner at times suggests its function in Christian baptism (it rains on the night Benjy's name is changed), there are also many significant intimations of its erotic quality. Bathing, in particular, as evoked in the novel, seems to prompt a kind of soft, sensuous, almost sensual intimacy between water and flesh, and to prurient eyes the spectacle of this tender complicity may become both a scandal and a temptation. In the insidious caress of water, in the way it reveals the body in its embrace, there is something all but immodest which, even in the early childhood scene at the branch, disturbs and alarms young Quentin. For him, who then begins to act as guardian of Caddy's "honor," the sight of his sister and of the drenched dress clinging to her body is no longer an innocent spectacle. And when he slaps her for having undressed, he introduces by this very gesture the first suspicion of evil into a hitherto intact childhood world.

In Quentin's reminiscences and reveries, flesh and sex are repeatedly linked to suggestions of dampness and fluidity, and as the hour of his death draws nearer, it almost seems as if the waters were slowly rising, submerging his mind and memory, bringing him ever closer to the instant of his drowning. Thus, in the long breathless memory sequence in which he relives his poignant encounter with Caddy at the branch and his subsequent meeting with Dalton Ames near the bridge (185–203), water saturates the whole atmosphere with a silent drizzle. Quentin inhales the smell of the rain, breathes in the scent of honeysuckle wafted on the humid warmth of twilight. And out of all this mugginess emerges the body of his nymph-sister—water made flesh:

> . . . I ran down the hill in that vacuum of crickets like a breath travelling across a mirror she was lying in the water her head on the sand spit the water flowing about her hips there was a little more light in the water her skirt half saturated flopped along her flanks to the waters motion in heavy ripples going nowhere renewed themselves of their own movement I stood on the bank I could smell the honeysuckle on the water gap the air seemed to drizzle with honeysuckle and with the rasping of crickets a substance you could feel on the flesh (186).

As in Faulkner's early sketch "Nympholepsy," woman's body—"her hips," "her flanks"—is associated wtih running water, and as Quentin watches his sister lying there, he cannot help thinking back to the day long past when as a little girl she had soiled her dress and drawers: "do you remember the day damuddy died when you sat down in the water in your drawers" (188). Quentin himself is aware of the symbolic relationship between the two scenes; in retrospect the childhood episode acquires a premonitory meaning, Caddy's muddy drawers becoming a symbol of her physical and moral defilement, of what Quentin considers to be an indelible stain on her honor: her fall from sexual innocence. This irremediable loss is the focal point of Quentin's obsession, an obsession eagerly feeding on every sense impression: the sight of flowing water, the smell of rain and honeysuckle, the chirp of crickets, shadows, warmth, moisture, everything melts into "a substance you could feel on the flesh." It is clear that Quentin's obsession, as it is described here, is by no means the abstract, disembodied mania for which it has been all too often mistaken by critics. Experienced at first in the sultry profusion of immediate sensations, the traumatic shock is relived by Quentin's memory with hallucinatory vividness and intensity.

There is no Proustian reunion, though, for Faulkner's hero. Caddy risen out of the past through the sortileges of memory is not Caddy recaptured. Memory only serves to exacerbate a sense of irrevocable loss. The past is recollected in fever and pain, never in tranquillity, and the camera obscura of memory turns out to be a torture chamber. It is never a shelter; happy memories have no place in it. As far back as it can reach, Quentin's memory encounters a Caddy *already* all but lost: as if she had resented her brother's jealous vigilance from the outset and were impatient to flee from the prison of innocence in which he would forever keep her, she is always seen rebelling against his demands, always on the point of running away. In this respect, the scene of the muddy drawers—one of the earliest among the childhood incidents recalled in his monologue—is equally prophetic: it marks the beginning of the ineluctable movement which is to separate him from his sister. From this childhood scene to Caddy's wedding, nearly all the fragments of the past which erupt into Quentin's mind are related to Caddy's gradual "betrayal," and each of his painful memories reenacts one moment in the process of her desertion.

Presence in absence, nearness in distance, nothing perhaps better sums up the paradox of Quentin's haunted memory than *odor*. A subtle emanation from things and beings, odor, as Jean-Paul Sartre writes, is "a disembodied body, vaporized, remaining entire in itself, yet turned into volatile essence."[18] Like memory, it is a diffuse presence, a felt absence, a tantalizing intimation of being. Like symbols, it acts by indirection, through allusion and suggestion: to the extent that it always has the power to evoke something other than itself, to point an absence, one might consider it a "natural" metaphor. Small wonder, then, that the fragrance of *honeysuckle* is the most pregnant and most poignant symbol in the Quentin section.

Quentin associates Caddy with the odor of honeysuckle, just as Benjy associated her with the smell of trees. But whereas in the first section "she smelled like trees" functions as an index to Caddy's sexual innocence and vanishes as soon as the latter is compromised (see, for example, the perfume incident, 48–51), the meaning of honeysuckle in Quentin's monologue changes as Caddy changes, and its scent is irremediably corrupted when it comes to reek in Quentin's nostrils as the smell of her sex and sin. It is noteworthy that the term "honeysuckle," which occurs approximately thirty times in section 2, is nowhere as frequent as in the scene immediately following Quentin's discovery of his sister's loss of virginity (185–203): the scent of honeysuckle then becomes the pivot in a shifting complex of sense impressions. After blending into the uncertain grayness of twilight (119), it combines with the humidity of the atmosphere (189), "coming up in damp waves" (192) or drizzling like the rain (191). Through the cross-play of synaesthesia, honeysuckle is made to encompass and condense the entire field of sensory experience: something at once smelled, seen, and felt, it suffuses the whole scene. Yet, while metamorphosing and expanding across space, the smell also seems to flow back to Caddy as to its source, and Quentin refers to it as though it were a carnal secretion on the surface of her skin, a substance exuded from her flesh: "...the smell of honeysuckle upon her face and throat" (183); "...it was on her face and throat like paint" (188). Quentin thus comes to resent the cloying odor as a disturbing indiscretion, an almost obscene exuding of the innermost secrets of the flesh. Associated with Caddy's lovemaking in the swing by the cedars and eventually equated with Caddy herself, it symbolizes in his mind "the bittersweet mystery of sisterly sex"[19] as well as the unbearable scandal of its violation. It quickens his obsession, becomes the very emblem of his anguish and torment: "...after the honeysuckle got all mixed up in it the whole thing came to symbolize night and unrest" (211). In his confrontation with Caddy about Dalton Ames, his sister reminds him that he once liked the smell (190); now he hates it, cursing "that damn honeysuckle" (185; see also 190, 191). So hateful has it become to him that it even oppresses him physically, making him gasp for breath: "...I had to pant to get any air at all out of that thick grey honeysuckle" (188). The sweet "honey" of sisterhood,

which Quentin so avidly "suckled" in his childish greed, has thickened into a suf-
focating substance, and now has the bitter taste of loss.

Trees, water, twilight, honeysuckle—all the nature imagery related to Caddy,
so far from calling attention to itself as symbolic, seems to grow out of the soil of
subjective experience while being at the same time inextricably bound up with the
sensible world. It never hardens into the fixed patterns of allegory; its mobile and
manifold symbolism originates in the dynamic exchanges between a self and its
concrete environment. If some of these images run through several sections, they
can never be separated from the singular voice in whose discourse they occur:
they reflect the changing moods or the stubborn obsessions of a particular consciousness; they belong to the shifting landscapes of an individual mind.

Yet the central ambiguity to which all these images ultimately refer is that of
Caddy herself. Caddy, as we have already seen, is first and foremost an image;
she exists only in the minds and memories of her brothers. We can find out what
she represents for Benjy, Quentin, and Jason; we never discover what she actually
is. Hence her many and contradictory faces: she is in turn sister and mother, virgin
and whore, angel and demon; she at once embodies fecundity and foulness, the
nostalgia for innocence and the call to corruption, the promise of life and the vertigo
of death. She is in fact what woman has always been in man's imagination: the
figure par excellence of the Other, a blank screen onto which he projects both
his desires and his fears, his love and his hate. And insofar as this Other is a myth
and a mirage, a mere fantasy of the Self, it is bound to be a perpetual deceit and
an endless source of disappointment. Caddy, to borrow a phrase from Paul Claudel,
is "the promise that cannot be kept, and her grace consists in nothing else."[20]

Even so, she is more than the sum of these fantasy images. Faulkner's triumph
in creating Caddy is that her elusive figure eventually transcends the abstract
categories and rigid patterns in which her brothers attempt to imprison her, just
as she escapes any facile sentimentalizing or demonizing on the author's part. Not
that the reader is enabled to infer a "true" picture of Caddy from the information
he is given in the novel. There is little doubt, of course, that she possesses the
vitality, the courage, the capacity for love and compassion which her self-centered
brothers and parents so sadly lack.[21] It is quite obvious, too, that she is both the
tragic victim of her family and the unwitting agent of its doom. But to focus
exclusively on Caddy's assumed psychology or to dwell at length on her moral
significance is to miss the point. Caddy was elusive to her creator; so she is to her
brothers in the novel, and so she must remain to the reader. She cannot be
assessed according to the same criteria as the other characters. However complex
her characterization (and it is indeed more complex than has been generally acknowledged), Caddy belongs in the last resort to another space, to what might be
called the novel's utopia. "The true life is absent," Rimbaud wrote. In *The Sound
and the Fury* Caddy is a pathetic emblem of that desired other life, while her fate
poignantly confirms its impossibility in a world of alienation and disease.

Henry James thought that "a story-teller who aims at anything more than a fleeting success has no right to tell an ugly story unless he knows its beautiful counterpart."[22] The story of the Compsons is indeed "an ugly story"; Caddy, the daughter and sister of the imagination, the figure projected by "the heart's desire," is "its beautiful counterpart." Let us remember, however, that from the very beginning she was conceived of as "a beautiful *and* tragic little girl." Caddy is a dream of beauty wasted and destroyed. Her presence/absence at the center and periphery of the novel signals the unfulfillment of the writer's desire as well as the inescapable incompletion of his work. Caddy's beauty is the beauty of failure.

NOTES

[1] Reported by Maurice-Edgar Coindreau, in "Preface to *The Sound and the Fury*," *The Time of William Faulkner* (Columbia: University of South Carolina Press, 1971), p. 41. The autobiographical source of the Damuddy episode is presumably the funeral of Faulkner's grandmother, Lelia Swift Butler, in 1907. Faulkner was then ten years old—approximately the same age as Quentin's at the time of Damuddy's death in the novel.

[2] *The Time of William Faulkner*, p. 49.

[3] "An Introduction for *The Sound and the Fury*," *The Southern Review*, N.S., VIII (October 1972), 710.

[4] On this point, see "Fantasmes originaires," in Jean Laplanche and J. B. Pontalis, *Vocabulaire de la psychanalyse* (Paris: Presses Universitaires de France, 1967), pp. 157–59.

[5] In this connection it is also interesting to note the phonic kinship of *muddy* and *Damuddy*.

[6] "Fetishism" (1927), in *The Standard Edition of the Complete Psychological Works of Sigmund Freud*, ed. and trans. James Strachey (London: The Hogarth Press, 1964), vol. XXI, p. 154. All further references to Freud will be to this edition.

[7] Ibid., p. 155.

[8] *The Sound and the Fury* (New York: Jonathan Cape and Harrison Smith, 1929), pp. 20–21. All page references in my study refer to this edition.

[9] With regard to the Edenic connotations of the scene, it is noteworthy that in one of his interviews Faulkner confused Caddy's pear tree with an apple tree (see *Faulkner in the University*, ed. Frederick L. Gwynn and Joseph L. Blotner, Charlottesville: University of Virginia Press, 1959, p. 31). Some critics have pointed to further biblical connotations in the description of the scene in the novel: before Caddy climbs the tree, "a snake [crawls] out from under the house" (45), and a few moments later Dilsey says to her, "You Satan . . . Come down from there" (54).

[10] *Lion in the Garden: Interviews with William Faulkner, 1926–1962*, ed. James B. Meriwether and Michael Millgate (New York: Random House, 1968), p. 244.

[11] *Faulkner in the University*, p. 6.

[12] See also what Faulkner told Maurice-Edgar Coindreau: ". . . the same thing happened to me that happens to many writers—I fell in love with one of my characters, Caddy. I loved her so much I couldn't decide to give her life just for the duration of a short story. She deserved more than that" (*The Time of William Faulkner*, p. 41). Faulkner's fascination with girls can be traced back to his earlier writings. Among the figures anticipating Caddy one might mention Juliet Bunden (in "Adolescence," an unpublished story written in 1922), Frankie (in an untitled and unpublished story seemingly written in 1924), Jo-Addie (in "Elmer," the uncompleted novel begun in 1925), the nameless girl who turns out to be "Little sister Death" (in "The Kid Learns," 1925), and Dulcie, the little heroine of Faulkner's tale, "The Wishing Tree" (1927). Most of the young female characters in his first three novels are also related to Caddy in some way or other, Patricia Robyn (*Mosquitoes*) being probably the one who bears the closest resemblance to her. The heroine of *The Sound and the Fury* is of course much more complex than any of these figures, and Faulkner's affective involvement with her has deep autobiographical sources. In creating her, he drew more than ever before on memories of his own childhood and adolescence. It seems safe to assume that Estelle Oldham, whom he had come to know as a little boy and with whom he fell in love as a young teen-ager, served as a model for Caddy. But so did Sallie Murry, the tomboyish cousin to whom, as Joseph Blotner points out, Faulkner "had been almost as close as a sister" (*Faulkner: A Biography*, New York: Random House, 1974, vol. I, p. 568). And one might do well to remember that Estelle also served as a model for the devastating portrait of Cecily

Saunders in *Soldiers' Pay*. Which is to say that Caddy, even though she rose out of the depths of Faulkner's private experience, is above all a literary creation.

[13]Further name-confusions are induced by the presence in the novel of two Quentins (uncle and niece), two Jasons (father and son), and by the change of the idiot's name from Maury to Benjamin. To consider this a perverse game on Faulkner's part is clearly beside the point. As Joseph W. Reed suggests, the name-confusions may be seen as an index to inbreeding and degeneracy (see *Faulkner's Narrative*, New Haven, Conn.: Yale University Press, 1973, p. 76). At a deeper level, however, they refer to the author's central concern with the precarious status of the self. Name-confusion leads to identity confusion. True, Faulkner's characters generally preserve recognizable features, but the device tends to blur the boundaries between them. What is at stake here is the very concept of *character* and its function in the novel. In this connection it is worth noting that in their theoretical writings several among the most experimental of contemporary European novelists have precisely called attention to Faulkner's disconcerting use of names. Nathalie Sarraute comments upon it in *L'Ere du soupçon* (Paris: Gallimard, 1956, p. 73), Michel Butor in *Répertoire* (Paris: Editions de Minuit, 1960, p. 252), Alain Robbe-Grillet in *Pour un nouveau roman* (Paris: Editions de Minuit, 1963, p. 28), and Ingeborg Bachmann makes it the main point of her essay on *The Sound and the Fury* ("Über *Schall und Wahn,*" in Gerd Haffmans, ed., *Über William Faulkner,* Zurich: Diogenes, 1973, pp. 127–29).

[14]The importance of this image and of the scene it heralds is confirmed by a study of the manuscript. Originally section 2 started thus: "One minute she was standing there. The next Benjy was yelling and pulling at her. They went down the hall to the bathroom and stopped there, Caddy backed against the door...." This page of the manuscript is reproduced in James B. Meriwether, *The Literary Career of William Faulkner: A Bibliographical Study* (Princeton, N.J.: Princeton University Library, 1961), illustration 11.

[15]Pp. 69, 99, and passim. See also p. 88: "Her hair was like fire, and little points of fire were in her eyes...."

[16]See pp. 5, 8, 22, 48, 50, 51, 54, 58, 88. The reversible metaphor *girl = tree* can be traced back to Faulkner's earliest work: in *The Marble Faun* poplars are compared to "slender girls"; girls are likened to trees in *Marionettes*, his early play, as well as in *Soldiers' Pay* and *Mosquitoes*.

[17]A similar ritual cleansing occurs in "There Was a Queen." See *Collected Stories* (New York: Random House, 1950), p. 741.

[18]*Baudelaire* (Paris: Gallimard, 1947), p. 201. My translation.

[19]The phrase is from Harry Modean Campbell and Ruel E. Foster, *William Faulkner: A Critical Appraisal* (Norman: University of Oklahoma Press, 1951), p. 54.

[20]*La Ville,* 2nd edition (Paris: Mercure de France, 1920), p. 307.

[21]For a full discussion of Caddy in psychological and moral terms see Catherine B. Baum, " 'The Beautiful One': Caddy Compson as Heroine of *The Sound and the Fury,*" *Modern Fiction Studies,* XIII (Spring 1967), 33–44; Eileen Gregory, "Caddy Compson's World," *Merrill Studies in* The Sound and the Fury, comp. James B. Meriwether (Columbus, Ohio: Charles E. Merrill, 1970), pp. 89–101.

[22]*Notes and Reviews* (Cambridge, Mass.: Dunster House, 1921), p. 226.

Douglas B. Hill, Jr.
FAULKNER'S CADDY

There are no extraneous characters in fiction. As far as the structure of a novel is concerned, every character depends upon every other. If a novelist accepts this condition as a challenge to his ingenuity, his work can take any number of directions. Dickens's method in a book like *Bleak House*—the arranging of dozens of characters into a structure so contrived that the least movement of the least significant of them causes it to topple into a new equilibrium—is one remarkable elaboration of the principle. What William Faulkner does with the Compson family in *The Sound and the Fury*, though accomplished with fewer actors, is no less remarkable. Readers of that work quickly become aware of the centrality of Caddy Compson to the complex structure that Faulkner has built. The novel revolves about her, focuses itself upon her. She never appears in the flesh, in the actual present time of any part of the book (unless Benjy's consciousness can be said to operate always in present time); yet in the way she is made to control the substance of each brother's narrative life, she gives each one, as a character and as a narrator, his reason for existence. It is as if Faulkner had determined to make Caddy the sole source of both human and structural energy in *The Sound and the Fury*, and proceeded to build his novel upon that plan.

Most readers would agree that *The Sound and the Fury* is not only intellectually stimulating but also, once its complexities have been met and absorbed, emotionally moving. Artifice abounds, but there is no effect of sterility, of mere brilliance. Faulkner's experiments with narrative consciousness and temporal order excite more than academic admiration. The reader feels he is involved with characters and with a human situation of great poignance, not just with a series of *tours de force*. How, precisely, does this come about? How does the reader move, or how is he led, from the technique to the emotion?

We can begin with two assumptions. The first is that the reader's emotional response to Caddy Compson is the measure of his emotional response to the novel. The second is that this response is essentially irrational, formed by the

From *Canadian Review of American Studies* 7, No. I (Spring 1976): 26–38.

reader's predisposition to accept uncritically the images and attitudes that the author presents to him, rather than examine them for what they actually are, or for what they may mean. This situation is complicated, as is our attempt to understand it, by the fact that Faulkner has given Caddy to the reader simultaneously as two types of literary experience. She is a human character, approached by the author from several different directions, and also by the reader, who puts his own preconceptions into his perception of her. She is at the same time a functional character and an element in the structure and sequence of the novel, a figure in the patterns that these make. It is to the first of these figures that the reader assumes he is responding: what we should observe is how the various images of the second figure both complement and confuse this response. If we can explore and then chart the connections between these two kinds of stimuli to the imagination, we should be able to understand some of the ways that Caddy, and through her the novel, work upon the reader.

We have to start with Caddy's place in the structure of the novel in order to get beyond it. We have to recognize, and understand the implications of, the differences between Faulkner's presentation of Caddy in the narrative and his presentation of Benjy, Quentin, and Jason. Each of the three brothers, as Faulkner has him create a character for himself through his distinctive first-person discourse, creates as well a character for Caddy. She does not define herself at all: she appears only in the recorded consciousness of each brother, and the reader has no first-person account of her own thoughts and perceptions. In this sense we can say that she is for the reader, for more than three quarters of the book, whatever Benjy, Quentin, or Jason seems to make her out to be. This is her subjective existence within the novel, her existence in their three minds. But of course this subjective reality, her reality for the narrators, is not all there is to Caddy: Faulkner also establishes, or lets the reader think he is establishing, a rich objective existence for her.

He accomplishes this task in several ways. First, he employs the convention of having her own words given as if verbatim by each of the three narrators. We might not even notice this, since it is such a common device, if the narrative difficulties of Benjy's section did not force us to question a number of our certainties about the privileges and possibilities of a fictional narrator. In addition, we have the characterizations and judgments of Caddy offered by her parents, by Dilsey and her family, and by Dalton Ames and Herbert Head, all of which again are recorded apparently word-for-word by the narrators. Then there is the measured and pictorial third-person narrative of the final section, which, though it touches Caddy only tangentially, has about it an air of sanity, and consequently authority, after so much unreason. In a similar way the Appendix, which for a quarter-century has formed, rightly or wrongly, an integral part of the reading experience of *The Sound and the Fury*, presents what would seem to be an elucidation or clarification of some of the novel's meanings, and thus implies reliability for the sketch of Caddy it contains. Finally, and most important though hardest to deal with, the reader himself establishes an independent objective existence for Caddy in his own mind by a process of negative inference. He creates her for himself, that is, by opposing his own insistence of what she must be to the (obviously to him) distorted pictures that Benjy and Quentin and Jason have painted. A figure of affectionate love (for Benjy), of awakening and aroused sexuality (for Quentin), of bitchiness (for Jason)— the reader knows that none of these is right, though he knows that none is totally wrong. So in unspoken argument to these three views he constructs his own Caddy, and with all the other so-called objective evidence to influence him, says that he has found the real Caddy, or at least a Caddy considerably less unreal than the one the brothers see. What the reader is also saying is that he has found *Faulkner's* real Caddy, the original conception of the child-girl-woman that nourishes the divergent and often apparently self-contradictory fictional characterizations.

To understand precisely how Faulkner has brought the reader to this imaginative discovery, we should examine how he gives Caddy an existence in the narrative structure that depends upon a variety of relations to time. If his efforts were to do nothing more than give her character depth, open it up to the working of memory, force the reader to see the difference between time (and Caddy) past and present, it would be significant. But we know that Faulkner's use of time is more complex than a straightforward recalling of vanished glories and lost opportunities, and clearly something more subtle than nostalgia affects the reader of *The Sound and the Fury*. There are elements in the texture of the novel that help to build the emotional power that Caddy projects, and we should isolate them; not only, it should be emphasized, to show Caddy's connection with time, but beyond this to discover what these elements reveal about Faulkner's conception of her and of women in general. To do this, we must look at the four sections of the novel, to see how Caddy appears in each, and to see if her distinctive features reflect either a consistent authorial attitude towards her character or a consistent structural pattern. Only in this way can we find and fully describe the woman Faulkner has visualized and the ways he has brought that vision into his novel.

It is useful at the outset to distinguish Benjy's chapter from the two that follow it in terms of the sexual vantage-point at which each of the three narrators stands. Benjy gives Caddy to the reader primarily from a pre-sexual point of view. Except for his one disastrous venture outside the gate, and the weekly carriage-rides to the cemetery, Benjy, regardless of his chronological age, lives in, and has his consciousness formed upon, the safe childhood world within the fences that enclose the property of his family and their immediate neighbors. By contrast, Quentin views Caddy from a sexual transition-point between child and man, with the awakening knowledge and accompanying fantasies and guilt of the adolescent. His narrative is centered upon the time in and around Jefferson just before Caddy's marriage, ranging back to the end of their childhood on the Compson place, and forward to his year at Harvard. And in the third section, Jason looks at his sister from a point that could almost be called post- or anti-sexual. His world is Jefferson, all business and self-denial of emotion: home is only where he eats and sleeps. It does not matter what Caddy's actual age seems to be in any part of the narratives— a child and less often a young woman in Benjy's, almost always a girl or young woman in Quentin's, a grown woman in her infrequent appearances in Jason's. What is important is that Faulkner has fixed each of his three narrators in a separate and self-consistent sexual phase, has made each see Caddy in his mind *from* a consistent sexual age—Benjy a child, Quentin an adolescent, Jason a man.

Faulkner is able to freeze Benjy, and consequently the objects of his perception, in a sort of permanent childhood by means of his manipulation of the time-sequence of the narrative. For Benjy all time is one: Faulkner has him make no discrimination between events that occur in the past and those that occur in the present. A stimulus from the real present—April 7, 1928—may lead Benjy to a chronologically subsequent impression; more likely it will lead him to a whole set of stimuli and responses from the near or distant past, any one of which may in its turn lead him backwards or forwards in chronological time. By making Benjy's strongest sensory impressions—clustered about roughly a dozen incidents—rise from the years when Caddy was a child, and by making his narrative return to these again and again, Faulkner reinforces that image of her as a child in a way that a more straightforward chronology could not accomplish.

The importance of this time-scheme for the reader's understanding of Caddy is apparent when we realize the skill Faulkner has concentrated upon her characterization as a child in these first hundred pages. Benjy as a narrator can only register phenomena and his physical reaction to them (crying or not-crying), yet out of the seeming jumble of associations that Faulkner weaves together in his narrative a surprisingly full picture of Caddy comes forth. Childish and motherly qualities blend equally in her. She plays with Benjy, involves him in her conspiracies, and balances her maternal tenderness for him against Jason's precocious meanness. In her perception of his helpless agony she is far more adult than Benjy's true mother: she is able like Dilsey simply to be concerned for him and to care for him. It is a touching portrait, and its poignance is increased by its unpretentiousness. Faulkner does not force this Caddy upon the reader, but rather lets her develop naturally out of the context Benjy records. All the details are presented unsentimentally: the reader takes them to be accurate, since he accepts the convention that Benjy cannot alter, in transmitting, anything that he perceives—that his senses connect to a brain that cannot think.

The Caddy Faulkner creates here is, in both her roles, child and mother, an almost entirely non-sexual figure. The dominant scene in the chapter—the episode at the branch when Caddy muddies her drawers—has in Benjy's narrative only a slight and unavoidable implication of innocent childhood sexuality, nothing more: what comes later, in Quentin's section, gives it its powerful sexually symbolic meaning. Benjy moans—quite believably in the context—because Caddy is "all wet and muddy behind,"[1] not because he is aware of Faulkner's metaphorical connotation of moral stain or doom. It is the same with the odors that Benjy recognizes as belonging to Caddy. For him she smells, in her child-state, like trees or grass, a reassuring smell, like a mother's for her child (Mrs. Compson, we might recall, usually smells of camphor). He cries then when he first smells perfume upon her simply because it is a different odor: the associations for the reader of perfume with sexuality do not necessarily occur immediately, but become attached by what he learns later.

Though Benjy remains mentally a child (or something less than a child) for the duration of his narrative, Caddy does not, and as she matures we can see a change in Faulkner's characterization of her. Benjy must still react to his world in the same manner, and give the reader a record of his reactions, but one of the essential facts of that world has changed, in a way that the character Faulkner has created for him cannot even appreciate, let alone communicate. Faulkner must find a method of showing that change in Caddy consistent with the narrative limitations he has placed upon Benjy; he must put Benjy in situations his response to which will give Caddy's sexual maturity the emphasis that he, Faulkner, wishes it to have. Therefore when the mature Caddy appears, Benjy's reactions to her must announce a sexual implication they have not had before: Faulkner must use him to register Caddy's loss of sexual and moral innocence. Benjy moans now not because of a smell or a touch, or the lack of them, but because, Faulkner would have the reader understand, Caddy is an adult, is no longer virginal and pure. On these occasions Faulkner's touch seems heavy: he makes Benjy reproduce scenes (which his physical presence has usually precipitated) like Caddy's washing her mouth with soap to cleanse it of the kisses she has received, or her becoming sexually excited before Benjy as Charlie touches her, or her running away from her wedding. All of these scenes, we should realize, depend considerably upon male fantasies of female behavior. Since as she is portrayed as a child Caddy is pure, free both from sexuality and from stereotyped characterization, the inference we may draw is that for Faulkner the sexuality causes the stereotyping.

What is remarkable here is not simply that there are two versions of Caddy in the first section of the novel, the child and the woman, and that Faulkner's conception and presentation of the second figure involve clichés of male attitudes; but that the existence of the second Caddy does not rob the reader of his impression of the first. Indeed it is the remembrance of that fully realized childhood that modifies, even controls, the reader's response in the later sections. Caddy grows away from childhood in the course of Benjy's narrative, and he loses her; so, in the sense that his later characterization of her is not as precise, not as discerning, does Faulkner. But for the reader that child never wholly vanishes: the organization and rhythm of time in the narrative keep the smell of grass and trees as strong for him as the perfume, make the child as real for him as the woman. And the reader, who understands time as Benjy cannot, can measure the distance Caddy has traveled in her passage of years, even if he is not aware immediately of all that it seems to mean for Faulkner.

In Quentin's section time is both form and content. Faulkner arranges the details of this chapter as he does in Benjy's, making their temporal interrelations appear to be a product of the mind of the narrator rather than of actual chronology. The time-sequence is somewhat more straightforward than that of Benjy's narrative, and for the most part easier to follow. The hypothetical present—June 2, 1910—

is much clearer and more fully drawn; the episodes from the past that well up into Quentin's thoughts are fewer in number if no less intense; Quentin himself is aware of time and at least some of its meanings for him. Faulkner weaves threads of time into the monologue, into the images and events that it contains, and makes them control Quentin's consciousness and thus the entire section. The bells and clocks of Cambridge, the remembered school-bell of his childhood, lengthening shadows on the grass and water—these all mark off the final hours of Quentin's life for him. In addition to such formal structures of time, Faulkner develops through Quentin an attitude towards Caddy and towards all female sexuality that has its basis in an intellectualizing of the relation of woman and time. This attitude is the force behind the events—both past and present—of Quentin's section, and beneath whatever meanings Faulkner brings out in the confrontations between Quentin and his father.

Quentin's narrative takes in a large number of incidents, but there are really only a few main subjects—sisters (Caddy and the little immigrant girl), honor, virginity, sexual desire, time—and they are closely interconnected. Time—chronological time—is the central fact. By a process time controls a girl-child becomes a woman: the "little sister" of Quentin's last day is an analogue, in more than words, to the child Caddy before she becomes sexually mature. After that physiological event, woman is even more directly a slave to time: she is then, as Mr. Compson puts it, a "delicate equilibrium of periodical filth between two moons balanced" (p. 159). For Quentin sexuality is a function of time: stop time—break the watch—or separate oneself from it—isolate Caddy "out of the loud world" (p. 220)—lie in the quiet water beyond the sound of bells—and the little sister cannot become the woman. Only thus, destructively, can sexual time be stopped. Virginity, as Faulkner has Quentin conceive of it, is simply a phenomenon of honor—sexual honor—in time. All that separates the dirty little sister (either one) from the soiled woman who is Caddy is a few years. In the second half of the chapter especially, when in Quentin's consciousness images from the past (his furtive sexual fumbling in the barn with Natalie, his struggle at the branch over Caddy's submission to be kissed by a "town squirt," his father's aphorisms about women) flood into the present (his adventures with the little girl and her loaf of bread), we can see how pervasively these assumptions are operating.

Faulkner's conception of adult female sexuality is effective for the reader in Quentin's section chiefly because of its relation to this overall emphasis on time: when we isolate his attitudes about women from their context in Quentin's time-ridden consciousness, we find them to be less convincing. With Benjy's section there is little incentive to attempt such analysis, since the emphasis there upon Caddy as a child raises few such questions in the reader's mind. With Quentin, however, that relatively pure, unsexual childhood is represented mainly by the immigrant girl (even in this there is the irony of his being accused of molesting her); among the images of Caddy those of adolescence are in control. These are the images we must examine, since it is through them that Faulkner works most patently to establish Caddy as a romantic figure. As we are aware, a romantic figure is not necessarily the same as a tragic figure, and in Faulkner's notions of female sexuality we can see why this part of the portrait of Caddy, superficially alluring though it may be, lacks the originality and the stature—and the possibility for tragic depth— of the portrait of her as a child.

Faulkner has Quentin and Jason—and to the degree we have remarked, Benjy—assume a sexual basis for the way women are and act. This attitude seems to belong not just to the particular character's created pose, but to Faulkner as well: nowhere does he specifically contradict or oppose it. It appears to be as fundamental to his view of the adult Caddy as it is to Quentin's and Jason's, though of course their versions are exaggerated in line with their respective characters. The basic assumption involved here is not very different from that which underlies a common male heterosexual erotic fantasy—the assumption that every woman, no matter what her age or background or social position, conceals within her a lustful sexual animal. This is the first half of the fantasy, and it seems responsible for a considerable part of the picture of Caddy in Quentin's section; the second half, that the male hero need only act upon his knowledge of this secret in order to unleash the animal, is not worked out explicitly in the actions of either Quentin or Jason. But by suggesting the existence of this masculine role in what the two brothers say about Caddy (Quentin even tries to make his father believe that he has actually performed it), Faulkner not only forces the reader to be aware of the role but allows him to conspire in it himself in his own imagination, in his own private emotional response to Caddy.

This conventional erotic impulse runs through all of Quentin's memories of the crucial encounters with his sister and determines the attitude towards her that Faulkner establishes for him: "did you love them Caddy did you love them When they touched me I died" (p. 185). When Faulkner has Quentin feel the pulse in Caddy's throat and say the name "Dalton Ames" (pp. 202–3), the fantasy is exemplified precisely. Faulkner uses scenes like this to justify Caddy's claim—accepted by Quentin, of course, as it appears to be accepted by Faulkner, and to a large extent by the reader—that she is somehow hereditarily doomed—and doomed as much because she is a woman as because she is a Compson. "Im bad anyway you cant help it," she says, and Quentin replies, "theres a curse on us its not our fault is it our fault" (p. 196). This equation may work for the reader—it is hard to deny its influence—but we should not mistake how Faulkner sets it up. He is simply using a version of a familiar male sexual fantasy to strike a sympathetic chord in the reader. Attempts at more precise psychological insights into Caddy's character as a young woman are avoided in favor of these male erotic stereotypes: she is in this respect not much different from the typical heroine-object of pornographic fiction. Faulkner's prose in these passages may be evocative, but the image it evokes is, as far as sexuality is concerned, a commonplace.

There is a temptation to see in the wisdom offered by Mr. Compson a view of women that opposes Quentin's excesses, and to assume that Faulkner is thereby balancing them. But the father undercuts the son only selectively, and his attitudes, though expressed in a manner that may be more to our liking—and we might suspect closer to Faulkner's—have no more real weight than Quentin's adolescent ones. Mr. Compson is more urbane than his son, but his philosophizing about female sexuality, as Quentin recalls it, has its ultimate source in an almost identical conception of women:

> Because women so delicate so mysterious Father said. Delicate equilibrium of periodical filth between two moons balanced. Moons he said full and yellow as harvest moons her hips her thighs.... Then know that some man that all those mysterious and imperious concealed. With all that inside of them shapes an outward suavity waiting for a touch to. (p. 159)

This sort of idealizing, with its traditional idea of woman as mystery—a force beyond man's knowing waiting to be awakened—is not as dramatically sexist as Quentin's, but it does no more for the reader's understanding of Caddy as a unique human being who happens to be female. If Mr. Compson's attitude seems less stereotyped than Quentin's it is because it has more style: in substance it is only a decadent, cynical version of the same point of view.

Where Mr. Compson appears most successfully to counter Quentin is in his perception of the meaning of his son's preoccupation with honor: here he offers an antidote to Quentin's romantic idealism. Mr. Compson's comments are often pungent: "Because it means less to women... it was men invented virginity not women" (p. 96); "Women are never virgins. Purity is a negative state and therefore contrary to nature" (p. 143). His parting advice to Quentin appears especially incisive: "You cannot bear to think that someday it will no longer hurt you like this... no you will not do that [commit suicide] until you come to believe that even she was not quite worth despair perhaps" (pp. 220–1). But if his comments are sometimes acute, they are also sometimes facile and occasionally ("it used to be a gentleman was known by his books; nowadays he is known by the ones he has not returned"—p. 99) simply banal and windy. This should caution us against taking his analysis of Quentin's predicament, or his ideas about women, to be wholly congruent with Faulkner's. But if we cannot accept Mr. Compson's views as the moral equivalent of Faulkner's, we should at least remark their overall artistic effect, the way they serve to carry on and explore, by presenting alternatives, the relation to time in which Faulkner has Quentin place Caddy. Primarily because of this relation, because Caddy is made a focus of the meaning of time—for both Quentin and his father—she succeeds in this chapter in affecting the reader. The representation of her sexuality—her portrait as a woman—seems on its own terms, when we analyze the attitudes that go into it, not nearly so effective and substantial.

By the end of Quentin's section, an image of Caddy has been so solidly established for the reader that the bitterly negative characterization of her that Jason presents does not alter it, but rather serves to convince the reader that what he has seen before is correct. This occurs partly because Jason's Caddy—"once a bitch always a bitch"—is completely at odds with Benjy's and Quentin's, and partly because even in its almost total negation his Caddy is based upon the same conception of woman that we have identified earlier. Jason's attitudes towards Caddy, and towards women in general, are in many respects no more than unpleasant versions of his father's, but where Mr. Compson seems to be all words, a disembodied speaker of epigrams, Jason, both because of his function as a narrator and because of the comic vitality of the character Faulkner gives to him, is a distinct presence. His father is nihilistic and cynical, Jason is sardonic and brutal: his father expresses disillusion, a sort of amused world-weariness; Jason expresses nastiness. He is characterized, and characterizes himself, by a cold, sadistic strain of the Compson malady, the inability to work out a normal human relation with another person: he simply refuses to allow himself to demonstrate affection or respect or even tolerance for anyone but himself.

This condition reveals itself in, and seems to be partly caused by, his peculiar brand of family pride. Faulkner makes Jason appear to believe in a sort of self-centered masculine code, one part male supremacy and one part regional, racial, and social xenophobia. This code has its icons—"my mother's good name," "the position I uphold," "pride," "discretion"—to all of which Jason must pay verbal homage. It is also deeply rooted in his thoroughgoing faith in the values of the past: for Jason the present is a period of penance that he must endure, and the future only a distant hope. His reaction to the carnival-worker who runs off with his niece and his money is typical of his attitude: "the first thing I saw was the red tie he had on and I was thinking what the hell kind of man would wear a red tie" (p. 289).

Jason's sense of honor, Faulkner suggests throughout the chapter, is no less deluded, no less debilitating than Quentin's. And if the energies that shape it arise, as they do for Quentin, from Jason's warped view of the past, so, likewise, the focus of those energies is the same, his failure to accept and deal with his own or anyone else's sexuality. Jason fears sex as much as Quentin does: what Faulkner once again implies, through him, is the sexual origin of Caddy's and all women's behavior. Jason's is an uglier version of the mystique than Quentin's—his remarks about his "whore" Lorraine, his suggestion that his niece would behave properly if only she were neutered like Benjy—and the ugliness is part of the personality Faulkner has created for him. The sexist assumption remains, however, as with Quentin, even when we subtract for characterization; it seems to have its root in Faulkner's own attitudes about women.

Jason's failure to respond to other human beings is exhibited most clearly with Caddy, of whom he is obviously jealous for the love, difficult of expression though it may be, that she has inspired in Benjy and Quentin, Mr. Compson, and even Dilsey. Faulkner intensifies the reader's knowledge of that failure by letting him see that for Jason this same love might have been possible, that Caddy offers the chance but Jason refuses to take it. In a scene he recalls—in the cemetery after their father's funeral—Jason comes closest to admitting an understanding of Caddy, and consequently of himself: "I didn't say anything. We stood there, looking at the grave, and then I got to thinking about when we were little and one thing and another and I got to feeling funny again, kind of mad or something..." (p.

252). He suppresses this feeling, but for the reader his subconscious reaction to Caddy, and more important an image of Caddy herself, the Caddy that Faulkner wants the reader to sense Jason cannot see, are brought out. The reader has almost no concrete evidence in Jason's chapter for this Caddy: he simply imagines her for himself, opposing her to the negative comments and generalizations that Jason offers him, and remembering the Caddy he thinks he has seen in the two previous sections.

We can observe a similar process affecting the reader in the way Faulkner uses Jason's attitude towards his niece Quentin to reinforce this positive image of Caddy. The time-sequence is again critical here. Caddy's daughter exists for Jason, of course, in the actual present time of the chapter—April 6, 1928—but as important as her own character and actions is the way she serves to bring Caddy into that present, and keep her there, both for Jason and for the reader. More than just memory is at work: by having Jason give Quentin to the reader as little more than a nymphomaniac teen-ager, tormented by her family's lack of love and understanding, Faulkner not only makes the reader recall Caddy, but somehow renews his belief—a belief attained in the various ways we have seen—in her essential goodness. Faulkner explains in the next section what the girl means for Jason: "If he could just believe it was the man who had robbed him. But to have been robbed of that which was to have compensated him for the lost job, which he had acquired through so much effort and risk, by the very symbol of the lost job itself, and worst of all by a bitch of a girl" (pp. 383–4). "Just like her mother," Jason says at one point (p. 267), and in the ways that she is—for Jason, misunderstanding both women in the novel's present time—and is not—for the reader, judging from outside this narrative time—all Jason's hostilities and hatreds working through the girl Quentin illuminate the figure of Caddy who stands behind her. Thus once again the reader makes a positive inference from the negative images offered him by a distorting narrator. But just as before, that positive image is no less idealized and conventionalized, no more specific—as far as the implied and expressed attitudes that form it are concerned—than the negative ones. The reader merely gains a few more stereotypes of female sexuality to complement those he has already been presented with.

Two sections of the book remain to be examined. The "Dilsey" chapter has usually been treated as a sort of conclusion, a final word from the author speaking at last in his own voice. The woman who is our main concern here—Dilsey—has a curious effect upon the reader's sense of Caddy. As Faulkner portrays her— loving, wise, strong—she recalls features of the child-mother Caddy of Benjy's section. Like that Caddy she is sexually safe, unthreatening; as an aged black servant, almost sexless (the opening description makes this apparent), she seems to be for Faulkner a person rather than an abstraction, real rather than ideal, just as Caddy the child is with Benjy, and to a slighter degree the little immigrant girl with Quentin. She is presented in a wealth of precise and symbolically unweighted detail: her relations with her families—both black and white—contrast with all the failures and perversions of love and affection the reader has observed in the preceding chapters. And, interestingly, she is not involved with time, either as perceiver or object, in any of the complex distortions we have noted earlier. Instead, as has often been pointed out, she is the one character who can deal with time on normal terms: she can read the "enigmatic profundity" of the one-handed kitchen clock. Now in view of all this, she might be expected to emerge as the dominant female figure in the novel. But although Dilsey is a powerfully affecting character in her own right, neither she nor the narrative she figures in detracts, for the reader, from the image of Caddy he has already created for himself.

The chief reason for this is paradoxical: she does not take away from Caddy simply *because* she is such a clear contrast to her. It is as if Faulkner by the end of the book has given the reader two women of equal power—the one, Dilsey, presented in a documentary narrative style and, the reader feels, objectively knowable; the other, Caddy, presented subjectively and apprehended by the reader in some of the less than wholly rational ways we have discussed. It should not seem strange that the subjective portrait, by the nature of its very subjectivity—its mystery and its potentiality—survives as the more compelling.

The emphasis Faulkner gives to images of maternal love also helps to keep Caddy before the reader in the final section. Dilsey herself is of course a mother, to three generations of Compsons as well as two of her own family; the divine counterpart to her secular motherhood—the Virgin and her Child—figures prominently in the climactic sermon in the Negro church. For the reader these images reflect Caddy, however faintly, both as a child, with Benjy, and as a woman, in her own ill-fated venture at maternity. We can see a further connection, incidental perhaps but nonetheless effective, between the Virgin Mary and Caddy, inasmuch as the aura that surrounds each can be considered the creation of man's impulse to idealize the woman—on the one hand the product of his spiritual, on the other of his sexual fantasies (though we can assume that each partakes to a substantial degree of the other). Certainly the figure of Caddy, as the focus of the energies of the novel, develops a presence that can be called, in strength if not in tone, almost religious. This seems to be especially true of the final chapter, which that presence infuses even though Caddy herself neither appears nor is mentioned by name in it.

It is unwise to make very much use of the Appendix as a tool for interpreting what Faulkner has done with Caddy, just as it is unwise to be excessively attentive to any author's statements about the meaning of his own work. Still, the Appendix has been a part of the book since 1946,[2] and has been turned to by a whole generation of readers seeking a clearer understanding of the novel. Since it is the reader's response to Caddy we are trying to describe, and since the Appendix affords examples of a romantic view of Caddy as extreme as any in Quentin's section—passages that obviously must influence the reader—it would seem arbitrary to ignore it.

The Appendix abounds in stock female characterizations: the Jefferson librarian, a "mousesized and -colored woman who had never married" (Melissa

Meek); the "homeless young women" in the bus terminal, following the soldiers, "pausing only long enough to drop their foals in charity wards or police-stations and then move on again"; even Dilsey, now grown old and feeble in Memphis, with "the black hands which, like the women of her race, were still as supple and delicately shaped as they had been when she was thirty or twenty or even seventeen." Caddy, as Faulkner presents her here, takes her place among these stereotypes. Her last chronological appearance in the book—she has "vanished in Paris with the German occupation, 1940"—is in a magazine photograph, posed with a German staff general (the year is now 1943), her face "hatless between a rich scarf and a seal coat, ageless and beautiful, cold serene and damned." If the implications of this reference, and the direct statement that concludes it, were not enough, Faulkner's language everywhere in the Appendix, but especially where it touches Caddy, is less precise, more inflated, than in the novel itself, even than in Quentin's narrative. Phrases like "the waiting willing friendly tender incredible body of his beloved," "life . . . with all its incomprehensible passion and turmoil and grief and fury and despair," "the frail doomed vessel of its pride and the foul instrument of its disgrace"—these are Faulkner vague and portentous, trying to force the reader to infer more than he is really being told.

In view of all this, we might think that the Appendix, whether read first or last or at some point between, would caution the reader to meet the Caddy of the fiction with a few thoughtful questions. Its conventional characterizations and loaded language should put him on his guard for writing of a similar nature in the novel. But it doesn't seem to work this way. Instead the Appendix makes the reader accept the Caddy of the novel even more unquestioningly; its almost direct statements serve to verify for the reader the picture of Caddy that he wants to construct from the narratives of the three brothers.

We have looked at Caddy in each of the parts of *The Sound and the Fury* with the aim of discovering the reasons for her power to animate and control the reader's emotional response to the book. We should now summarize our findings and consider a few of their implications. Seen as a woman, Caddy appears to be formed out of stereotyped male assumptions and attitudes. As an adolescent and as an adult, insofar as Faulkner's portrayal of her sexuality is concerned, she is little different from the heroine of pulp romance or pornography. Beautiful, mysterious, passionate—she might be the object of a sexual daydream. Despite the apparent triteness of the specific details of her characterization in her sexual role, Caddy is able to move the reader and pull him into the human situation of the novel. Certainly the reader's cultural conditioning makes it difficult for him not to respond in some measure to these stereotypes, at the same time that it blinds him to what is actually happening to him. Within the novel itself, however, as we have seen, lie specific, tangible reasons for her power. Faulkner has of course given Caddy the central position in his narrative and psychological structure. In addition, and this is where we have directed our attention, he has involved her—as idea, image, and character—in his preoccupation with the meaning of time, with the relation of past and present, in such a multitude of ways that the reader's emotional response to her character is intensified and enriched at every turn.

It would seem then that *The Sound and the Fury,* in the concerns that it centers upon, is really about time not people. The child in Benjy's section, the young girl in Quentin's, the mature woman in Jason's—as he meets each of these versions of Caddy the reader reacts to the meaning of time as much as to the female figure this meaning surrounds. Caddy's immense poignance as a woman, the emotional impact she has upon the reader, should properly be understood to come from the novel's complex temporal or elegiac sensibility rather than from its relatively simplistic and shallow sexual sensibility. Time, not sexuality, is the key to her force as a character: it is the way Faulkner is successful in spite of the limitations in his human portrait of her. In her sexual role the adolescent and adult Caddy is, as we have seen, little more than an abstraction, a sort of popular formula. In her temporal role she is an abstraction, too, but here this suffices, since time itself, as Faulkner conceives of it, is the generative abstraction: the demanding richness of the latter replaces, for the reader in the act of reading the novel, the inadequacy of the former.

If this is a correct analysis, it is not intended to be a disparagement: observing clearly how and why Faulkner succeeds and fails with Caddy should make us marvel the more at the way his exploration of time and change carries all before it. We should not be upset to discover that, as far as Caddy is concerned, he has given us something other than what first appears, for through understanding our response to her—difficult as it may be to delineate it precisely—we get to the central meanings of the book. Faulkner in Quentin's section describes a bird's song— "invisible, a sound meaningless and profound" (pp. 168–9). We may read this as a metaphor for Faulkner's accomplishment with Caddy and time: as a woman her characterization is relatively meaningless, offering only surfaces; as a symbol of and a focus for time, it is profound, opening upon depths of meaning that justify our fullest response and respect.

Caddy, we have to conclude, is a female character neither in the classic style of a Dorothea Brooke or an Isabel Archer, nor in the modern one that informs the best of the numerous recent novels by and about women. Compared to the humanity, the psychological reality, the fully-imagined womanhood, of such fictional women as these, there is very little substance to Caddy; yet her capacity to draw and hold the reader is fully equal to theirs. We should be aware now that most of this power comes from her place in the narrative and temporal structure of the book, not from her characterization as a woman. As a child she is sketched with great sensitivity and insight in a few strokes—she is alive and unique for Faulkner and for the reader: once she matures sexually she is stereotyped and romanticized. It appears that Faulkner was able to achieve the necessary detachment from his personal sources of inspiration to create a "beautiful and tragic little girl,"[3] and to create in her a remarkable elegy for childhood. At the same time, however, he was unable to achieve an equivalent detachment from his cultural situation— his feeling for the disappearance of the old South and the old America—to create a tragic woman, a woman tragic in herself. We may wonder that an artist can make use of a sense of personal loss more effectively than a sense of a larger, more generalized tragedy, but reflection should suggest that this is nearly always the case. The artist can work out of his private grief and longing, but he cannot escape his time. We should understand then that Faulkner's approach to Caddy reflects both how clearly he is of his time and place, and how, if he cannot perhaps surmount the conditions they present to him, he can illuminate the predicament and the struggle to extricate himself from it.

NOTES

[1] *The Sound and the Fury* (New York: Random House, 1929, 1956), p. 21. Subsequent quotations will be identified in the text, when necessary, by parenthetical page reference to this edition.

[2] The Appendix introduces the Modern Library edition, published first in 1946. The Vintage edition, based upon a photographic reproduction (1956) of the first printing, places it last.

[3] See Faulkner's recently recovered introduction to the novel (prepared in 1933 for a limited edition that was never published). Edited with a note by James B. Meriwether, *Southern Review*, NS 8 (1972), 705–12. Reprinted with a slightly different note, *New York Times Book Review* (5 Nov. 1972), p. 1. Quoted in part (four of five typescript pages) in Michael Millgate, *The Achievement of William Faulkner* (New York: Random House, 1965), p. 26.

Steve Carter

CADDY AND QUENTIN: ANIMA AND ANIMUS ORBITED NICE

But still I watched them spinning, orbited nice,
Their flames were not more radiant than their ice.
—JOHN CROWE RANSOM, "The Equilibrists"

In comparing the applicability of Freudian and Jungian concepts to Faulkner's work, Irving Malin concludes that although Freud's ideas are reflected in Faulkner—in particular, the Oedipal conflict and the struggle between the ego and the super-ego—Faulkner is actually "closer to what Jung represents."[1] For Faulkner's work as a whole, this evaluation probably has validity; but for some of Faulkner's novels, especially some of the early novels like *The Sound and the Fury*, it is harder to see how Malin can be right. In *The Sound and the Fury*, the Freudian elements are obvious and have been discussed in depth by Carvel Collins, Harry Campbell, Ruel Foster, and many others. Lawrance Thompson's opinion can perhaps be taken as typical of those writers who view the Freudian ontology and symptomatology as critical to the effects achieved in the novel. Thompson states that, in *The Sound and the Fury*, "Faulkner counterbalances the pessimistic psychological determinism of Freud against the optimistic Christian concept of freely willed action."[2]

One of the principal reasons for the prevalence of Freudian interpretations is the Quentin section—Section Two. Faulkner once called Quentin an "educated half madman," and in his long "stream-of-consciousness" narration in Section Two, Quentin lives up to Faulkner's characterization.[3] The section is replete with Freudian imagery and symbolism, and Quentin himself sounds like one of Freud's clinical cases. Faulkner, who admitted he was aware of Freud's ideas before writing the novel (though he insisted he had never read Freud), probably did make use of Freud's ideas in this section.[4] Always an eclectic, he would naturally have made use of what came to hand to portray Quentin on the verge of suicide.

The early Freudian readings, however, led to some misreading of the central characters. Thus, when Catherine Baum, in her important revaluation of Caddy,

From *Hartford Studies in Literature* 12, No. 2 (1980): 124–42.

argues that Caddy should be viewed as the central and truly tragic figure in the novel, she takes issue with some of those critics who have looked at the characters from a Freudian perspective. Carvel Collins, she says, wrongly sees Caddy as representing the "libido" and as having a personality twisted from the normal;[5] Charles Anderson is not fair to Caddy in characterizing her as a "promiscuous nymphomaniac";[6] and Lawrence Bowling is not accurate either in saying that Caddy is "a naturalist and never rises above her natural state."[7] In reality, Baum argues, Caddy should be seen as representing "selfless love," and her tragedy viewed as the central fact of the novel. "The wasteful loss of Caddy's great capacity for compassion and sacrifice," Baum states, "makes her fate the most unbearable and tragic doom in *The Sound and the Fury.*"[8]

Such a view certainly agrees more closely with Faulkner's intentions and provides a needed corrective for an excessively pessimistic analysis of the novel's characters. Faulkner said he intended the book's central character to be Caddy and that it was she who prompted him to write the novel in the first place. "She was the beautiful one," he said.[9] But Baum's view of Caddy may also be an incomplete one. Baum herself admits there is "an obscurity surrounding [Caddy's] character,"[10] and many other readers have been struck by the same "obscurity." Walter Slatoff, for example, points out that "the reader is never really enlightened about her character"; he watches her suffer, but gains "little insight into why she behaves as she does or how she feels beyond the moment."[11]

Baum's reading of Caddy as the truly tragic figure in the novel may also, to some extent, lessen the impact of Quentin as a character. Despite his obvious ineptitude and instability, Quentin still serves as an important *persona* and voice for Faulkner, and even comes close to being a tragic figure himself. Faulkner's characterization of Quentin as an "educated half madman" sounds a little like Joyce's comment about his own *persona,* Stephen Dedalus: "I haven't let this young man off very lightly, have I?" Joyce is supposed to have remarked to Frank Budgeon.[12] Faulkner may have been similarly unfair to Quentin. As Harry Campbell points out, all that keeps Quentin from being a tragic figure is his weakness.[13]

Another possible reason for Quentin's lack of appeal as a character—just as it may be a reason for Caddy's "obscurity"—is the Freudian terminology used to understand him. A better way of looking at Caddy's and Quentin's character is provided by some of the Jungian psychological concepts which Malin is convinced are highly appropriate to Faulkner's corpus. One attempt at a Jungian reading of the novel has, in fact, been made by Kathryn Gibbons.[14] Her study, like most of the psychological studies of the novel, concentrates on Quentin; but her comments also suggest a possible indirect means of approaching Caddy's personality through the use of Jung's "anima-animus" concept (the "syzygy").

Caddy, as Gibbons states, can be seen as Quentin's "anima"—the female figure who, for a man, is the "personification of the collective unconscious."[15] The "anima" is met with, Jung contends, either in dreams or, if a man "projects" his unconscious feelings onto some real woman, in the real world. Quentin, Gibbons argues, has done precisely this: he has projected his inner feelings about this numinous, emotion-laden, archetypal figure onto his sister so that she becomes a personification of all that *Woman*—taken as an abstract concept—means to him. What Gibbons suggests but never actually states, however, is that Quentin may also be taken as Caddy's "animus," Jung's male equivalent of the "anima"; and if the two are indeed mutually complementary personalities after the pattern of the "syzygy"—if, like the two lovers in Ransom's poem, they are "orbited nice," their fates and personalities inextricably intertwined—then by understanding Quentin as an "animus" figure it may be possible to understand both brother and sister more completely.

The clearest indication of the extraordinary nature of the relationship between Caddy and Quentin is seen in the way each is preoccupied with the other. In Quentin's case this preoccupation is obvious. His obsession with his sister is almost certainly psychotic. His claim of having committed incest with her, though rejected as false by the elder Compson (his father) and by Faulkner himself (in the "Appendix," published after the novel), nevertheless indicates the extent of the obsession. The dialogue that takes place between Quentin and his father—in which Quentin makes his claim of having committed incest and in which his father denies and rationalizes this claim—shows dramatically how much emotional force is behind Quentin's obsessive fantasies.[16]

And just as he is preoccupied with Caddy, so Caddy is preoccupied with him. On one occasion, for example, Herbert Head, eventually Caddy's first husband, tells Quentin that Caddy

> talked about you all the time up there at the Licks [the vacation spot where Herbert and Caddy had met in 1909] I got pretty jealous I says to myself who is this Quentin anyway I must see what this animal looks like because I was hit pretty hard see soon as I saw the little girl I dont mind telling you it never occurred to me it was her brother she kept talking about she couldnt have talked about you any more if you'd been the only man in the world. (p. 113)

The intensity of the love that Caddy and Quentin have for one another is stated directly by Faulkner himself in the "Appendix"; and Faulkner's language strongly suggests Jung's "anima-animus" concept. Like Quentin's father, Faulkner denies that Quentin's love for Caddy is an incestuous physical desire. Quentin, Faulkner says,

> loved not his sister's body but some concept of Compson honor precariously and (he knew well) only temporarily supported by the minute fragile membrane of her maidenhead ... loved not the idea of the incest which he would not commit, but some presbyterian concept of its eternal punishment: he, not God, could by that means cast himself and his sister both into hell, where he could guard her forever and keep her forevermore intact amid the eternal fires. (p. 411)

What is indicated by Faulkner here—and what is supported in numerous ways by the text of the novel itself—is that Quentin's love for Caddy is actually a love of certain concepts; that is, in Jungian terms, his love for her is energized by, and founded upon, unconscious "primordial images." He is actually "projecting" onto Caddy his own unconscious feelings about *Woman* in the abstract. Caddy serves as his "anima."

In the same way, Faulkner's description in the "Appendix" of Caddy's love for Quentin indicates that Caddy's love is founded upon the same kind of "primordial images" as Quentin's. The language Faulkner uses closely parallels the language he uses in describing Quentin's love for Caddy. Her love is also a love of abstract "concepts" (though she is also described as loving Quentin himself in addition to the concepts he represents to her). In her case, these "concepts" represent certain unconscious feelings about *Man* in the abstract. Caddy, according to Faulkner,

> Loved her brother despite him, loved not only him but loved in him that bitter prophet and inflexible corruptless judge of what he considered the family's honor and its doom . . . she loved him . . . accepting the fact that he must value above all not her but the virginity of which she was custodian and on which she placed no value whatever: the frail physical stricture which to her was no more than a hangnail would have been. (p. 412)

Like Quentin, Caddy is really concerned with certain concepts. What she loves in Quentin is what he represents to her: the certain boundaries of law and tradition which the Compson family needs if it is to endure. Jung once described archetypes as dry river beds to which water "may return at any time."[17] Quentin's neurotic conception of *Woman* in the abstract, his neurotically-conceived "anima," is much like one of these dry river beds. In his world, the water of life is always damned up somewhere upstream. In Caddy's world, the water is always flowing. Quentin is aware of *Woman* only as an abstraction; Caddy is aware of *Man* only as a physical reality. Both Caddy's flowing water and Quentin's river bed of abstractions would seem to be necessary to nourish and sustain the Compson family life. The river bed without the river is dead; but the river without the definite boundaries of the river bed can only waste itself.

In a sense, the complementarity of Quentin and Caddy reflects the relationship between men and women in all Faulkner's novels. Women are associated with physical life in the earth and with its concrete and practical expressions; men, with spiritual-mental activities. Cleanth Brooks, among others, has noted this characteristic differentiation between the sexes in Faulkner. In Faulkner's works, he states, "the men are romantic, obsessed with their foolish codes, quixotic schemes and violent follies. It is the women who are practical, concerned with the concrete actualities and committed, undeviatingly to first principles."[18] Quentin, from this perspective, can be seen merely as a latter-day radical expression of the masculine concern with mental-spiritual constructs or codes, while Caddy can be seen as a radical expression of the feminine interest in the immediate and practical concerns of life.

Faulkner's presentation of the male-female dichotomy parallels very closely Jung's description of the "anima" and "animus" and of men and women in general. In Jung's terminology, Caddy's psychology could be said to be "founded on the principle of Eros, the great binder and deliverer," while Quentin's psychology could be said to be based on "Logos . . . as his ruling principle."[19] "Whereas logic and objective reality," Jung states, "prevail in the outer attitude of man, or are at least regarded as an ideal, in the case of woman it is feeling."[20] And he adds, in discussing "individuation": "The woman is . . . aware that love alone can give her her full stature, just as man begins to discern that spirit alone can endow his life with its highest meaning."[21] Quentin and Caddy are radical examples of these two poles of behavior. Quentin pursues "spirit" to such a degree that he loses his sense of "love"; Caddy pursues "love" to such a degree that she eventually loses sight of the spiritual ideals which would sanction and harmonize love's expression.

Jung uses the terms "love" and "spirit" in this case to try to define the differences between men and women and to show how the path to fulfillment differs for each. The most important aspect of the male-female polarity, however, is the way the sexes interact or interrelate. When the interaction is positive and fruitful, the sexes "complement" one another, each supplying that which the other lacks; when the interaction is not positive, each tends to project onto the other his own negative qualities—his own "shadow." When the projection is even more unconscious and even more associated with pure concepts or "primordial images," it is then connected with the qualities (either positive or negative) of the "animus" or "anima." Jung explains:

> One might assume that projections like these, which are so very difficult if not impossible to dissolve, would belong to the realm of the shadow—that is, to the negative side of the personality. This assumption however becomes untenable after a certain point, because the symbols that then appear no longer refer to the same but to the opposite sex, in a man's case to a woman and vice versa. The source of projections is no longer the shadow—which is always of the same sex as the subject—but a contrasexual figure. Here we meet the *animus* of a woman and the *anima* of a man, two corresponding archetypes whose autonomy and unconsciousness explain the stubbornness of their projections.[22]

That Quentin's "projections" are many and stubborn is clear. In his long stream-of-consciousness monologue—Section Two—he often broods on the nature of the man-woman polarity. His broodings reveal his projection of both those feelings connected with his "shadow" and those connected with his "anima." Quentin is clearly in the grip of his "anima"; and this fact seems to suggest—if Caddy and Quentin are truly complementary personalities—that Caddy likewise struggles with the negative aspects of her "animus." Indeed such can be inferred from her actions and speeches in the novel. Her inner world—the world of her memories and feelings—is never directly revealed, but in her case the thought world is of lesser importance anyway. She immediately "acts out" her feelings so that her outer world becomes a mirror reflection of her inner world; and her actions show her to be the direct antithesis of Quentin.

One way of understanding the mutual projection and complementarity of Caddy and Quentin is provided by Jung in an essay in which he uses the words "love" and "power" in speaking about the opposite poles of femininity and masculinity. "Where love rules," he states, "there is no will to power; and where power predominates, there love is lacking. The one is the shadow of the other."[23] Quentin and Caddy are extreme examples of these two opposites. Quentin expresses the "power" side of his personality—that is, he constantly attempts to "master" and dominate his environment and himself. He represses, and remains unconscious of, his "love" side, his physical and earthly nature. Because he does so, he is left without a means of coming into contact with the earth. By the time of his Harvard sojourn, he has become an almost bodiless intellect controlled by the "primordial images" of his personal and collective unconscious—those images connected with the earth and the physical which he has denied and repressed. This is his condition in the long, pre-suicide, Section Two monologue with its recurrent images of eclipsed time, darkness, and putrefaction.

Caddy, on the other hand, expresses in extravagant measure the "love" side of her personality. She manifests at one time or another almost every shade and variation of "love," from near Platonic affection and devotion to purely physical sexuality. Her love for Benjy seems entirely unselfish; her love for Quentin seems likewise sincere despite being unjustified; her devotion to her mother and family was very possibly, in the case of her first marriage at least, such as to cause her to sacrifice her real feelings for the sake of the family's honor.

At the other end of the spectrum are her many physical "loves" which, except perhaps for her first affair, could hardly be called Platonic. In her first affair, her feelings are almost certainly sincere. Quentin asks her to reveal her feelings about Dalton Ames in one particularly dramatic episode and receives an appropriate response. She does not answer Quentin in words but does what is for her even more honest and revealing: she allows him to feel her pulse when her lover's name is mentioned. "Do you love him Caddy?" Quentin asks, and her response is to take his hand and hold "it flat against her throat." "Now say his name," she instructs Quentin, and when he does, "her blood surged steadily beating and beating against my hand" (202–203).

Caddy is not able to express the "power" side of her personality as easily. Perhaps largely because of Quentin's extreme attitudes, she represses that side of the personality that Quentin expresses: the disciplining and controlling qualities of the will and the intellect. She has no "code" by which to live. But it is not so much the Compson "code" which Caddy rejects, as it is Quentin's life-denying way of expressing that "code." Quentin does attempt to express a certain Compson nobility, a respect for tradition and a firm discipline. He plays the part of the "inflexible corruptless judge," but his methods are hardly calculated to excite admiration. His smearing of mud on Caddy following the Natalie episode shows why his crude, anti-physical, and abstract idealism has been said to be a cause of Caddy's promiscuity. Finding nothing to admire in Quentin's crudeness, she rejects that for which Quentin "seems" to stand—a life-destroying and life-denying abstract idealism. But at the same time she rejects that which, in his own bumbling way, he is attempting to express—a masculine power and control over life.

In Jung's terms, the result of her rejection of that which Quentin represents is that she "projects" onto Quentin all those feelings with which the "power" side of her psyche (the "animus") is freighted, so that these feelings become a part of her "shadow." Being in the grip of her "animus," Caddy is "infected" and is forced to meet in the outer world those psychological factors of which she is unconscious in her inner world. "One encounters projections," Jung points out, "one does not make them";[24] and in speaking of the "anima" and the "animus," Jung explains that the power of the archetypes "grows in proportion to the degree that they remain unconscious. Those who do not see them are in their hands, just as a typhus epidemic flourishes best when its source is undiscovered."[25]

Caddy's "infection" by her "animus" helps to explain her penchant for affairs with men who display a great deal of "power" over, or "mastery" of, the external world. Two of the men in her life—the rich and "extremely eligible" Herbert Head and the "minor movingpicture magnate"—exemplify two aspects of this masculine mastery of the outer world. In these cases, masculine "power" is measured in terms of money and prestige. A more sinister aspect of masculine "power" is exemplified by two other men in her life: the gangster-like Dalton Ames and the Nazi officer (the "handsome lean man of middle-age in the ribbons and tabs of a German staffgeneral") with whom Faulkner leaves Caddy in his "Appendix."

Caddy's inability to master or dominate life—her "powerlessness"—is seen often in the novel. In addition to her inability to control her physical desires, she is powerless to control or even influence the direction of her family's fortunes. The episode which most dramatically portrays her powerlessness in family affairs occurs when she attempts to bribe Jason into allowing her to see her illegitimate daughter. After finally agreeing to allow her to "see" Quentin (her daughter) in return for an ample sum of money, Jason drives rapidly past Caddy in a hack allowing her merely to catch a glimpse of her daughter through the window. Caddy runs vainly after the hack in the rain, helpless in the face of her brother's callousness and treachery.

From a Jungian standpoint, however, a paradox is at work. Both Caddy and Quentin are driven by neurotic needs and desires; yet their "neuroses" drive them to try to express the psychological qualities they lack. Thus, they often seem to be both unconscious victims and conscious creators of their fate. Caddy's powerlessness seems to be a result, not so much of her refusal to *seek* power, as of her own Compson lineage, both her physical-mental make-up and her environment. In spite of her many attempts to exert power over herself and over others, she is thwarted by overpowering biological needs and by her cultural milieu. She constantly *seeks* "power," though what she seeks may be more shadow than substance. In her childhood games, Quentin recalls, "She never was a queen or a fairy she was always a king or a giant or a general" (215). She is driven, like many of the tragic figures in literature, by her own inner "daemons" to oppose the established conventions of her environment and the Compson tradition, but her very opposition is actually an attempt to achieve wholeness, both for herself and her family. Like Quentin, she is actually trying to express a positive aspect of the Compson heritage. Her energy and passion are worthy of her passionate and energetic forebears, though she misdirects and mis-channels these energies. She is up against the "divine pair," the "syzygy," that psychological power which is often at the root of tragedy. These two "archetypes," Jung remarks, "possess a fatality that can on occasion produce tragic results. They are quite literally the father and mother of all the disastrous entanglements of fate and have long been recognized as such by the whole world."[26] Just as Quentin's attempts to "dominate" and "master" fail because he lacks certain feminine qualities—warmth, feeling, sensibility—so Caddy's attempts to enrich life by means of her passion and energy (a secondary meaning of the word "power") fail because she lacks certain masculine qualities— abstract thinking, detachment, objectivity.

Yet, paradoxically, as Jung would argue, for both Caddy and Quentin, "Neurosis is really an attempt at self-cure . . . an attempt of the self-regulating psychic system to restore the balance."[27] They both are attempting to break the grip of the "syzygy" by expressing that which will make them whole. By her frantic promiscuity, Caddy is seeking to achieve a "mastery" of, and "power" over, her life; and by his obsessive introspection and frequent bursts of audacity, Quentin is seeking to get in touch with his feelings. Jung would argue, as Irving Malin points out, that "coming to awareness" involves a confrontation with certain opposing principles or "archetypes."[28] Understood in this light, the motives of both Caddy and Quentin are heroic. Caddy is trying to acquire, by confronting the "opposing principles" in her outer experience, that which will cure her "powerlessness" and give her what she would like to believe Quentin possesses: a stern discipline and a standard for behavior—in other words, a "code" by which to live. When she fails to achieve this, by failing to accept and integrate Quentin's "concept of Compson honor"—however misguided his expression of that concept—she is destroyed and the Compson family is destroyed along with her. She lacks that faith in a sustaining tradition which Quentin possesses in excess. Neither she nor Quentin is able to find a balance between faith in tradition and loving commitment to life— the kind of balance Dilsey found by means of her religious faith. Caddy and Quentin are not among those who "endure."

Quentin, like his father, seems congenitally incapable of psychological balance. He seems largely responsible for driving Caddy toward her radical and tragic— and likewise "unbalanced"—life style. But he is probably no more culpable than the other family members or Caddy herself; and his numerous attempts to express nobility, strength, and kindness indicate his unrealized potential for heroism. He, too, is trying to gain wholeness by meeting and integrating certain "opposing principles." An unconscious content, according to Jung, "can only be integrated when its double aspect has become conscious and when it is grasped not merely intellectually but understood according to its feeling value."[29] Quentin's numerous fights to preserve or protect what he considers "virtue," however futile, indicate his desire to gain more than a purely intellectual appreciation of value. He would like to experience the "feeling values" of life that Caddy experiences. Even his obsessive intellectuality can be seen as an attempt to get into touch with his feelings. Quentin belongs to that personality category Jung has designated by the word "feeling." Like "thinking," "feeling" is "a *rational* function," Jung explains;[30] the "feeling" type, however, is concerned not with what a thing is, but with "what a thing is *worth*"—in other words, with values.

> The feeling type . . . when he gets sophisticated and somewhat neurotic . . . is disturbed by thoughts. Then thinking appears in a compulsory way, he cannot get away from certain thoughts. . . . He is caught by his thinking, entangled in certain thoughts; he cannot disentangle because he cannot reason, his thoughts are not movable.[31]

Quentin is not really a tragic figure (though by comparison with the "completely inhuman" Jason, he almost seems so). He fails to achieve tragic stature because of his utter and ludicrous ineffectuality. Yet Caddy's life, too, is an exercise in futility. Quentin's life style is merely the direct opposite of hers and at the same time a logical complement. He eventually becomes all Logos; she, all Eros. His life is spent in an attempt to stop time long enough to discover value and meaning: failing to achieve this, he chooses suicide. Caddy's life is spent in an attempt to become one with the flow of life itself. Failing to find any solid boundaries for the flowing river of her life, she eventually wastes her natural energies and turns to stone. In the "Appendix," Faulkner describes her as "ageless and beautiful, cold serene and damned" (415).

Caddy seeks to acquire "wholeness" by drawing to herself men of power and self-control; Quentin seeks to enforce wholeness by controlling everything outside himself—other men, Caddy, and even "time" itself. Separately, Caddy and Quentin are "unbalanced"; but considered as a pair, they are "orbited nice." To view them merely as pathological misfits does not do justice to them or to the social drama of which they are a part. Unquestionably, both Caddy and Quentin are mentally and emotionally unstable, and certain Freudian concepts do indeed help to understand their lack of equilibrium; but their psychological condition has implications beyond the clinical. Like Jung's "anima-animus" pair, they may be seen as "irreconcilable opposites" who come to embody "every conceivable pair of opposites that may occur: hot and cold, light and dark, north and south, dry and damp, good and bad, conscious and unconscious;"[32] Caddy and Quentin come to stand as timeless symbols, chiseled in marble, of Jung's mythological "divine pair."

NOTES

[1]"Faulkner and Two Psychoanalysts," in *William Faulkner: An Interpretation* (New York, 1972), pp. 79–99.
[2]*William Faulkner: An Introduction and Interpretation* (New York, 1963), p. 49.

[3]Frederick L. Gwynn and Joseph L. Blotner, eds., *Faulkner in the University* (New York, 1965), p. 95.

[4]Jean Stein, "William Faulkner" interview, in Malcolm Cowley, ed., *Writers at Work: The* Paris Review *Interviews* (New York, 1958), p. 137. Faulkner also admitted to a conversational acquaintance with Joyce and Frazer in the same interview.

[5]"A Conscious Literary Use of Freud?," *Literature and Psychology*, III, iii (1953), 3. Collins elaborates his Freudian hypotheses in several other articles too: "The Interior Monologues of *The Sound and the Fury*," *English Institute Essays, 1952* (Columbia Univ. Press, 1953), pp. 29–56; "The Pairing of *The Sound and the Fury* and *As I Lay Dying*," *Princeton Univ. Library Chronicle*, 18 (Spring 1957), 115–123.

[6]"Faulkner's Moral Center," *Etudes Anglaises*, 7 (1954), 57.

[7]"Faulkner and the Theme of Innocence," *Kenyon Review*, 20 (1958), 476.

[8]Catherine B. Baum, " 'The Beautiful One': Caddy Compson as Heroine of *The Sound and the Fury*," *Modern Fiction Studies*, 13 (Spring 1967), 44.

[9]Gwynn and Blotner, p. 6.

[10]Baum, p. 33.

[11]*Quest for Failure: A Study of William Faulkner* (Cornell Univ. Press, 1960), p. 151.

[12]Frank Budgeon, *James Joyce and the Making of* Ulysses (Indiana Univ. Press, 1960), p. 51. "Many writers have written about themselves," Joyce continued. "I wonder if any one of them has been as candid as I have?" There is a good deal of Faulkner in Quentin though Faulkner probably would have been less candid than Joyce in admitting the connection.

[13]Harry M. Campbell, "Experiment and Achievement: *As I Lay Dying* and *The Sound and the Fury*," *Sewanee Review*, 51 (Spring 1943), 314.

[14]"Quentin's Shadow," *Literature and Psychology*, 12 (Winter 1962), 16–24.

[15]C. G. Jung, *Analytical Psychology: Its Theory and Practice* (New York, 1970), p. 99.

[16]*The Sound and the Fury* (1929; rpt. New York, 1956), pp. 219–222. Echoes and allusions to this father-son dialogue are scattered throughout. All subsequent references to the novel are from this edition, including quotes from the "Appendix," and are cited by page number in the text.

[17]*Essays on Contemporary Events*, trans. Elizabeth Welsh, Barbara Hannah, and Mary Briner (London, 1947), p. 12.

[18]*The Yoknapatawpha Country* (Yale Univ. Press, 1963), p. 107.

[19]*Contributions to Analytical Psychology*, trans. H. G. and Cary Baynes (London, New York: 1928), p. 175.

[20]*Psychological Types or The Psychology of Individuation*, trans. H. Godwin Baynes (London, New York: 1923), p. 595.

[21]*Contributions to Analytical Psychology*, p. 185.

[22]Ibid.

[23]Quoted in *Psychological Reflections: An Anthology of the Writings of C. G. Jung*, ed. Jolande Jacobi (New York, 1961), p. 87.

[24]"Aion," in *Psyche and Symbol*, ed. Violet S. de Laszlo (New York, 1958), p. 8.

[25]Ibid., pp. 20–21.

[26]Ibid., p. 20.

[27]*Analytical Psychology: Its Theory and Practice*, pp. 189–190.

[28]*An Interpretation*, p. 90.

[29]"Aion," p. 30.

[30]*Analytical Psychology: Its Theory and Practice*, p. 12.

[31]Ibid., p. 18.

[32]*Psychology and Alchemy*, trans. R. F. C. Hull, vol. 12, *Collected Works of C. G. Jung* (New York, London: 1953), p. 192.

Linda W. Wagner

LANGUAGE AND ACT: CADDY COMPSON

The centrality of Caddy Compson to *The Sound and the Fury* is one of those critical commonplaces that may become blurred through the years. Every reader respects Caddy's importance; Faulkner himself told us the book was about Caddy. It began with the image of the child in the tree, muddy drawers clearly in view, and grew into his most important and most moving novel.[1] Most of the criticism on *The Sound and the Fury,* however, has seemed to find Caddy less interesting than Faulkner's characterizations of Quentin, Jason, Benjy, and even Dilsey. There are comparatively few studies that deal primarily with Caddy, and even fewer that suggest Faulkner's actual means of creating this central figure.[2] This essay hopes to discuss the latter area, with special attention to Caddy's role as language-creator and giver.

There is little question that Caddy dominates the novel. She opens the book (in the "caddie" scene and two flashbacks about Caddy and Benjy); she is central to all the Benjy section, much of the Quentin section, and then—in the form of her daughter Quentin, but in her own voice—much of the Jason section and Part IV. Like Addie Bundren in *As I Lay Dying,* Caddy motivates nearly all the action of the novel. What is most brilliant about Faulkner's methods of fixing her so prominently is that his manner of characterizing her changes with each section of the novel, and that his narrative method in each section is particularly appropriate both for the brother "narrating" that section *and* for the role Caddy plays in that brother's life.

In Book I, Caddy is presented aurally and sensually. She is the voice Benjy hears as well as a comforting and loving presence. She is also a pleasant, natural odor and a predominant visual image for Benjy. Caddy's chief importance for Benjy, however, who cannot speak except in bellows of pain, is that of creator and conveyor of language. Caddy attempts to create language for Benjy; she also translates—correctly—his non-verbal communication into meaningful language for the rest of the family, and for himself.

From *Southern Literary Journal* 14, No. 2 (Spring 1982): 49–61.

Because the Benjy section appears first, and was written first, the portrait Faulkner gives of Caddy is almost completely positive. With Benjy, Caddy is consistently gentle, loving, and teaching. Unlike Mrs. Compson, the ironic mother of the novel, she never reproves him. Caddy rather attempts to reach Benjy and to give him the means of reaching others. In fact, the first scene Faulkner gives us of Caddy and Benjy illustrates her positive, sympathetic role: "Uncle Maury said not to let anybody see us, so we better stoop over. Stoop over, Benjy. Like this, see?"[3]

Caddy uses repetition so that Benjy will understand that there is a name for the action; but more importantly, she herself participates in the action. She is one with Benjy, instead of giving him commands as her mother and Jason do ("You, Benjamin!"). She also uses his name, a diminutive form, lovingly, both the first and second-given names, with no distinction. In Caddy's speech, all Benjy's names become loving.

Throughout their one-sided dialogue (for Benjy at this point in his life appears to make no sound whatever), Caddy's method remains the same—repetition of key words, repetition of Benjy's name, touch and action to accompany and illustrate language, support. Her patience is remarkable, and Faulkner points out repeatedly that Caddy is only a child herself (seven at one point). "Keep your hands in your pockets. Or they'll get froze. You don't want your hands froze on Christmas, do you." Whenever Caddy talks to Benjy, she moves to his level—stooping, bending over, as when she comes home from school in the next scene:

Caddy was walking. Then she was running, her book-satchel swinging and jouncing behind her.
"Hello, Benjy." Caddy said. She opened the gate and came in and stooped down. Caddy smelled like leaves. "Did you come to meet me." she said. "Did you come to meet Caddy. What did you let him get his hands so cold for, Versh" (5).

A more important function for Caddy in the scenes with Benjy is her attempting to bring him to speech. She gives him definitions: "'It's froze.' Caddy said, 'Look.' She broke the top of the water and held a piece of it against my face. 'Ice. That means how cold it is'" (13). She uses repetition of and emphasis on key words, always in an encouraging context. She expects Benjy to learn to speak:

"What is it." Caddy said. "Did you think it would be Christmas when I came home from school. Is that what you thought. Christmas is the day after tomorrow. Santy Claus, Benjy. Santy Claus. Come on, let's run to the house and get warm." She took my hand and we ran through the bright rustling leaves (6).

With the mastery of the imagist poet he was, Faulkner sets this warm scene between Caddy and Benjy immediately in juxtaposition with a scene between Benjy and Mrs. Compson. As a mother, Caroline Compson is a complete failure, but the true irony of her ineptitude is shown less in her dealings with Benjy than in Caddy's comments *on* those dealings. Faulkner gives Caddy a multiple role—both participant and observer-narrative voice; no other character in the novel has these dual roles. Mrs. Compson has hovered over Benjy, pitying herself and him and calling him "poor baby." Directly after this scene, Caddy takes Benjy into the hall and contradicts her mother:

> "You're not a poor baby. Are you. You've got your Caddy. Haven't you got your Caddy?" (8).

Caddy rejects the maudlin and useless sympathy which only debilitates; she will teach Benjy so that he can live and speak for himself.

Three other events occur in this brief scene. Caddy is physically close to Benjy ("Caddy knelt and put her arms around me and her cold bright face against mine"); she has the characteristic odor Benjy loves ("Caddy smelled like trees"); and she appoints herself as his salvation—she, in short, gives us the plot of the novel in nine words: " 'You've got your Caddy. Haven't you got your Caddy?' "

Faulkner structurally has shaped the Benjy section of *The Sound and the Fury* so that Caddy's presence or absence does create or diminish Benjy's life. The first scene in this kaleidoscope of visual images is that of the golfers approaching Benjy across the former Compson pasture. The first spoken language in the novel is "Here, caddie." With the mention of Caddy's name, Benjy's own wound begins. (We do not hear it, but everyone else in range does: " 'Listen at you, now.' Luster said. 'Aint you something, thirty-three years old, going on that way...'" (1). So important was the mention of Caddy to be that in the manuscript version of this scene Faulkner did not include Benjy's age or the fact that it is his birthday: the only reason for this initial scene is to show Benjy's reaction to the sound of Caddy's name. (In the manuscript version, *Caddie* is capitalized when the golfer speaks the word.)[4]

The first scene, then, gives us Benjy's lament, and his lament is not for the downfall of the Compson family or lineage but—much more directly and per-sonally—for the loss of Caddy. The first flashback, a structural decision of equal import as to what will be the opening scene, is of Caddy and Benjy together, doing something as equals, with Caddy instructing Benjy. The second flashback is Benjy waiting by the gate for Caddy, a poignantly charged image, for we see him often—fenced in, captive, waiting for a release that never comes. Because Caddy, and Caddy's ability to reach Benjy through language, might have saved Benjy from his tragic fate of inaction, her loss is the most important single happening of the novel.

The scene of Benjy's waiting for Caddy also shows Benjy's ability to manipulate the family. He has gotten himself outside in time to meet her; without language, he has conveyed his needs well enough that people have responded. Caddy is his motivation. We see very few acts on Benjy's part throughout the novel; by the present time of the book he is cast only as a reactor, and his chief reaction is to mourn. When he was a child, however, Benjy did show initiative.

In these early scenes, Faulkner also shows the advantage of Caddy's responsible behavior toward Benjy. She knows what the child means, wants, and feels. Others in the family do not, partly because they do not communicate directly with him.

When Mrs. Compson wants information about Benjy, she asks Versh instead of Benjy: " 'Is he cold, Versh?' " A simple touch would have told her; instead she receives false information. Mrs. Compson talks *at* Benjy (as she later talks at Jason, Quentin, and Dilsey), but she does not listen: speech for her is monologue, self-aggrandisement. Her "sympathy" for Benjy, in the most loving scene between her and her young retarded son, is all self-pity.

After Faulkner has opened the novel with these clearly positive scenes of Caddy's interaction with Benjy,[5] set against the negative interaction of other people—adults who might be expected to be nurturing forces in Benjy's life—the mastery of his structure begins in earnest. He alternates scenes in which Benjy's fear that Caddy will leave is set against a more tranquil moment; the impending tragedy keeps before us Benjy's present role as mourner (and the obvious plight of the Compson family, once it has banished Caddy). Most of the flashbacks are those in which Caddy is heading toward banishment—the branch scene where Faulkner portrays her defiance, the funeral scene with Caddy in the tree, and Caddy's wedding, her actual leaving. All the scenes give the reader a wealth of information about the entire Compson family, including Quentin and Jason, who will become lead characters in sections II and III; but their particular impact in the Benjy section is their characterization of Caddy. (What happens to Quentin and Jason is of little interest to Benjy, for he had very little contact—emotional contact—with them; his center, his life, is Caddy and her presence or absence.)

In the relatively long branch scene, for example, the relationship between Caddy and Quentin has often been discussed, but it is very possible that Faulkner placed that scene as prominently and as early as he did because in it for the first time Caddy threatens leaving. As she flaunts to Quentin, " 'I don't care. . . . I'll run away. . . . I'll run away and never come back' " (21). Benjy begins to cry; Caddy tells him to hush; he does. But later he cries again, and Caddy knows he is remembering her threat. She reassures him, coming near and squatting in order to speak to him (" 'Hush now.' she said. 'I'm not going to run away.' So I hushed. Caddy smelled like trees in the rain").

All reassurances fail, however, and Faulkner's incremental use of Benjy's alarm when Caddy's look or smell changes—first with her hat; then her perfume; then with kissing, and finally with the sex act—is an effective barometer for her gradual maturity. In each of these scenes, Caddy understands Benjy's alarm and tries to correct the problem. Regaining her virginity is, however, not so easy as giving Dilsey her perfume and so the Benjy section must end by mirroring Benjy's despair. Caddy is gone, lost to the Compsons forever, and Faulkner gives us that image in a juxtaposition as dramatic as the moment Benjy finds his voice:

> "What you seeing." Frony whispered.
> *I saw them. Then I saw Caddy with flowers in her hair, and a long veil like shining wind. Caddy, Caddy*
> "Hush." T. P. said, "They going to hear you. Get down quick." He pulled me. Caddy. I clawed my hands against the wall Caddy. T. P. pulled me (46–7).

Faulkner takes us from the children watching Caddy in the tree on the haunting day of Damuddy's death to the poem of Benjy's recollection of Caddy in her wedding veil (a section that sounds very much like Quentin's prose, and is the only direct recounting of Benjy's memory of the wedding) to T. P.'s worries that Benjy's voice will give them away. It could well be that Caddy's wedding is the first time Benjy has made his sound. As a child, he had cried and people tried to quiet his crying, but I find no earlier indication that the bellowing Benjy produces by the time of the novel proper existed before this scene, Caddy's wedding. If this were the first time Benjy had made these loud and mournful noises, that would explain Quentin's and T. P.'s attempts to move him physically out of the vicinity of the wedding. The speculation that Benjy "found" his voice at Caddy's wedding makes emotional sense because, bereft of her, he has no other way of expressing his great loss.

From this point on, for approximately the last third of the Benjy section, Faulkner gives scenes in somewhat more rapid order to show Caddy in more dimensions of her role. She protects Benjy from Jason, gives him the important objects of comfort (which are also classic identity symbols—fire, mirrors, and the red and yellow cushion), and does battle for him with his mother. In the latter conflict lies the heart of Faulkner's indictment of the Compson family as family: that they allow themselves to be dominated by the least loving of the adults, Caroline Compson, a woman motivated only by social pressure and status. When Caddy insists that her mother hold Benjy, Caroline refuses; when Caddy tries to carry Benjy to her mother, Caroline reprimands Caddy ("You'll injure your back. All of our women have prided themselves on their carriage. Do you want to look like a washerwoman."); when Caddy calls her brother *Benjy* rather than *Benjamin,* Caroline reproves her for being "vulgar." The long skirmish between Caddy and Caroline over Benjy's name serves as culmination of the conflict between love and discipline, between understanding Benjy's needs and providing him with unnecessary conflict. Faulkner depicts Caroline from Benjy's point of view as a third person— *she,* in contrast to Caddy, who is usually named:

> "Look at me." Mother said.
> "Benjamin." she said. She took my face in her hands and turned it to hers.
> "Benjamin." she said. "Take that cushion away, Candace."
> "He'll cry." Caddy said.
> "Take that cushion away, like I told you." Mother said. "He must learn to mind."
> The cushion went away.
> "Hush, Benjy." Caddy said.
> "You go over there and sit down." Mother said. "Benjamin." She held my face to hers.
> "Stop that." she said. "Stop it."
> But I didn't stop and Mother caught me in her arms and began to cry,

and I cried. Then the cushion came back and Caddy held it above Mother's head. She drew Mother back in the chair and Mother lay crying against the red and yellow cushion.

"Hush, Mother." Caddy said. "You go upstairs and lay down, so you can be sick" (77–8).

The scene confirms Caddy's earlier contention when she told her mother she need not bother with Benjy: "I like to take care of him." The first section closes with the apt description of sleep, Benjy going to sleep beside Caddy, "thinking" of things in language Caddy had provided for him: "Then the dark began to go in smooth, bright shapes, like it always does, even when Caddy says that I have been asleep" (92).

Faulkner's tactic in the Quentin section is very different from that in Benjy's. Caddy hardly appears for the first third of the section, but Quentin then is approaching his impending suicide rationally. As he draws nearer the act, Caddy's importance to his life, and death, must be acknowledged, and we not only see images of her; we also hear her voice. Father's voice had dominated the first half of Quentin's section, and it will also the ending scene, but the only emotionally moving events in Quentin's life had to do with Caddy and with his mother, or perhaps with the gap where his mother might have been.

Quentin seldom refers to Caroline Compson. What he attempts to do with Caddy, rather than recognize his love for her, is create a fetish of her virginity.[6] His references to Little Sister Death, to Saint Francis, and to the phrase "had no sister" begin in the second paragraph of his section and continue throughout it. Quentin's method of distancing himself from his pain is to refer to Caddy as "a sister" rather than "my sister": he seldom ever uses her Christian name.

Just as in Benjy's section, one central event in Quentin's is Caddy's marriage. By page three of the second section, Faulkner has quoted from the wedding invitation. It seems fitting that for Quentin the awareness of Caddy's marriage is abstract, verbal, anticipatory; whereas for Benjy, awareness was immediate. He looked through a window and saw Caddy in her wedding veil; he did not use, or even know, the word *wedding*. But Benjy's release was also real and immediate, whereas Quentin's is a smoldering, denying stance that, even at the point of his death, refuses to admit fully its source.

Before Quentin and Caddy interact in any flashback within the Quentin section, Faulkner gives the reader many episodes from the marriage and courtship—Benjy's bellowing, Quentin's hatred for Caddy's intended husband. Set among the many references to Caddy's wedding, however, is a sustained scene in which Caroline Compson denounces all her children except Jason, and suggests to her husband that he take the three so that she and Jason can go off alone and start over. Quentin, consequently, has been abandoned by both mother and sister.

To reinforce this situation, the first appearance of Caddy in this section shows her concern for everyone except Quentin. The scene begins "Are you going to look after Benjy and Father" and continues with her description of the "something terrible in me sometimes at night I could see it grinning at me" (139), a vision Quentin wants to know more about. Her confession that she is sick, that she can take care of Benjy again after it's over, leaves Quentin only further mystified and closed out. He insists on touching her, on being intimate with her; and Faulkner's denouement of that later branch scene shows again how thoroughly Caddy knows her family:

> it wont take but a second just a second then I can do mine I can do mine then
> all right can you do yours by yourself
> yes the blades long enough Benjys in bed by now (189)

Dominant as she has always been, Caddy surmises that once she is dead, Quentin will be unable to kill himself, and then his guilt and grief will be immense. His reference to Benjy points to her almost obsessive responsibility for the youngest brother, responsibility that—like that for her own child—she must relinquish, unwillingly, for the sake of the family pride.

As Faulkner presents this montage of dialogue between Caddy and Quentin throughout the latter half of the Quentin section, images of pain (Quentin's broken leg) and frustration (sex play with Natalie, smells of the honeysuckle near Caddy and her lovers) underlie the more explicit problem—Caddy's pregnancy and the need for her marriage. Woven through that memory is the dual narrative of the Bland travesty of mother-son love and Quentin's "salvation" of the non-speaking little girl. Quentin's need to protect, to assume the parental role, fails once again, with his fight with Bland echoing his fight with Dalton Ames; and his arrest for child molesting putting the ironic close to his role as self-assigned protector of sisters. The culmination of his frustration and abandonment occurs not in a scene with Caddy, however, but in the compelling glimpse of the family relationship: "if I'd just had a mother so I could say Mother Mother" (213), prefacing the scene after the wedding:

> *After they had gone up stairs Mother lay back in her chair, the camphor handkerchief to her mouth. Father hadn't moved he still sat beside her holding her hand the bellowing hammering away like no place for it in silence* When I was little there was a picture in one of our books, a dark place into which a single weak ray of light came slanting upon two faces lifted out of the shadow. *You know what I'd do if I were King?* she never was a queen or a fairy she was always a king or a giant or a general *I'd break that place open and drag them out and I'd whip them good* It was torn out, jagged out. I was glad. I'd have to turn back to it until the dungeon was Mother herself she and Father upward into weak light holding hands and us lost somewhere below even them without even a ray of light... (214–15).

Caddy as king or giant or general extends Quentin's confusion about his role, but the real problem for him—and for the other children—is the abdication of the parental role by both mother and father, to illness and withdrawal, and to alcoholism: "us lost somewhere below even them."

Faulkner's method within the Quentin section was to deflect almost all Quentin's anguish which would have been directed to his mother, so that the primary image is a sexual one, the primary conflict that between sister and brother, over—ironically—the responsibility for the family. Quentin's feeling of being responsible for Caddy is very much like Caddy's feeling of being responsible for Benjy; they are both assuming roles that have been relinquished by their parents. And his method of presenting both Caddy and Caroline changes dramatically. Both are much less in evidence, are represented chiefly by surrogate figures rather than through flashbacks, and are seldom seen or heard. Faulkner's treatment here tends to emphasize that Quentin's *role* is of primary importance to him—Quentin as son, Quentin as protector of younger sisters—a somewhat different identity than Quentin as person of feeling and emotion.

By Part III, the Jason section, Faulkner's method has once again changed.[7] Here Caddy is in evidence only through flashbacks and only in those which present her as a mother. She still dominates Jason's consciousness because she is one source of his income as well as the source of his irritation in the person of her daughter Quentin. Much of Jason's life consists of manipulations of Caddy's money and her child. In the latter conflict, that between Jason and the niece Quentin, Caddy's correspondence (her "voice" through letter, as illustrated early in the Jason section) is often the point of contention. If not that, Jason then carps about Quentin's identity as a female and a "bitch." Faulkner achieves the merging of Caddy's character and that of her daughter through his use of pronouns without referents (*she, her*) and the devastating opening line of Jason's section, "Once a bitch always a bitch, what I say" (223). Jason's ironic concern about family "honor" is the motivation for much of his sadistic behavior toward both Caddy and Quentin; and in that posture he echoes the remaining power of the family, that of his punitive mother.

Now armed with a "huge bunch of rusted keys on an iron ring like a medieval jailer's," Caroline Compson controls her family by locking it up. She still employs her self-pitying rhetoric, but the lock and key—though ineffectual—is the real source of her authority. Faulkner has moved to the depiction of the Compson family as Caroline and Jason (the Bascomb line) accompanied by Ben (whose name has been shortened to the curt monosyllable since Caddy's leave-taking) and the remainder of Dilsey's family. The ruin of the Compson family is clear—none of the Compsons remains. Once Quentin runs away, any hope of survival—much less of nobility or redemption—disappears. Dilsey's Easter refrain, "I seed de first en de last," does not begin until after Quentin leaves.

Faulkner's presentation of Caddy emphasizes this ruin. Omnipresent in the Benjy section, Caddy was the voice and touch of genuine caring. In her conflicts with her mother, chiefly over the care of Benjy, she showed the strong moral conviction that meant hope for the Compson line. By the Quentin section, however, Caddy was wrapped in her own problems, but her concern for both Benjy and her father still dominated most of her dialogue. Forced out of the family by her mother's perverted sense of virtue, she tried to make Quentin responsible for Benjy's care. Caddy appears much less in the second section than she had in the first; she has also grown into adolescence. If she was a child and a pre-adolescent in much of the Benjy section, by the time of Quentin's monologue, she is nearly seventeen.

The result of Caroline Compson's mania for keeping up appearances is the tragedy of the Jason section. Caddy appears seldom, and then only in macabre attempts to see her child; but the voices of both Ben and her daughter Quentin establish her absence. Interaction among the remaining family members makes clear that the source of love has long since disappeared. Caddy is now a mother, and the few words she does speak (in the funeral scene, to Jason) are touched with clarity and maturity. She wants desperately to have her child, but she accepts the reality of her life and allows Jason to keep Quentin.[8] She has few choices— none, in fact, because of the obtuse and self-righteous behavior of her mother.

By the fourth section of the novel, Caddy is represented only by Ben's laments and by the final scene, the penultimate image of the novel, on the golf course. As he had opened the novel, Faulkner chose to close it with the sound of the golfer's voice repeating "caddie," and Benjy's voice bellowing its own hollow echo. There are no flashbacks in the fourth section; there is no image of Caddy anywhere at all, and even the child who carried on her presence has disappeared. The results of Quentin's action dominate Part IV, but Quentin does not appear in that closing segment.

Structurally, then, too, Faulkner is casting his message about the Compsons in terms of Caddy's absence. The stark lives of the Compsons, the weariness of the worn Dilsey, and the impending doom that hovers over the family on Easter of 1928 are all answers to the question of what has happened to Caddy. Caroline's punitive judgments, her banishment of both child and child's name, have led the family into the impasse that has no culmination—only further sound (that of Benjy) and further rage and fury (that of Jason and, subdued, Caroline). The ironic return to "order" that closes the novel cannot change the direction of the entire fourth section. It only points more directly at the false rhetoric and equally false value system of the remaining Compsons. To quiet Benjy may be one primary pur- pose of their existence, just as to maintain a good reputation excused Jason's vindictiveness toward Quentin. In Faulkner's eyes, however, both are unworthy goals.

The initial promise of the novel—imaged in Caddy's generous love for Benjy, Quentin, her father—dwindled into mere endurance. Caddy, labeled *whore,* is separated from her family and from her own family, her daughter. That separation, however, has been the result of the family's action, not of external forces: the Compson family has damned itself in its allowing Caroline to mete out punishment. One might say that the villain of the novel (Mrs. Compson), like the hero (Caddy), has been portrayed obliquely. Neither Caddy nor Caroline has a monologue or section entire, but each is portrayed so clearly from the characterizations of the three brothers that further portrayal would be redundant. As Douglas B. Hill, Jr., comments about Caddy: "The novel revolves about her, focuses itself about her. . . . in a way she is made to control the substance of each brother's narrative life, she gives each one, as a character and as a narrator, his reason for existence."[9]

Linguistic theory would define the narrator of any fiction as the person whose speech act dominates the telling of the fiction,[10] yet Caddy and Caroline Compson are in many ways essential narrators of the Compson story. So much of their language, so much of their verbal presence, emanates through the novel that they are clearly and vividly drawn. Rather than being given one section, they take the novel entire.[11]

But that they are also antagonists determines much of Faulkner's structure as well. Caddy, the positive character, gradually, and perhaps predictably, disappears. Caroline, the repressive and punitive character, looms larger and larger as the novel continues and the years pass. Caddy's gentle and helpful voice has vanished by the fourth section of the book; and even Mrs. Compson's voice was replaced by the harsh clang of her keys. Language—meaningful language—has been replaced by sound (Benjy's) and fury (Jason's), and from those expressions will come only further waste. At this stage in Faulkner's career, his women characters were the sources of both promise and disappointment; they were his central figures even though he could handle them only through indirect presentation. Within a decade, he moves to male characters who can act purposefully and who can express themselves fluently. Such characters as Bayard Sartoris, V. K. Ratliff, and Chick Mallison are the better because of his experimentation with Caroline and Caddy Compson; but even if they were not, Faulkner's achievement in *The Sound and the Fury* is reason enough for that experimentation.

NOTES

[1]William Faulkner, *Faulkner in the University,* eds. Frederick L. Gwynn and Joseph L. Blotner (Charlottesvillle, Virginia: The University Press of Virginia, 1959), p. 6. See "Preface to *The Sound and the Fury,*" trans. George M. Reeves, *Mississippi Quarterly,* 19 (1966), pp. 107–15 and "An Introduction to *The Sound and the Fury,*" in *A Faulkner Miscellany,* ed. James B. Meriwether (Jackson: University Press of Mississippi, 1974), p. 158. Joseph Blotner's *Faulkner: A Biography* (New York: Random House, 1974) should be the starting point for any reading of this novel.

[2]Many treatments are helpful, among them John Earl Bassett, "Family Conflict in *The Sound and the Fury,*" *Studies in American Fiction,* 9 (Spring, 1981), 1–20; Eileen Gregory, "Caddy Compson's World," *The Merrill Studies in* The Sound and the Fury (Columbus, Ohio: Merrill Co., 1975), 89–101; Douglas B. Hill, Jr., "Faulkner's Caddy," *Canadian Review of American Studies,* 7 (Spring, 1976), 26–38; John L. Longley, Jr., " 'Who Never Had a Sister': A Reading of *The Sound and the Fury,*" *Mosaic,* 7 (1973), 35–54; Gladys Milliner, "The Third Eve: Caddy Compson," *Midwest Quarterly,* 16 (April, 1975), 268–75; M. D. Faber, "Faulkner's *The Sound and the Fury:* Object Relations and Narrative Structure," *American Imago,* 34 (Winter, 1977), 327–50; Judith Wittenberg, *Faulkner: The Transfiguration of Biography* (Lincoln: University of Nebraska Press, 1979); Gary Lee Stonum, *Faulkner's Career: An Internal Literary History* (Ithaca, N.Y.: Cornell University Press, 1979); David Williams, *Faulkner's Women, the Myth and the Muse* (Montreal: McGill–Queen's University Press, 1977) and David Minter, *William Faulkner: His Life and Work* (Baltimore: The Johns Hopkins University Press, 1980).

[3]William Faulkner, *The Sound and the Fury* (New York: Vintage, 1946), p. 3. Hereafter cited in text.

[4]University of Virginia Faulkner Collection, manuscript of *The Sound and the Fury.*

[5]As Arthur F. Kinney points out in *Faulkner's Narrative Poetics: Style as Vision* (Amherst: University of

Massachusetts Press, 1978), Benjy's memories are not merely of Caddy but "Caddy and Benjy . . . the center of Benjy's perceptual life; his memories revolve . . . around his relations with her and her absence from him" (140).

[6] I concur with several other critics, most strongly with Panthea Reid Broughton in *William Faulkner: The Abstract and the Actual* (Baton Rouge: Louisiana State University Press, 1974), 115–17.

[7] Olga Vickery was the first to point out the similarities between Benjy and Quentin, in that they maintained a rigid concept of normalcy and refused to accept changes that time would mandate in *The Novels of William Faulkner: A Critical Interpretation* (Baton Rouge: Louisiana State University Press, 1959), 35–39; see also Kinney (149) and James Guetti, who adds Jason to the list in *The Limits of Metaphor: A Study of Melville, Conrad, and Faulkner* (Ithaca, N.Y.: Cornell University Press, 1967), 150–51.

[8] As Gladys Milliner points out, Caddy defies Southern tradition by becoming a mother: "She is the only one of the Compson children to produce a child, because she is the only Compson with the spirit of life within her," *Midwest Quarterly,* 16 (Spring 1975). John Longley, Jr., concludes that "Caddy's tragedy is that she will never find anyone commensurate with her own capacity to love: not father, mother, brothers, or lover," *Mosaic,* 7 (1973).

[9] Douglas B. Hill, Jr., *Canadian Review of American Studies,* 7 (Spring, 1976), 26.

[10] Among recent treatments of this point is that by Nomi Tamir, "Personal Narrative and Linguistic Foundation," *PTL: A Journal for Descriptive Poetics and Theory of Literature,* 1 (1976), 403–29 and Ann Banfield, "Narrative Style and the Grammar of Direct and Indirect Speech," *Foundations of Language,* 10 (1973), 1–39.

[11] As M. D. Faber concludes, Caddy doesn't need a section of her own because "Caddy, in the deepest psychological sense, is *in* the men," *American Imago,* 34 (Winter, 1977), 327. Faber sees Mrs. Compson's as "the central role in the tragedy of Quentin, indeed, in the tragedy of all the Compson children" because of her clearly "pathogenic behaviours" (p. 341).

Cleanth Brooks

THE SOUND AND THE FURY

The structure of *The Sound and the Fury* is complex. To begin with a small but obvious matter, the novel does not open with Friday, April 6, and go on in chronological sequence with the flashback to 1910 coming somewhere within the sequence. Instead, we move from Holy Saturday, 1928, back to June 1910, then on to Good Friday, 1928, and end with Easter Sunday, 1928.

Greater confusion yet is to come. I have said that the novel opens with the monologue of Benjy the idiot. As we begin the novel, its title is immediately pertinent. We are reading what is literally a tale told by an idiot, for Faulkner is borrowing from Macbeth's great speech in which the Scottish king cries out that life itself is a "tale / Told by an idiot, full of sound and fury, / Signifying nothing." In accord with his own purposes, Faulkner seems to have deliberately begun his novel with the most incoherent of the four sequences, presenting his reader with a puzzle to unravel rather than a narrative exposition of the general situation out of which the narrative of the novel is to develop. The reader may well believe that Faulkner is ordering his sequences in the worst possible way.

Yet the testimony of thousands of readers amounts to an endorsement of Faulkner's method. Certainly the reader is confused as he works through the first section of the novel. Since he is compelled to experience the world as Benjy has to experience it, he finds himself in a topsy-turvy world in which the past and the present intermingle, and in which the principle of cause and effect simply does not exist. Faulkner evidently wanted his reader to participate in Benjy's experience of time and reality which means that the reader participates in Benjy's confusion. Yet—and here is where the testimony of thousands of readers becomes relevant— curiously enough most readers, even on a first reading, discover that they learn a great deal about the Compson family. They have been immersed in the family situation, they know what it feels like to live in this household.

Many of the particular references and events in Benjy's monologue are bound to be puzzling to the reader. But some of these will become clear as one reads

From *William Faulkner: First Encounters* (New Haven: Yale University Press, 1983), pp. 44–60.

on into the other sections and finds them mentioned again. Besides, there is nothing to prevent the interested reader's returning to Benjy's section after completing the book—we usually have to reread any intricate poem several times—and there may be a real pleasure in the recognitions that come from these rereadings.

Faulkner was quite aware of the burden he was imposing upon his reader. Though he saw no alternative to his general strategy, he suggested to his publisher certain special devices. Because Benjy makes no distinction between a past and a present event, and because, in addition to references to the present (that is, April 7, 1928), there are references to some dozen time strata in which past events occurred, Faulkner urged that Benjy's section be printed in different color inks, a particular hue to indicate a different segment of time to which Benjy was referring.

Since this matter may be confusing, let me illustrate. Open a copy of the Vintage Book edition, mark the passage beginning with the first line of page 1, "present." Then on page 3, mark the passage printed in italic, "A–3"; mark the passage in roman type that follows on page 3, "A–1"; mark the small block in italic on page 5, "present"; and mark the passage in roman type beginning with the last two lines on page 5 and ending with the block in italic on page 8, "A–2." The "A" passages refer to an especially cold day, December 23, 1909.

If we want to straighten the time sequence out, we might read passage A–1 (p. 3), and go right on to A–2 (pp. 5–8), and then back to A–3 (p. 3). Read consecutively, the sequence of events is thoroughly coherent. Benjy wants to go outdoors. In spite of the cold, he is finally allowed to do so. Caddy then returns from school and greets her little brother. But Uncle Maury calls Caddy aside and entrusts her with a letter she is to deliver to a neighbor. Having dismissed Versh (who ordinarily looks after Benjy), Caddy takes Benjy along with her on her walk to the neighbor's house. They have to get there by crawling through a barbed wire fence on which Benjy promptly snags his coat and so has to be freed by Caddy.

But why did Benjy's mind jump from April 7, 1928 (where the novel starts on page 1) to December 23, 1909? Because Luster, who is now looking after him, takes him through a gap in a fence and Benjy catches his clothing on a nail and Luster has to free him. The connection is " 'Cant you never crawl through here without snagging on that nail' " (ll. 2–3, p. 3) and *"Caddy uncaught me,"* and so forth (l. 4, p. 3).

Benjy's mind is now very much on Caddy, and his memories of the cold day before Christmas Eve. When Luster—we are once more back to April 7, 1928— complains *"What are you moaning about,"* the answer is Caddy. In fact, in a moment Benjy's mind (if you can call it a mind) is back with Caddy again, as we move to A–2 at the bottom of page 5.

Before the notion of printing in different color inks had been broached, Faulkner had already made use of the switch of typefaces in his manuscript to signal to the reader a shift in the time level, and this device was retained and so presented in the published text. Just how Faulkner meant to use his colored inks, we do not know. Perhaps he meant to print the A section (December 23, 1909) in red; the time of Mr. Compson's death (April, 1912) in blue; the time of Benjy's grandmother's death (in 1898) in green; the present in black; and so on. But since there may be a number of references to the same time level—there are twenty to the date (November 1900) on which Benjy's name was changed from Maury—and since Benjy does not necessarily get all the references to a time level in their proper sequential order—remember that the three A references we used in our illustration went A–3, A–1, and A–2—he might still have had to use some changes in typeface besides the colored-ink differentiation. Presumably, this was what Faulkner planned to do, but the publisher was not willing to use the dozen or more different colors required by Faulkner's proposal, and so Faulkner wrote to his friend Ben Wasson: "I'll just have to save the idea until publishing grows up to it."[1]

Yet I must not make Benjy's section seem more difficult than it is. Upon opening the book for the first time, the reader should not treat Benjy's monologue as a puzzle to be worked out rather than as a piece of fiction to be savored and enjoyed. If the reader later should want to contemplate the detail of a piece of brilliant literary engineering, help is at hand. Let him or her look at Edmund Volpe's careful dissection in *A Reader's Guide to William Faulkner* or read the article by George R. Stewart and Joseph M. Backus in *American Literature.*

For most readers, and especially for first readers of this novel, it is better to be content with experiencing the general quality of Benjy's world, the confusions in it that cause his sense of baffled helplessness, and the poignance for him of the loss of the one person who genuinely loved him and tried to comfort him, his sister Caddy.

Though Benjy is almost subhuman in so many respects, he retains certain aspects of his humanity. He retains a dim awareness of the lost Caddy, whom he has not seen for many years now. When he hears golfers call out "caddie" as they play on the course that adjoins the Compson property, the word recalls Caddy to him. He has his own fetishes and talismans: one of Caddy's discarded slippers, bits of glass with which he plays, flowers to hold in his fist, the flicker of flames in the fireplace.

Yet I would misrepresent matters if I suggested that Faulkner's interest in Benjy was a coldly clinical interest in his primitive psychology. Faulkner is interested in Benjy because he tells us something about humanity at large and because he represents the human being reduced to its ultimate dimensions and essentials. In short, Faulkner uses Benjy not to debunk humanity, but to affirm its distinctive quality and value. Benjy calls forth love, and in his own manner he is able to return love.

One fruitful way in which to consider Benjy is to see how he is related to the realm of time. As we have already remarked, events of thirty years past have for him the same immediacy as events of thirty seconds past. In fact, Benjy may be said to live in what is a virtual present. He has no real past and no real future. Benjy's experiences on this plane are very much like an animal's or at least like what we suppose an animal's to be: his life is in effect timeless. He has associations, patternings, habitual couplings of experience just as a dog or a horse has them:

the sight of flames somehow soothes him; the sound of Caddy's name stirs him to a vague but aching disquiet. But he has no ordered past to which he can consciously turn. This is what one means by saying that Benjy lives in a virtual present.

There is another and related way of regarding Benjy. He lives in a world of primitive poetry. Everything is concrete. Abstractions are beyond him and so is conceptual language in general. He responds to events in their immediacy. He does not sort them out and reorganize them as most of us do, albeit unconsciously. In this matter, then, Benjy is not so much a mere animal as a very primitive savage.

To repeat: he exists in a world of primitive poetry, whereas the rest of us distinguish between the prosaic, routine aspects of our lives and the poignant and significant moments. Let me illustrate: when Benjy says to himself, as he does continually, "Caddy smelled like trees," he is not trying to be poetic, though his comparison will seem poetic to most of us. Benjy does not even know what he means by saying this beyond the fact that in some wonderful way Caddy does smell to him like a tree. We can analyze his metaphorical language if we like. We can say that to Benjy, Caddy smells like a natural, organic plant that has its own dignity and unforced beauty. No wonder that Benjy becomes frantic when Caddy first puts on perfume; the new odor somehow seems to violate her integrity and inner nature since it is artificial, synthetic, unnatural. This is the way in which we might undertake to explain Benjy's violent reaction. But such words would be ours. Benjy is incapable of such articulation, but that is not to say that his inarticulate response is at odds with our interpretation.

I have been insisting on Benjy's limitations, deficiencies, and confusions. In addition, an attentive reading of Benjy's monologue can also give us some sense of the quality of the Compson household: a father, defeated and cynical, who drinks too much; a mother who lacks maternal feeling; a chronic unhappiness between the mother and father; a worthless uncle, Mrs. Compson's brother, who is a sponge, an encumbrance, and a disgusting caricature of the cultivated gentleman; and the four children. And how different the children are: Quentin, the eldest, hypersensitive, ineffectual, unsure of himself; Caddy, the daughter, sweet, natural, loving, brave, and desperate to break out of this hopeless gloom; and Jason, crass, hard, contemptuous of his father and his elder brother. Jason regards his sister as a plain bitch and his idiot brother as simply a nuisance, a family disgrace, a probable obstacle to the worldly success that he craves. If poor Benjy's helplessness in this hopeless situation and his inability even to understand it come home to us, then section one of the book has already done the most important part of its work even if many particular details remain obscure.

Quentin's monologue (section two of the novel) is very different from Benjy's. The thoughts he expresses are those of a highly literate, intelligent, and sensitive young man. Yet Quentin's monologue, like Benjy's, has its own difficulties. In the first place, he is talking to himself—or simply meditating, if you prefer—and he is not taking time to explain his meditations to any outsider. (For him, there are no outsiders: the reader simply overhears his thoughts.)

Benjy cannot explain and, of course, feels no need to explain. Quentin does not need to explain to himself. Thus, there are cryptic allusions to some of his experiences about the exact nature of which we can only guess: to an accident in which Quentin's leg was broken; to a fight that Quentin had with a schoolmate over something that the schoolmate had said about their young woman school-teacher; and so on. But certain matters of importance to which Quentin's mind keeps returning are clear enough, especially his concern for virginity—for his own, but far more importantly, for Caddy's loss of her virginity and her pregnancy and hurried marriage to provide a name for her expected child. Also important are his feeling that his mother is no mother at all and his several conversations with his cynical father who evidently had heavily influenced Quentin's thinking, but who was able to offer him no consolation and no real guidance. Most of all, we shall find, Quentin is obsessed with a certain code of honor which he feels he must not violate, and with death, as a refuge, a way out of a hopeless situation, and an offering of peace to his tormented spirit.

But before we go further into Quentin's monologue, it may be helpful to compare him with his brother, Benjy, in the matter of their relation to time and in relation to the kind of language they use. Let us begin with the matter of time. Benjy lives in a virtual present and knows neither past nor future; Quentin lives in the past. It is the past which obsesses him and from which he sees no way to extricate himself. The Quentin who is talking to himself in section two is living the last day of his life. He has resolved to drown himself. His life has essentially ended. During these last hours, he is simply killing time until it is time to kill himself.

In a very real sense, Quentin has long been obsessed by the past. He has, for example, refused to accept the fact that his relation to Caddy is bound to change as she becomes a young woman and seeks a mate and a life of her own. He has an impossible wish, nothing less than to arrest the movement of time. Many years ago, Jean-Paul Sartre compared Quentin's situation to that of a man sitting in a speeding convertible automobile and looking backward. Such an observer cannot see where the car is going, nor can he see clearly what is immediately before his eyes as he looks backward. Objects near at hand are too blurred for him to see. The only things that achieve real form and perspective for him are things far down the road in the receding distance.[2]

Sartre's comparison is excellent. About all that Quentin can see clearly are certain things in the past. Unfortunately Sartre ascribed this situation to Faulkner's characters generally—which is absurd. But it does fit Quentin's perspective perfectly.

As to language: if Benjy's internal monologue has the virtues of a simple, primitive, barbaric poetry, Quentin's reminds one of the decadent poets of the 1890s. In the first place, Quentin's poetry is very "literary." It is mannered and quite consciously "poetic," but it is also languid, tired, and world-weary.

The fact is that Faulkner as a very young man came under the spell of English poets like Swinburne and Wilde and of French poets like Verlaine. He was, in time, to shake off the world-weary cadences and find his true poetry in his own energetic and muscled prose; but his fictional character, Quentin, has not shaken himself free of such poetry and why should he? The date of his death is 1910. The real point is that Quentin *is* world-weary. His language thoroughly suits his attitudes and psychic condition.

This last observation brings us to the reason for Quentin's suicide. Why has he decided to put an end to his life? I shall propose no simplistic answer, for Quentin is a complex character and the reader needs to respect his complexity. It is not enough, for example, to find Quentin's motive in the fact that he is disconsolate because the Compson family, a family of aristocratic pretensions, has gone to seed, and that his native land is a defeated, poverty-stricken part of the country. It is perfectly true that the family as we see it in *The Sound and the Fury* is in poor estate, and Quentin is fully conscious of its desuetude, but I find little evidence in his long monologue that he is much concerned about the loss of his family's past glories. I can recall only one reference to such glories and even that one merely glances at them. The reference (on p. 125) has to do with something else: Mrs. Compson's insecurity and her hostility toward her husband's family. The fragment in question reads: "do you think so because one of our forefathers was a governor and three were generals and Mother's weren't."

Quentin does come of decayed gentry and he is deeply Southern, but he does not commit suicide for either of these reasons, or for the combination of the two. At least two of Quentin's friends at Harvard are from the South. Gerald Bland is the wealthy Kentuckian who takes—or at least his vapid mother takes—his Southern heritage very seriously. His other friend, Spoade, is from South Carolina, and so Mrs. Bland approves of him, but she cannot forgive him for "having five names, including that of a great English ducal house."

But neither of these young men shows any suicidal tendencies. They are not melancholy at the defeat of the South and in fact are happy-go-lucky. Bland has done so well that Quentin has come to believe that God is not only "a gentleman and a sport; He is a Kentuckian." Even in Jefferson, Mississippi, where the gentry are not as wealthy as Bland or as noble in blood as Spoade, they seem able to bear their fate without too much repining. Within his own family, Quentin is the only one who ever thinks of taking his life.

We shall come closer to Quentin's basic motive for taking his life if we pay attention to his mother. She has somehow withheld her love from her children, all except the loathsome Jason, whom she regards as lacking the selfishness and "false pride" of the Compsons and who is more like her own people.

In his meditations on this last day of his life, Quentin touches on this matter very specifically. Quentin, thinking of his mother, says of his family, "Finished. Finished. Then we were all poisoned." Again, he says to himself, "If I could say Mother. Mother." He is conscious of the fact that he has no mother. Most pointed of all is his memory of an illustration in a book that he and Caddy used to look at (p. 215), a picture of a "dark place into which a single weak ray of light came slanting upon two faces lifted out of the shadow." The picture used to enrage Caddy as a child. She would say, *"if I were King... I'd break that place open and drag them out and I'd whip them good."* The sentiment is characteristic of Caddy. But Quentin's reaction is just as characteristic of him. He broods on the picture, turning back to look at it "until the dungeon was Mother herself she and Father upward into weak light holding hands and us lost somewhere below even them without even a ray of light." It is a measured indictment, uttered to himself, not in heat or in anger, but simply in weary, utter hopelessness.

The impact of the family situation on Caddy is just as drastic, but she reacts in a different way. Looking for warmth, joy, life itself, Caddy loses her virginity to a handsome young man, a stranger in town named Dalton Ames. Later she becomes promiscuous. There is something morbid in the relationship for Caddy, for she is to tell Quentin later: *"There was something terrible in me sometimes at night I could see it grinning at me . . .* through their faces. . . ." (p. 138)

Quentin is crushed by Caddy's fall. He has invested too much in his sister's honor. Quentin's father tellls him that he is taking it too hard. He remarks that "It's nature is hurting you not Caddy," and further, "it's because you are a virgin: dont you see? Women are never virgins. Purity is a negative state and therefore contrary to nature." But this is cold comfort to Quentin who yearned to keep Caddy inviolate, or if she must be violated, would want to be the violator himself. If he and she could only commit incest, they would become pariahs, exiled by the world and so somehow safe from the world, or as Quentin puts it in one of his more exalted moods, they would be punished together in some chamber of hell, wrapped in the same "clean flame."

This is all extravagant enough, but Quentin is a very special case. His psyche clearly has been twisted and he has been very badly hurt in spirit. He is lonely, estranged, afraid of reality, and still virginal about sex. Finally, his sense of honor is quixotic. Don Quixote was one of Faulkner's favorite literary characters. A good number of the characters in Faulkner's novels resemble the Don in one way or another, and Faulkner is willing to regard them, from time to time, as comic, if at the same time, somehow pathetic.

Quentin does conform to the Quixote type, but Faulkner never laughs at him. It is a real achievement that he has so managed matters that it never occurs to the reader to laugh at him either. In part, the reason is that Faulkner has brought the reader so fully into Quentin's mind that he participates in Quentin's agonies and compulsions.

One further point has to be made. For all of Quentin's pathos, he is not a gloomy psychopath or given to sorrowful whining or filled with self-conscious Byronic melancholy. He actually goes about the preparations for his death with a kind of sober cheerfulness. He has not lost his sense of humor. He can even smile at himself as a brother who could not take proper care of his own sister and who gets falsely arrested on a charge of molesting another man's sister. Quentin is perceptive, alert, and even shows a certain wisdom. Consider, for example, his definition of the word *nigger:* "a nigger is not a person so much as a form of behaviour; a sort of obverse reflection of the white people he lives among." Or consider his remark on the name of his sister's seducer: "Dalton Ames. It just missed gentility. Theatrical fixture. Just papier-mâché. . . ." Or note the quiet relish he takes in his black friend Deacon's answer to the question "Did any Southerner ever play a joke on you?" In his answer Deacon shows himself a diplomat and yet at the same time a realist: "They're fine folks. But you cant live with them." (Deacon was then living in Cambridge, Massachusetts.)

What I take to be the fatal wound inflicted on Quentin's spirit is relived by him in full detail on this last day of his life. During the past summer Quentin had tried to assume the role of the protective brother. When he found that Dalton Ames had seduced Caddy, he approached Dalton with the words: "I've been looking for you two or three days," and proposed that they meet at the bridge over the creek at one o'clock.

Caddy heard Quentin asking T. P. to saddle his horse for one o'clock, and when Caddy asked Quentin what it was that he planned to do, he replied: "None of your business whore whore" and told T. P. he had changed his mind and would walk.

Dalton is waiting at the bridge and Quentin then gives him his ultimatum: he is to leave town. When Dalton says nothing responsive to this, Quentin specifies that he has "until sundown to leave town." And when asked what he will do if Dalton does not, Quentin says, "Ill kill you dont think that just because I look like a kid to you . . ." But Dalton simply asks him how old he is and finally gives him a piece of advice: "listen no good taking it so hard its not your fault kid it would have been some other fellow." When Quentin asks Ames whether he ever had a sister, the reply is *"no but theyre all bitches."*

Quentin tries to strike him, but Dalton catches in succession both his hands, then manages to hold Quentin's wrists in one hand and swiftly pull out his pistol. He drops a piece of bark on the stream and, having let the bark drift down, shatters it with one shot, and then disintegrates two of the pieces with two more shots. Dalton reloads the three empty chambers and hands Quentin the gun, telling him that he will need it in view of what he has threatened. Quentin says "to hell with your gun" and again tries to strike Dalton, but "then it was like I was looking at him through a piece of coloured glass." Quentin inquires of Dalton: "did you hit me?" Dalton tells him yes, and, holding Quentin up on his feet, asks him how he feels, proposes lending him his horse to get home, and when Quentin declines the offer, rides off.

But Quentin, now sitting with his back against a tree, knows that Dalton "had not hit [him,]" that he had "lied about that for her sake too and that I had just passed out like a girl. . . ."

Meantime, Caddy rides up on Quentin's horse. Having heard the shots, she is frantic for Quentin's safety, but having found that her brother is unhurt, she insists that she must leave at once, for she has got to catch Dalton and ask his pardon. Her commitment to her lover is absolute. She is relieved that Quentin is all right, but to her he is simply her little brother (though in years he is the elder) and she makes it plain that she resents her little brother's meddling in her affairs.

The total experience for Quentin is emasculating. Quentin has had it proved to him that he cannot live up to what he takes to be the old heroic code, the code of a man of honor. He cannot protect his sister from any handsome transient who means to enjoy her. No one, including Caddy herself, takes him seriously. It has been argued that if Quentin had not interfered, Caddy would have married Dalton Ames and her life would not have been ruined. But Quentin has surely judged this situation correctly. Dalton means it when he says that women are all bitches. He is not the marrying kind. In any case, neither in his eyes nor in Caddy's has Quentin provided any real interference. Had Dalton wanted to marry her, he could have taken her off with him at any time. Quentin did not break up a true-love affair and, as we have seen, could not have done so had he wished.

What about Mr. Compson? What responsibility does he have for what happened to Caddy and to Quentin? A great deal, for Quentin, it becomes clear from his monologue, confided much of his anguish to his father and took with real seriousness his father's counsel. Mr. Compson is a kindly man. He loves his children, including Benjy. But he has probably never been a very effectual man, and by the time we meet him in *The Sound and the Fury,* two years before his death, he has failed his children and obviously lost control of the family situation. He is now a beaten man, worn down, and all too ready to take refuge in his decanter of bourbon.

He is not without wit. His brother-in-law, that outrageous fake Southern gentleman, is for him a constant source of merriment—if scarcely innocent merriment. The skepticism and cynicism that he affects is probably genuine enough. But in spite of his show of cynicism about Caddy, he is deeply hurt by her promiscuity. For this, there is plenty of proof. Caddy tells Quentin: "Father will be dead in a year they say if he doesn't stop drinking and he wont stop he cant stop since I since last summer." She is, of course, alluding to her affair with Dalton Ames. What Mr. Compson believes and what he has tried to instill in Quentin is a version of stoicism. One is not to whimper, not to bemoan his fate, but to endure it like a man.

Quentin's father once tells him that "we must just stay awake and see evil done for a little while its not always." Mr. Compson, by the way, did not get this sentiment out of his well-thumbed copy of Horace or even out of the bourbon bottle, but via Faulkner who took it from poem 48 of A. E. Housman's *A Shropshire Lad.* (In the mid-1920s Housman had become Faulkner's favorite poet, and one of the traits in Housman that Faulkner admired was what Faulkner called "the splendor of fortitude.") Lines 11–12 of poem 48 read as follows:

> Be still, be still my soul; it is but for a season:
> Let us endure an hour and see injustice done.

Mr. Compson is obviously paraphrasing these lines when he tells Quentin that we are asked just to "stay awake and see evil done for a little while[.] its not always," but Quentin replies that it does not even have to be a little while "for a man of courage."

When Mr. Compson asks whether he considers that expedient (in other words, suicide) a manifestation of courage, Quentin answers, "yes sir dont you." Mr. Compson refuses to take a stand on the matter, observing that "every man is the arbiter of his own virtues." But Quentin suspects that his father does not believe that he is serious about taking his own life and his father admits that he does not take Quentin's threat seriously.

Mr. Compson turns out to be a really shrewd psychologist. He tells his son "you cannot bear to think that someday it will no longer hurt you like this now" and he goes on to predict that Quentin will not take his life "until [he comes] to believe that even she [Caddy] was not quite worth despair."

Does Quentin finally drown himself because he has come to believe that Caddy was not worth despair? or is it because he fears that if he waits long enough his present despair will indeed die into apathy? We are not told, but his memory of this conversation with his father takes us down to the last page of Quentin's monologue. All that remains—one long paragraph—has to do with such mundane matters as Quentin's need to leave a letter for Shreve in their room, and his washing his teeth and brushing his hat, for Quentin is as meticulous about his final appearance as any Japanese warrior preparing to commit hari-kari. Quentin means at least to die like a gentleman and man of honor.

I have spent perhaps too much time discussing Quentin's character and the motives that expressed themselves in his life, and more importantly in his death. I have suggested that though Quentin is a thoroughly Southern type, his death is not really occasioned by the breakup of the Old South so much as by the breakup of an American family wrecked by parental strife and lack of love. Moreover, I have suggested that Quentin is a very special case—hypersensitive, idealistic, lonely, and almost absurdly romantic—even though in the novel Faulkner has been careful not to make him absurd.

Yet in stressing matters of this sort, I have not spoken in any detail of the power of the writing, sentence by sentence, or the dramatic force of some of the great scenes such as that in which Quentin proposes that he and Caddy commit suicide together and actually holds a knife to her throat. Most of all, I have failed to deal adequately with the atmosphere of the whole monologue, its deeply resonant and sustained quality of anguished suffering as Quentin gets through his last day, literally killing time, for he is quite contemptuous of time. Quentin has already abandoned his watch, having broken it and thrown it in a convenient garbage can. Alive in his head on this final day are the passionate memories of events, situations, confrontation, physical objects, and even sounds and odors of the past such as the smell of honeysuckle which from time to time gets mixed up with everything. Quentin's disastrous past surges and resurges through his head.

He cannot purge his mind of it. Since he can see no future for himself, there is no way out of the past, no way to redeem it; any Christian solution is meaningless to this intense, sad, and terribly honest young man. Having no future, he is indeed condemned to live with his past. He believes the only way out is death.

Oscar Wilde tells us that life imitates art. Maybe so, maybe not. But sometimes there *is* an uncanny resemblance between reality and fiction. A few years ago I read a very moving account of a young man of our time who, because he felt he had nothing to live for, though his body was healthy and though he had a good job and—whether or not he realized it sufficiently—loving parents and friends, resolved to kill himself. He went about it as quietly and methodically as Quentin did. The young man in question, however, had never read *The Sound and the Fury*.

One further note on life's imitating art. On one of the bridges spanning the Charles River in Cambridge, there is a small plaque commemorating Quentin's death on June 2, 1910. It was placed there several years ago by three admirers of *The Sound and the Fury* for whom Quentin's death in the river had become a real happening.

NOTES

[1]Michael Millgate, *The Achievement of William Faulkner* (New York, 1966), p. 94.
[2]See *Three Decades of Faulkner Criticism,* ed. F. C. Hoffman and Olga Vickery (Ann Arbor: University of Michigan Press, 1960) for an English translation of Sartre's "A Propos de *Le Bruit et la furor,*" *La Nouvelle Revue Française* (52).

Max Putzel

COMING TO THE
SACRIFICE

All three Compson brothers betray the author's impressions, however exaggerated and distorted, of his father and brothers. You might say that each, too, reflects his maker, in a fun-house mirror. If so, it is all the more clear that Caddy stands for his Other and theirs as well. She is the common center of their orbits, their gravitational pull, the wavering family self-image. For Faulkner himself she is what Psyche is to Poe, the Oversoul to Emerson, Una to Spenser. We may feel free to make what use we can of biographical evidence linking the author's family to the Compsons. To approach Caddy in so pedestrian a way would be discourteous to say the least. Anyway, such evidence as we might adduce would be irrelevant. For Caddy is in no sense a representation of some somatic female.

The three brothers perhaps symbolize what is interior to the writer's ego or superego, his troubled night thoughts. If that fact tricks us into using them as a key to personal dilemmas of his which are none of our concern anyhow, all the more important to see Caddy as a key only to his life of the imagination. She is sheer artifice controlled by the modes and devices of fine art, and as such she belongs to the art of her time. Constant references to Caddy as Faulkner's "heart's darling" are a misuse of a nice phrase he turned to accommodate a sensitive undergraduate. It is no help to our understanding of her aesthetic reality, her true worth. She is outside of the frame enclosing her brothers and parents and Dilsey, distinct in kind. Bleikasten finds a neat analogy likening her to Eurydice, the lost beloved almost recaptured, forever evasive and forever drawing us back to Hades and nonentity.[1]

As a poetic construct rather than a person, Caddy has a poetic life of her own. Certainly she is no kin to Faulkners or Oldhams. Her family tree is a burning bush within a budding grove, not some common orchard variety. On the literal level we see her first as a charmingly willful, naturally wild little girl; then as a rebellious, promiscuous young woman in the throes of puberty; finally as a lost outcast, a heartbreaking, bereft mother, a wraith. None of these human shapes,

---

From *Genius of Place: William Faulkner's Triumphant Beginnings* (Baton Rouge: Louisiana State University Press, 1985), pp. 163–74.

however much we feel their reality, defines her essence or her place in the history of art.

To discover the source of Caddy Compson's appeal to our sympathy, her hold on our affection, we must depart from the literal. She exists on the symbolic level where Virgil leads his poet guest from hell through purgatory. But as Caddy fades out of the plot, becoming no more than a recollection of recollections, it will be Dilsey who leads us higher, as Beatrice alone could guide Dante, "uscendo fuor della profunda notte."

Caddy is a product of the twenties, a time of almost unprecedented eclecticism when the arts intermingled. To see her in context with her time is not to reduce her to the stature of a local or transient figure. Like any object of fine art, she has to be seen in relation to her period before we evaluate her, along with La Gioconda or a favorite Renaissance madonna, not for an age but for all time. Hers was a period when a new Gothic revival and a new classicism came into headlong collision with strident modernism. Instead of the tangled discord one would expect, all three joined in sprightly dance. The novel fuses these three tendencies, then surprisingly concludes with a hymn—a paean of rhapsodic Christian fundamentalism. Quentin is a relic of chivalric ideals. Jason is realistic, modern, with all the noisy vulgarity and hollow cynicism that can imply. Benjy and Dilsey are primitives, while Caddy is just as surely a figure cast in the purest classic mold.

"You, Satan."

It is understandable that Dilsey should order her down from the forbidden tree in those terms. For Caddy belongs alongside cloven-footed demigods, survivors of medieval Christianity still showing the mark of their Dionysian origin. Gresset reminds us of Faulkner's persistent addiction to Swinburne and the *symbolistes*.[2] She steps out of the limp suede covers of Stephen Phillips' *Marpessa,* "wounded with beauty in the summer night," partaking both of Faulkner's callow youth and his artistic coming of age, the time of Diaghilev's greatness: *Le Sacre du printemps.*

When that marvelous ritual ballet burst on the world at the Théâtre des Champs Elysées just before the Great War, Jacques Rivière greeted it in the *Nouvelle Revue Française* as a work that "modifies the very source of our aesthetic judgments." He predicted it would soon be counted among the greatest works of art. After the review he returned to his theme in a studied essay concluding that this masterpiece was a fragment of the primitive world still flourishing, "a rock full of holes whence emerge unknown beasts busy with indecipherable and outmoded actions from a time long gone by."[3]

Following the war, the ballet rocked London audiences. T. S. Eliot in his London letter to the *Dial* called Stravinsky, its composer, the greatest hit since Picasso, adding that the music had an effect like *Ulysses* "with the best contemporary illustration." Diaghilev was the supreme master of the eclectic, and Eliot points out another correlative. "The Vegetation Rite upon which the ballet is founded remained, in spite of the music, a pageant of primitive culture," he writes. It had special appeal to anyone who had read works like *The Golden Bough*. Stravinsky seemed to transform "the rhythm of the steppes into the scream of the motor horn, the rattle of machinery, the grind of wheels, the beating of iron and steel, the roar of the underground railway, and the other barbaric sounds of modern life." One year later, readers of the *Dial* (Faulkner perhaps among them) would open to a frontispiece representing in the post-Cubist manner a Gothic interior. On the facing page they would encounter beneath Greek and Latin epigraphs *The Waste Land*. Eliot's poem was the leading feature of that issue. It resounds loud and clear especially in the Quentin and Jason sections.[4]

Eliot's mention of Picasso recalls the other great genius of the time who, like Diaghilev, Stravinsky, Joyce, and Eliot himself, epitomizes the eclectic. Picasso and Faulkner have striking similarities and equally striking differences. Unlike Faulkner, Picasso was precocious both artistically and sexually. Yet as one examines room after room of his erotica in Barcelona, noting the classic purity of female figures so seductive, so sexy, one is struck by the fact that most of their male admirers (like those of Velázquez and Goya) are fully dressed. Picasso is forever the voyeur, Faulkner the eavesdropper.

In his artistry Picasso surpassed his father while yet a boy and could draw a classic figure to rival Ingres. Like Faulkner, he borrowed or stole from every period and any contemporary, yet experimented relentlessly. His one true innovation, cubism, dates from the time of life when Faulkner was still polishing *The Marble Faun*. At that stage in each of their lives his sophistication contrasts blatantly with Faulkner's provincialism, yet neoclassicism recurs with both. By the early twenties of the century Picasso had squeezed cubism dry and returned to classicism in innumerable graphics like those at Arles. Faulkner would similarly soon cast off the stream-of-consciousness rhetoric invented for *The Sound and the Fury*.

Like Faulkner, Picasso was attracted by youthful beauties of both sexes. He was incapable of love for anything but his art. That young man leading the horse is as fetching as the delicate child acrobat balancing on her huge ball beside a brutish Caliban, a seated giant. She reminds me of that gaggle of young girls Faulkner invented in the course of his search for Caddy Compson. Caddy herself would find it hard to resist any of Picasso's pitiful boy waifs with their big, sad, Spanish eyes. I think particularly of one who reappears often in so many of the master's canvases and etchings, the wistful littlest brother in the *Family of Saltimbanques*, a painting, by the way, that inspired the great fifth *Duineser Elegie* of Rainer Maria Rilke published in 1923. Doesn't that boy have a hint of young Quentin, too, in his dark gaze? But by the time Faulkner discovered Quentin, Picasso had changed styles again. He was doing illustrations for the classics, the *Metamorphoses* and *Lysistrata*.

Now consider another of Eliot's suggestions. Perhaps Faulkner himself did. Already familiar with Sir James Frazer in the one-volume 1922 edition of *The Golden Bough* Phil Stone owned, Faulkner might well have found there at least the situation needed to turn Quentin and Caddy into figures of high tragedy.

"Who does not know Turner's picture of the Golden Bough?" Sir James begins. "The scene, suffused with the golden glow of imagination in which the divine mind of Turner steeped and transfigured even the fairest landscape, is a dream-like vision of the little woodland lake of Nemi—'Diana's Mirror,' as it was called by the ancients." And he goes on to recount the myths of the Nemian Diana and her nymph Egeria "of the clear water," and to remind us that their sparkling stream "as it ran over the pebbles is mentioned by Ovid, who tells us that he had often drunk of its water." "Legend had it," Frazer continues, "that Virbius was the young Greek hero Hippolytus, chaste and fair, who . . . spent all his days in the greenwood chasing wild beasts with the virgin huntress Artemis. . . . Proud of her divine society, he spurned the love of women, and this proved his bane." Hippolytus became the victim of the sea god and was destroyed, but his myth lived on, and he became a saint in the Roman calendar, whose martyrdom is still celebrated on August 13, "Diana's own day." Frazer teaches us that Artemis, later so chaste, had once been a goddess of fertility, and so "must necessarily have a male consort." "These hapless lovers were probably not always mere myths," he continues, "and the legends which traced their spilt blood . . . were no idle poetic emblems of youth and beauty fleeing as the summer flowers." Artemis-Diana, he explains, was friendly to life, a goddess of childbirth. But her priests at Nemi were doomed like Hippolytus to a bloody end, each in turn hunted down and murdered by his successor, a human sacrifice. One thinks of Picasso again, the brave bulls and doomed horses, the Minotaurs.[5]

In a chapter whose title, "The Sacred Marriage," oddly suggests the Keble hymn that plagues Quentin, Frazer goes on to add that, because of her function as goddess of childbirth, incest was particularly repugnant to Diana and her worshipers. Where incest had occurred, expiatory sacrifices had to be offered up in the Nemian grove lest—as in Eliot's poem—sterility overtake the land.[6]

So all these esoteric references are not as far afield as at first they might seem. Fear of incest haunts Quentin.

At the outset I warned against too glib an acceptance of Faulkner's late explanations of early works. Here is a case in point. Some ten years after the event he told Maurice-Edgar Coindreau how Caddy came into being. While writing a short story about a group of children sent away the day of their grandmother's funeral he fell in love with one of the characters. Because Caddy deserved more than a short story he expanded her tale into a novel. Years later, in the justly famous *Paris Review* interview, he elaborated on this account. "It began with a mental picture of the muddy seat of a little girl's drawers, in a pear tree." He went on to tell how that image was replaced "by one of the fatherless and motherless girl climbing down the rainpipe." Then, having tried three times to tell the same story, once through each of the brothers, he decided to "fill the gaps by making myself the spokesman."[7]

One has the impression that by now Faulkner had told the story of how he invented Caddy and fell for her so often that the details of his retelling overshadowed the novel in his recollection. Just as he forgot that Miss Quentin shinnied down the same tree her mother once shinnied up, so he implies that Quentin might have told his niece's story, too, though he died before she was born. Most important, he forgot that Part Four of the novel, the Dilsey section, does not tell Caddy's story, hardly mentions her. These innocent deceptions are, of course, unimportant unless one substitutes them for what stands in the text.

Just as Benjy had been prefigured in "The Kingdom of God," so Caddy was sketched again and again in a variety of fictions, some symbolic, some naturalistic, long before she muddied those panties. His "heart's darling" she may have been, but that phrase was thought up the year after the *Paris Review* interview, not thirty years before. Long ere Caddy came, he created Cecily Saunders and Emmy of *Soldiers' Pay,* but even they and their faun-infested wonderland came late in the procession of proto-Caddys. I once tried to trace the *Ur*-Caddy through a dozen crass juvenilia.[8] At best they were teetering stepping stones in the path that leads to the creekside colloquy between Quentin and Caddy which comes after the accusation scene in the manuscript. But how crude the language in which they are clothed—if they are clothed. For most of these nymphoid nudes—Frankie or Emmy or Juliet—are all creatures of adolescent reverie, and all are but feeble forerunners of the loved one.

Like Frankie in one of three early sketches, Caddy leads an admirer to premature death, personified as a little sister. Like another of them, she accepts her unlawful pregnancy with intransigent gratefulness and no trace of regret. A "girl of spirit," this other Frankie is deserted by a young mechanic who longs to drive racing cars, but she glories in her prospective motherhood. The moon goddess figures in that tale and also in the early poem "Adolescence," which hints at the familiar twilight setting:

> Within the garden close, whose afternoon
> To evening languishing is like to swoon,
> A diana. . . .[9]

Drunk in a gondola beside his Venetian whore, Elmer still dreams of an odorless "Diana-like girl with impregnable integrity, a slimness virginal and impervious to time." The short story fragment telling how Elmer loses his virginity with a demi-vierge named Ethel, who, once pregnant, serenely marries somebody else, anticipates the Natalie episode in *The Sound and the Fury.* That ends, of course, with Quentin rolling in a hog wallow, smearing Caddy's "hard turning body" with filth, then suggesting they both wash in the branch "and the water building and building up the squatting back the sloughed mud stinking surfaceward."[10]

In the scenes of epicene girlhood, water is always an ambivalent symbol. Like Elmer's beloved only sister Jo-Addie, Caddy is a hardbodied tomboy. Like Juliet in the short story also named "Adolescence," and Miss Zilphia Gant in the tale named for her, and Emmy in *Soldiers' Pay,* these prototypes of Caddy's pubescence are anything but depraved. They are all innocence even when discovered sleeping naked beside boys next to swimming holes. Like Caddy all are alienated, too, by the nasty suspicions of angry, mean-minded elders. Their crises lead up to that bizarre episode when Quentin is charged with seducing the little Italian girl walking beside a swimming hole squirming with naked boys, the afternoon before he drowns. Symbolic or naturalistic, all these girls, like Diana or Egeria, are figures of ancient libido, of fertility rites, ominous premonitions of sexual secrets associated with girlhood innocence and boyhood fears—of what? Perhaps of sex itself and the secret of life. Perhaps of the chill, wet hand of death.[11]

We must resist the temptation to trace these visions to specific incidents in the author's childhood, his friendship for a shy little girl at school or his affection for the girl cousin with whom he attended one grandmother's funeral in the course of the half year when they also lost the other grandmother they called Damuddy. Bleikasten, Blotner, and others have explored each clue, and I have rummaged through the same heap of attic furniture for traces of the Ur-Caddy. But in the end I come back to the Attic original, the primordial nymph, waiting maid to the moon goddess bathing in the Nemian pool.

Like Egeria, Caddy is the tutelary nymph of a Compson domain fraught with doom, partly of her own making. Lolita of the New South she may be, but we must remember that Lolita is a nickname for Maria de los Dolores, Our Lady of Sorrows. Whoever else Caddy may represent, she and her name are alike enigmatic. Perhaps she is simply the embodiment of Faulkner's Genius of Place.[12]

Perhaps, too, she is related to Eliot's hyacinth girl: "Your arms full, and your hair wet." Such a vision is found on the last page of the hand-lettered, illustrated bibelot Faulkner gave Helen Baird after she announced her engagement to a rival in 1926. Mayday, as it is called, tells of an archaic knight who contemptuously resists the blandishments of three princesses and ends by drowning himself to join "one all young and fair and white, and with long shining hair like a column of fair sunny water," who makes young Sir Galwyn think of spring and honey and sunlight— and hyacinths, of course. She is the sister of Hunger, known also to the knight's other fellow traveler, Pain. This allegory is more complex than The Wishing Tree. I read it as a parable of the artist's struggle to defend his Dionysian sofa, battleground of the imagination, against the soft peace of the Apollonian double bed. Both Collins and Brooks have emphasized the undoubted indebtedness Faulkner has to medieval pastiches by James Branch Cabell. They pass over another component, the tale's transparently false frivolity. Mayday lapses constantly into the slangy jargon of College Humor, one of the cheap magazines to which Faulkner submitted potboilers.[13]

Of greater importance are its illustrations. Where Faulkner's earlier drawings were frank imitations of Aubrey Beardsley or of John Held, Jr., popular cartoonist of flappers and sheiks, Mayday is ornately adorned. It has illuminated capitals and line drawings reminiscent of the symbolistes and even the pre-Raphaelites but also three exquisite watercolors. Their style shows that Faulkner was aware of the more sophisticated manner which Boris Anisfeld, earlier one of Diaghilev's protégés, brought to the decor of the Metropolitan Opera's production of The Blue Bird. That fact suggests another important poet whose example Faulkner drew on not only for fairy tales but for the theme of the children (including Caddy) in The Sound and the Fury. The paintings bring up the possibility that Faulkner actually attended the opera or at least saw reproductions of its costumes and sets—Anisfeld's first opportunity to emerge from the shadow of better-known Diaghilev designers like Léon Bakst and Aleksandr Benois.[14] The direct influence of Maurice Maeterlinck is more certain.

The Belgian dramatist had won his Nobel Prize, while Faulkner was still in knickerbockers, partly on the strength of the dramatic production of *The Blue Bird* staged by Stanislavsky and later put on in Paris. Several years later, while still serving lackadaisically as postmaster, Faulkner was apparently the target of a lighthearted student hoax that persisted for some months. The student journal to which he had been contributing made him out to be one of three presidents of a Bluebird Insurance Company set up to guarantee the happiness of undergraduates and save them from the dullness of their professors. Clearly the bluebird of Maeterlinck's masterpiece had by 1924 become a well-worn topic of jovial badinage.[15]

The suspicion of Maeterlinck's influence is heightened when we come to examine the various manuscripts (some sedulously corrected by hand) of the booklet Faulkner wrote for Estelle's little daughter Victoria as a birthday gift in 1927. *The Wishing Tree* (posthumously published in the *Saturday Evening Post* and a few days later in a children's format by Random House) closes as does *Mayday* with a reference to Saint Francis. Again the saint is concealed by multi-colored birds that swirl upward, but in the fairy tale he does not introduce a young man to his little sister Death, as he does in one of the *Times-Picayune* sketches and in *Mayday*. (The reference to death as a sister seems to have haunted Faulkner, who must have encountered it in the canticle where the saint also personifies his ailing body as Brother Ass and begs its pardon for the indignities an ascetic life has heaped on it.) The details of the myriad birds and talking tree are Maeterlinck's. But it will be remembered that the children Mytyl and Tyltyl do not, like Dulcie, get a bluebird in the end. The bird is as elusive as Caddy; when caught, Maeterlinck's bluebirds die. In the end the little neighbor girl in *The Blue Bird* (like one of the children to whom Faulkner presented his *Wishing Tree*) is left empty-handed. Even Tyltyl's dove gets away from her. Faulkner's little neighbor Margaret Brown, who got one copy of his book, had cancer and was fated soon to die.

The booklet Faulkner made for Victoria and also gave Margaret betrays other preoccupations alien to Maeterlinck. If we turn to its opening we encounter an astonishing phallic dream, more suggestive of the mysteries of Eleusis than of the Victorian nursery tale Faulkner must have thought he was writing. His little heroine, who has a name like Dilsey's and also a black nurse like her, awakens on her birthday morning to find she is still dreaming. Dulcie dreams she is a fish "rising through the warm waters of sleep" and then she dreams she is awake. But "it was like there was still another little balloon inside her, getting bigger and bigger and rising and rising. Soon it would...pop out and jump right up against the ceiling. The little balloon inside her got bigger and bigger, making all her body and her arms and legs tingle."[16]

On Dulcie's illusory awakening she finds a strange boy standing quizzical and challenging at her bedside. And if hitherto we only suspected that Faulkner got his inspiration from Maeterlinck, now we know. "Name's Maurice," he replies curtly. But *The Wishing Tree*'s resemblance to *The Blue Bird* flickers, comes and goes. And though resemblances to persons and situations in *The Sound and the Fury* or *Alice* and her looking-glass world are worth exploring, it is the end of *The Wishing Tree* that really matters. Dulcie gets a present—a bluebird—but the children in Maeterlinck's play have discovered that bluebirds cannot be captured; that they die when you touch them. The Belgian poet's classic has myriad philosophic implications, but Faulkner's tale can be summed up with a simple moral: if you are kind to helpless things you will need no magic to get your wish.[17]

Caddy Compson is not so simple. She resembles the afterimage of an ecstatic dream, a very orgasm, that dies with the return of consciousness. She leaves us only the retreating, fading spectral image of all we know in youth that is purest pleasure and pain, sheer magic, but beyond recall. Then, unlike little Dulcie but much like Sir Galwyn and poor Caddy, we too must face up to the ennui of life's dull ache and insatiable hunger.

NOTES

[1]André Bleikasten, *The Most Splendid Failure: Faulkner's* The Sound and the Fury (Bloomington and London, 1976), 66.

[2]Michel Gresset, "Le Regard et le désir chez Faulkner, 1919–1931," *Sud* (Marseilles), Nos. 14–15 (May, 1975), 12–61.

[3]Jacques Rivière, "Le Sacre du printemps," *Nouvelle Revue Française*, X (1913), 309–13. The essay, also entitled "Le Sacre du printemps," appeared ibid., 706–30. See also Blanche A. Price (ed. and trans.), *The Ideal Reader: Selected Essays by Jacques Rivière* (New York, 1960), 147.

[4]T. S. Eliot, letter, in *Dial*, LXXI (1921), 452–53; Eliot, *The Waste Land*, ibid., LXXI (1922), November issue.

[5]Sir James George Frazer, *The Golden Bough: A Study in Magic and Religion* (abridged ed.; 1922; rpr. New York, 1935), 1–8, 141.

[6]Ibid., 141.

[7]*Paris Review* interview in Malcolm Cowley (ed.), *Writers at Work* (New York, 1960), 130–31.

[8]Max Putzel, "Evolution of Two Characters in Faulkner's Early and Unpublished Fiction," *Southern Literary Journal*, V (Spring, 1973), 47–63.

[9]"Adolescence," reproduced in Robert A. Wilson, *Faulkner on Fire Island* (New York: Phoenix Bookshop, 1979).

[10]*The Sound and the Fury* (New York: Random House, 1956), 172.

[11]Blotner includes the short story "Adolescence" in the *Uncollected Stories* (New York, 1979), 459–73, and provides helpful notes on it (p. 704) and on "Frankie and Johnny" (*Double Dealer*, January, 1925) and "The Kid Learns" (*Times-Picayune*, May, 1925) (p. 698). Cleanth Brooks couples "Miss Zilphia Gant" with the far more finished story "A Rose for Emily" in the most extensive analysis the former has been given: *William Faulkner: Toward Yoknapatawpha and Beyond* (New Haven, 1978), 152–64, 380–82. "Miss Zilphia" was published by the Book Club of Texas (Dallas) in 1932, with a preface by Henry Nash Smith, and rpr. in *Uncollected Stories*, 368–81.

[12]Caddy's given name, Candace, is not informative. It occurs in the New Testament (Acts 8:27) in an oblique reference to a *Kandake* or ruling queen of Ethiopia who invaded Egypt around 22 B.C. and was twice defeated by Petronius, the Roman governor. Strabo calls her a woman of manly spirit. There is no reason to suppose Faulkner attached any importance to the biblical reference to the queen's eunuch.

[13]See Carvel Collins, Introduction to Collins (ed.), *Mayday* (Notre Dame, 1978) and illustrations between pp. 58 and 59. Also Brooks, *Toward Yoknapatawpha*, 47–52, and passim. Faulkner submitted three stories to *College Humor* in 1930–31. On other potboilers, see James B. Meriwether, "Two Unknown

Faulkner Short Stories," *Recherches Anglaises et Américaines* (Strasbourg), IV (1971), 23–28. In this connection "Nympholepsy" should be mentioned as a clue to the theme still evolving of death by water coupled with sexual fear.

[14]On Anisfeld, see John E. Bowlt, "Synthesism and Symbolism," *Forum* (St. Andrews, Scotland) (January, 1973), 36ff., and Stephanie Terenzio, Introduction to *Boris Anisfeld, 1879–1973: A Catalogue* (Storrs, Conn., 1979).

[15]Joseph Blotner, *William Faulkner: A Biography* (New York, 1974), I, 350–51. On Maeterlinck, see Pierre-Aimé Touchard, "Le Dramaturge," in Joseph Hanse and Robert Vivier (eds.), *Maurice Maeterlinck, 1862–1962* ([Bruxelles?], 1962), 323–429. Also *Noble Prize Library* (New York, 1971), 139–220.

[16]*The Wishing Tree* (New York, 1967), 6.

[17]Cf. Blotner, *Biography*, I, 541–42, 565, 573.

CONTRIBUTORS

HAROLD BLOOM is Sterling Professor of the Humanities at Yale University and Professor of English at the New York University Graduate School. He is a 1985 MacArthur Foundation Award recipient, served as the Charles Eliot Norton Professor of Poetry at Harvard University (1987–88), and is the author of eighteen books, the most recent being *Poetics of Influence: New and Selected Criticism*. Currently he is editing the Chelsea House series Modern Critical Views and Modern Critical Interpretations, and other Chelsea House series in literary criticism.

CATHERINE B. BAUM is a former instructor of English at Emory University.

SALLY R. PAGE is a former instructor in the Department of English at Duke University.

JOHN T. IRWIN is Chairman of the Writing Seminars at Johns Hopkins University. His work includes *American Hieroglyphs* (1980) and *The Heisenberg Variations* (1976), a volume of poetry published under the name of John Bricuth.

GLADYS MILLINER is a Professor of English at Southern University.

ANDRÉ BLEIKASTEN, Associate Professor of English at the University of Strasbourg, has written many articles in French and English on Faulkner and is the editor of *William Faulkner's The Sound and the Fury: A Critical Casebook* (1982).

DOUGLAS B. HILL, JR., is a member of the English Department at Erindale College, University of Toronto.

STEVE CARTER is a member of the English Department at Northwest Oklahoma State University.

LINDA W. WAGNER is a Professor of English and Associate Dean in the College of Arts and Letters at Michigan State University. Her work includes *Hemingway and Faulkner: Inventors/Masters* (1975) and *American Modern: Essays in Fiction and Poetry* (1980).

CLEANTH BROOKS is one of the premier critics of the twentieth century. Among his books are several studies of Faulkner as well as *Modern Poetry and the Tradition* (1939) and *The Well Wrought Urn* (1947).

MAX PUTZEL is a member of the Department of Germanic Languages at Indiana University Northwest. He is the editor of Sir Philip Sidney's *Astrophil and Stella* (1967).

BIBLIOGRAPHY

Adams, Richard P. *Faulkner: Myth and Motion.* Princeton: Princeton University Press, 1968.

Backman, Melvin. *Faulkner: The Major Years: A Critical Study.* Bloomington: Indiana University Press, 1966.

Bloom, Harold, ed. *Modern Critical Interpretations:* The Sound and the Fury. New York: Chelsea House, 1988.

————, ed. *Modern Critical Views: William Faulkner.* New York: Chelsea House, 1986.

Blotner, Joseph L. *Faulkner: A Biography.* New York: Random House, 1974. 2 vols.

Bowling, Lawrence E. "Faulkner: Technique of *The Sound and the Fury.*" *Kenyon Review* 10 (1948): 552-66.

Broderick, John C. "Faulkner's *The Sound and the Fury.*" *Explicator* 19, No. 3 (November 1960): 12.

Brooks, Cleanth. *On the Prejudices, Predilections, and Firm Beliefs of William Faulkner: Essays.* Baton Rouge: Louisiana State University Press, 1987.

————. "Primitivism in *The Sound and the Fury.*" In *English Institute Essays 1952.* New York: Columbia University Press, 1954, pp. 5–28.

————. *William Faulkner: Toward Yoknapatawpha and Beyond.* New Haven: Yale University Press, 1963.

————. *William Faulkner: The Yoknapatawpha Country.* New Haven: Yale University Press, 1963.

Broughton, Panthea Reid. *William Faulkner: The Abstract and the Actual.* Baton Rouge: Louisiana State University Press, 1974.

Coindreau, Maurice-Edgar. *The Time of William Faulkner.* Edited and translated by George McMillan Reeves. Columbia: University of South Carolina Press, 1971.

Collins, Carvel. "The Interior Monologues of *The Sound and the Fury.*" In *English Institute Essays 1952.* New York: Columbia University Press, 1954, pp. 29–56.

Cowan, Michael H., ed. *Twentieth Century Interpretations of* The Sound and the Fury. Englewood Cliffs, NJ: Prentice-Hall, 1968.

Edel, Leon. "How to Read *The Sound and the Fury.*" In *Varieties of Literary Experience,* ed. Stanley Burnshaw. New York: New York University Press, 1962, pp. 241–57.

Everett, Walter K. *Faulkner's Art and Characters.* Woodbury, NY: Barron's Educational Series, 1969.

Freedman, William A. "The Technique of Isolation in *The Sound and the Fury.*" *Mississippi Quarterly* 15 (1962): 21–26.

Fried, Barbara H. *The Spider in the Cup: Yoknapatawpha County's Fall into the Unknowable.* Cambridge, MA: Department of English and American Languages and Literatures, Harvard University, 1978.

Gold, Joseph. *William Faulkner: A Study in Humanism, from Metaphor to Discourse.* Norman: University of Oklahoma Press, 1966.

Gresset, Michael, and Noel Polk, ed. *Intertextuality in Faulkner.* Jackson: University of Mississippi Press, 1985.

Griffin, Robert J. "Ethical Point of View in *The Sound and the Fury.*" In *Essays in Modern American Literature,* ed. Richard E. Langford. DeLand, FL: Stetson University Press, 1963, pp. 55–64.

Grimwood, Michael. *Heart in Conflict: Faulkner's Struggles with Vocation.* Athens: University of Georgia Press, 1987.

Guérard, Albert J. *The Triumph of the Novel: Dickens, Dostoevsky, Faulkner.* New York: Oxford University Press, 1976.

Hall, Constance Hill. *Incest in Faulkner: A Metaphor for the Fall.* Ann Arbor, MI: UMI Research Press, 1986.

O'Connor, William Van. *The Tangled Fire of William Faulkner.* Minneapolis: University of Minnesota Press, 1954.

Parker, Robert Dale. *Faulkner and the Novelistic Imagination.* Urbana: University of Illinois Press, 1985.

Polk, Noel, and Kenneth L. Privratsky, ed. The Sound and the Fury: *A Concordance to the Novel.* Ann Arbor, MI: University Microfilms, 1980. 2 vols.

Reed, Joseph W. *Faulkner's Narrative.* New Haven: Yale University Press, 1973.

Sartre, Jean-Paul. "On *The Sound and the Fury:* Time in the Work of Faulkner." In *Literary Essays.* Translated by Annette Michelson. New York: Philosophical Library, 1957, pp. 79–87.

Schmitter, Dean Morgan, ed. *William Faulkner: A Collection of Criticism.* New York: McGraw-Hill, 1973.

Slatoff, Walter J. *Quest for Failure: A Study of William Faulkner.* Ithaca: Cornell University Press, 1960.

Snead, James A. *Figures of Division: William Faulkner's Major Novels.* New York: Methuen, 1986.

Thuckstun, William R. *Visionary Closure in the Modern Novel.* New York: St. Martin's Press, 1988.

Volpe, Edmond L. *A Reader's Guide to William Faulkner.* New York: Farrar, Straus, 1964.

Wadlington, Warwick. *Reading Faulknerian Tragedy.* Ithaca: Cornell University Press, 1987.

Waggoner, Hyatt Howe. *William Faulkner: From Jefferson to the World.* Lexington: University of Kentucky Press, 1959.

Wagner, Linda Welshimer, ed. *Four Decades of Faulkner Criticism.* East Lansing: Michigan State University Press, 1973.

Warren, Robert Penn, ed. *Faulkner: A Collection of Critical Essays.* Englewood Cliffs, NJ: Prentice-Hall, 1966.

Williams, David L. *Faulkner's Women: The Myth and the Muse.* Montreal: McGill–Queen's University Press, 1977.

Wyatt, David. *Prodigal Sons: A Study in Authorship and Authority.* Baltimore: Johns Hopkins University Press, 1980.

ACKNOWLEDGMENTS

"An Introduction to *The Sound and the Fury*" by William Faulkner from *Mississippi Quarterly* 26, No. 3 (Summer 1973), © 1973 by Jill Faulkner Summers, Executrix for the Estate of William Faulkner. Reprinted by permission of W. W. Norton & Company.

"Mirror Analogues in *The Sound and the Fury*" by Lawrance Thompson from *English Institute Essays 1952,* © 1952 by Columbia University Press. Reprinted by permission.

Excerpts from *Faulkner in the University: Class Conferences at the University of Virginia 1957–1958,* edited by Frederick L. Gwynn and Joseph L. Blotner, © 1959 by The University Press of Virginia. Reprinted by permission.

"Worlds in Counterpoint: *The Sound and the Fury*" by Olga W. Vickery from *The Novels of William Faulkner: A Critical Interpretation* by Olga W. Vickery, © 1959, 1964 by Louisiana State University Press. Reprinted by permission.

"Quentin's Responsibility for Caddy's Downfall in Faulkner's *The Sound and the Fury*" by Jackson J. Benson from *Notes on Mississippi Writers* 5, No. 2 (Fall 1972), © 1972 by *Notes on Mississippi Writers.* Reprinted by permission.

"Faulkner" by Mimi Reisel Gladstein from *The Indestructible Woman in Faulkner, Hemingway, and Steinbeck* by Mimi Reisel Gladstein, © 1974, 1986 by Mimi Reisel Gladstein. Reprinted by permission.

" 'Who Never Had a Sister': A Reading of *The Sound and the Fury*" by John L. Longley, Jr., from *The Novels of William Faulkner,* edited by R. G. Collins and Kenneth McRobbie (special issue of *Mosaic* 7, No. 1 [Fall 1973]), © 1973 by *Mosaic.* Reprinted by permission.

"The Problem of Time in *The Sound and the Fury*: A Critical Reassessment and Reinterpretation" by Douglas Messerli from *Southern Literary Journal* 6, No. 2 (Spring 1974), © 1974 by the Department of English, University of North Carolina. Reprinted by permission of The University of North Carolina Press.

"Caddy, Benjy, and the Acts of the Apostles: A Note on *The Sound and the Fury*" by Michael J. Auer from *Studies in the Novel* 6, No. 4 (Winter 1974), © 1975 by North Texas State University. Reprinted by permission.

"Caddy Compson's Eden" by Boyd Davis from *Mississippi Quarterly* 30, No. 3 (Summer 1977), © 1977 by Mississippi State University. Reprinted by permission of *The Mississippi Quarterly.*

"Faulkner's *The Sound and the Fury*: Object Relations and Narrative Structure" by M. D. Faber from *American Imago* 34, No. 4 (Winter 1977), © 1978 by the Association for Applied Psychoanalysis. Reprinted by permission of *American Imago* and the Association for Applied Psychoanalysis.

"Brothers and Sisters in Yoknapatawpha County" by Susan Gallagher from *Essays in Literature* 7, No. 2 (Fall 1980), © 1980 by *Essays in Literature.* Reprinted by permission.

"The Self's Own Lamp" by David L. Minter from *William Faulkner: His Life and Work* by David L. Minter, © 1980 by The Johns Hopkins University Press. Reprinted by permission.

" 'The Beautiful One' " (originally titled " 'The Beautiful One': Caddy Compson as Heroine of *The Sound and the Fury*") by Catherine B. Baum from *Modern Fiction Studies* 13, No. I (Spring 1967), © 1967 by Purdue Research Foundation. Reprinted by permission.

"The Ideal of Motherhood" (originally titled "The Ideal of Motherhood: *The Sound and the Fury*") by Sally R. Page from *Faulkner's Women: Characterization and Meaning* by Sally R. Page, © 1972 by Sally R. Page.

Excerpts from *Doubling and Incest/Repetition and Revenge: A Speculative Reading of Faulkner* by John T. Irwin, © 1975 by The Johns Hopkins University Press. Reprinted by permission.

"The Third Eve" (originally titled "The Third Eve: Caddy Compson") by Gladys Milliner from *Midwest Quarterly* 16, No. 3 (Spring 1975), © 1975 by *The Midwest Quarterly*. Reprinted by permission.

"Caddy, or The Quest for Eurydice" by André Bleikasten from *The Most Splendid Failure: Faulkner's* The Sound and the Fury by André Bleikasten, © 1976 by Indiana University Press. Reprinted by permission.

"Faulkner's Caddy" by Douglas B. Hill, Jr., from *Canadian Review of American Studies* 7, No. I (Spring 1976), © 1976 by *Canadian Review of American Studies*. Reprinted by permission.

"Caddy and Quentin: Anima and Animus Orbited Nice" by Steve Carter from *Hartford Studies in Literature* 12, No. 2 (1980), © 1980 by University of Hartford Studies in Literature. Reprinted by permission.

"Language and Act: Caddy Compson" by Linda W. Wagner from *Southern Literary Journal* 14, No. 2 (Spring 1982), © 1982 by the Department of English of the University of North Carolina at Chapel Hill. Reprinted by permission of The University of North Carolina Press.

"The Sound and the Fury" by Cleanth Brooks from *William Faulkner: First Encounters* by Cleanth Brooks, © 1983 by Yale University Press. Reprinted by permission.

"Coming to the Sacrifice" (originally titled "Coming to the Sacrifice: *The Sound and the Fury* II") by Max Putzel from *Genius of Place: William Faulkner's Triumphant Beginnings* by Max Putzel, © 1985 by Louisiana State University Press. Reprinted by permission.

INDEX